Coaching Youth Lacrosse

Second Edition

American Sport Education Program

Human Kinetics

Library of Congress Cataloging-in-Publication Data

Coaching youth lacrosse / American Sport Education Program. — 2nd ed.
    p. cm.
  ISBN 0-7360-3794-2 (soft cover)
  1. Lacrosse for children. 2. Lacrosse—Coaching. 1. American Sport Education
Program.
  GV989.17 .C63 2002
  796.34'7--dc21   2002005933

ISBN 0-7360-3794-2

Materials in chapter 4 are reprinted, with permission, from YMCA of the USA, 1999, *Coaching YMCA Winners Baseball and Softball* (Champaign, IL: Human Kinetics).

Managing Editor: Wendy McLaughlin; **Lacrosse Consultants:** Al Brown (Portsmouth, RI), Feffie Barnhill (Wilmington, DE), Richard Loper (Finksburg, MD), Ian Loper (Finksburg, MD); **Assistant Editor:** Kim Thoren; **Copyeditor:** Erin Cler; **Proofreader:** Julie Marx Goodreau; **Permission Manager:** Toni Harte; **Graphic Designer:** Fred Starbird; **Graphic Artists:** Kim McFarland, Tara Welsch; **Art and Photo Manager:** Dan Wendt; **Cover Designer:** Jack W. Davis; **Photographer (cover):** Bill Welch; **Photographer (interior):** Tom Roberts; **Illustrators:** Line drawings by Accurate Art, MAC art by Jennifer Delmotte; **Printer:** United Graphics

Printed in the United States of America   10 9 8 7 6 5 4 3 2

Human Kinetics
Web site: www.HumanKinetics.com

United States: Human Kinetics
P.O. Box 5076
Champaign, IL 61825-5076
800-747-4457
e-mail: humank@hkusa.com

Canada: Human Kinetics
475 Devonshire Road Unit 100
Windsor, ON N8Y 2L5
800-465-7301 (in Canada only)
e-mail: orders@hkcanada.com

Europe: Human Kinetics
107 Bradford Road
Stanningley
Leeds LS28 6AT, United Kingdom
+44 (0) 113 255 5665
e-mail: hk@hkeurope.com

Australia: Human Kinetics
57A Price Avenue
Lower Mitcham, South Australia 5062
08 8277 1555
e-mail: liaw@hkaustralia.com

New Zealand: Human Kinetics
Division of Sports Distributors NZ Ltd.
P.O. Box 300 226 Albany
North Shore City
Auckland
0064 9 448 1207
e-mail: blairc@hknewz.com

Contents

Welcome to Coaching!

Coaching young people is an exciting way to be involved in sport. But it isn't easy. Some coaches are overwhelmed by the responsibilities involved in helping athletes through their early sport experiences. And that's not surprising, because coaching youngsters requires more than bringing the balls to the field and letting them play. It involves preparing them physically and mentally to compete effectively, fairly, and safely in their sport, and providing them with a positive role model.

This book will help you meet the challenges *and* experience the many rewards of coaching young athletes. In this book you'll learn how meet your responsibilities as a coach, communicate well and provide for safety, use a highly effective method – the games approach – to teaching tactics and skills, and learn strategies for coaching on game day. We also provide three sets of season plans to guide you throughout your season.

This book serves as a text for ASEP's Coaching Youth Sport course. If you would like more information about this course or other ASEP courses and resources, please contact us at

ASEP
P.O. Box 5076
Champaign, IL 61825-5076
1-800-747-5698

www.asep.com

A Message From US Lacrosse

Welcome to lacrosse! As the national governing body of men's and women's lacrosse, US Lacrosse provides a leadership role in virtually every aspect of the sport, offering numerous programs and services to over 150,000 members and more than one million lacrosse enthusiasts throughout the United States. An important US Lacrosse initiative is the development of educational resources to support the sport's fast-paced growth.

Coaching Youth Lacrosse was developed as part of a comprehensive coaching education program to assist coaches at all levels of men's and women's lacrosse. The national program is one of many resources available to help you introduce and develop the sport. Be sure to visit the Web site of our partner, Positive Coaching Alliance (PCA), www.positivecoach.org, to help you make lacrosse a character-building experience for your youth players.

US Lacrosse would like to give special thanks to consultants Feffie Barnhill, Alfred Brown, Wendy Kridel, Abigail Burbank, Julia Mignatti, Jennifer Allen, Richard Loper, Ian Loper, and Karen Collins for their hard work in helping us create this valuable resource for youth lacrosse coaches. US Lacrosse would also like to thank the volunteers who helped review the book's original manuscript.

In addition, thanks to these organizations and people who participated in the photo shoot: MBNA America, LAX World, Sports Her Way, Mitch Whiteley and St. Paul's School, Mike Ferrell, M.C. McFadden, and Mike Thomas.

Thanks also to all of the models for demonstrating lacrosse skills for the book's photographs: Mike Thomas, Brian Carroll, Kevin Carroll, Jennifer Allen, Allyson Levy, Maureen Onda, Caitlyn McFadden, Breanna Stiff, Abbie Mitchell, Caitlin Whiteley, Jill Whitty, Katie Reese, and Kelly Taylor.

We thank you for your commitment to today's young athletes and wish you many wonderful experiences while coaching youth lacrosse. Good luck and have fun!

Steve Stenersen   Charles Simpson
Executive Director, US Lacrosse   Chair, US Lacrosse Youth Council

Key to Figures

⟶	Running
⇢	Passing
∿⟶	Cutting
☐	Defensive Player
○	Offensive Player
D	Defense
O	Offense
M	Midfielder
A	Attacker
C	Coach
G	Goalkeeper

chapter 1

Stepping Into Coaching

If you are like most youth league coaches, you have probably been recruited from the ranks of concerned parents, sport enthusiasts, or community volunteers. Like many rookie and veteran coaches, you probably have had little formal instruction on how to coach. But when the call went out for coaches to assist with the local youth lacrosse program, you answered because you like children and enjoy lacrosse and perhaps because you wanted to be involved in a worthwhile community activity.

Your initial coaching assignment may be difficult. Like many volunteers, you may not know everything there is to know about lacrosse or about how to work with children. *Coaching Youth Lacrosse* will help you learn the basics of coaching lacrosse effectively.

To start, let's take a look at what's involved in being a coach. What are your responsibilities? We'll also talk about how to handle the situation when your child is on the team you coach, and we'll examine five tools for being an effective coach.

Your Responsibilities As a Coach

As a lacrosse coach, you'll be called on to do the following:

1. **Provide a safe physical environment.** Playing lacrosse holds an inherent risk, but as a coach you're responsible for regularly inspecting the practice and competition fields (see the checklists for facilities, equipment, and support personnel in chapter 6).

2. **Communicate in a positive way.** You'll communicate not only with your players but also with parents, umpires, and administrators. Communicate in a way that is positive and that demonstrates you have the best interests of the players at heart. Chapter 2 will help you communicate effectively and positively.

3. **Teach the tactics and skills of lacrosse.** We'll show you an innovative "games approach" to teaching and practicing the skills and tactics young athletes need to know—an approach that kids thoroughly enjoy. We ask you to help all players be the best they can be. In chapter 5 we'll show you how to teach lacrosse skills, and in chapters 9 and 12 we'll provide multi-level season plans for girls and boys, respectively. In chapters 8 and 11 we'll provide descriptions of all the skills for girls and boys, respectively, you'll need to teach and information to help you detect and correct errors that players typically make.

4. **Teach the rules of lacrosse.** We'll ask you to teach your players the rules of lacrosse. You'll find the rules for girls' lacrosse in chapter 7 and the rules for boys' lacrosse in chapter 10.

5. **Direct players in competition.** This includes determining starting lineups and a substitution plan, relating appropriately to umpires and to opposing coaches and players, and making tactical decisions during games (see chapter 6). Remember that the focus is not on winning at all costs but in coaching your kids to compete well, do their best, and strive to win within the rules.

6. **Help your players become fit and value fitness for a lifetime.** We want you to help your players be fit so that they can play lacrosse safely and successfully. We also want your players to learn to become fit on their own, understand the value of fitness, and enjoy training. Thus, we ask you not to make them do push-ups or run laps for punishment. Make it fun to get fit for lacrosse, and make it fun to play lacrosse, so they'll stay fit for a lifetime.

7. **Help young people develop character.** Character development includes learning caring, honesty, respect, and responsibility. These in-

tangible qualities are no less important to teach than the skill of moving the ball well. We ask you to teach these values to players both by conducting team circles after every game and by demonstrating and encouraging behaviors that express these values at all times.

These are your responsibilities as a coach. But coaching becomes even more complicated when your child is a player on the team you coach. If this is the case, you'll have to take into account your roles as both a coach and a parent, and think about how those roles relate to each other.

Coaching Your Own Child

Many coaches are parents, but the two roles should not be confused. Unlike your role as a parent, as a coach you are responsible not only to yourself and your child but also to the organization, all the players on the team (including your child), and their parents. Because of this additional responsibility, your behavior on the lacrosse field will be different from your behavior at home, and your son or daughter may not understand why.

For example, imagine the confusion of a young boy who is the center of his parents' attention at home but is barely noticed by his father/coach in the sport setting. Or consider the mixed signals received by a young girl whose lacrosse skills are constantly evaluated by a mother/coach who otherwise rarely comments on her daughter's activities. You need to explain to your son or daughter your new responsibilities and how they will affect your relationship when coaching.

Take the following steps to avoid problems in coaching your child:

- Ask your child if he or she wants you to coach the team.
- Explain why you wish to be involved with the team.
- Discuss with your child how your interactions will change when you take on the role of coach at practices or games.
- Limit your coaching behavior to when you are in the coaching role.
- Avoid parenting during practice or game situations, to keep your role clear in your child's mind.
- Reaffirm your love for your child, irrespective of his or her performance on the lacrosse field.

Now let's look at some of the qualities that will help you become an effective coach.

Five Tools of an Effective Coach

Have you purchased the traditional coaching tools—things like whistles, coaching clothes, sport shoes, and a clipboard? They'll help you coach, but to be a successful coach you'll need five other tools that cannot be bought. These tools are available only through self-examination and hard work; they're easy to remember with the acronym COACH:

C – Comprehension

O – Outlook

A – Affection

C – Character

H – Humor

Comprehension

Comprehension of the rules, tactics, and skills of lacrosse is required. You must understand the basic elements of the sport. To assist you in learning about the game, we describe rules, tactics, and skills for girls in chapters 7 and 8, and for boys in chapters 10 and 11. We also provide season plans in chapters 9 and 12 for girls and boys, respectively.

To improve your comprehension of lacrosse, take the following steps:

- Read the sport-specific section of this book in chapters 7, 8, and 9 for girls and chapters 10, 11, and 12 for boys. Contact US Lacrosse for information on additional resources available to you (www.uslacrosse.org).
- Consider reading other lacrosse coaching books.
- Contact youth lacrosse organizations.
- Attend lacrosse clinics, including the annual US Lacrosse convention.
- Talk with more experienced lacrosse coaches.
- Observe local college, high school, and youth lacrosse games.

In addition to having lacrosse knowledge, you must implement proper training and safety methods so that your players can participate with little risk of injury. Even then, injuries may occur. And more often than not, you'll be the first person responding to your players' injuries, so be sure you understand the basic emergency care procedures described in chapter 3. Also, read in that chapter how to handle more serious sport injury situations.

Outlook

This coaching tool refers to your perspective and goals—what you are seeking as a coach. The most common coaching objectives are to (a) have fun; (b) help players develop their physical, mental, and social skills; and (c) win. Thus your *outlook* involves the priorities you set, your planning, and your vision for the future.

While all coaches focus on competition, we want you to focus on *positive* competition, keeping the pursuit of victory in perspective by making decisions that first are in the best interest of the players and second will help to win the game.

So how do you know if your outlook and priorities are in order? Here's a little test for you:

Which situation would you be most proud of?
   a. Knowing that each participant enjoyed playing lacrosse.
   b. Seeing that all players improved their lacrosse skills.
   c. Winning the league championship.

Which statement best reflects your thoughts about sport?
   a. If it isn't fun, don't do it.
   b. Everyone should learn something every day.
   c. Sport isn't fun if you don't win.

How would you like your players to remember you?
   a. As a coach who was fun to play for.
   b. As a coach who provided a good base of fundamental skills.
   c. As a coach who had a winning record.

Which would you most like to hear a parent of a player on your team say?
   a. Mike really had a good time playing lacrosse this year.
   b. Nicole learned some important lessons playing lacrosse this year.
   c. Willie played on the first-place lacrosse team this year.

Which of the following would be the most rewarding moment of your season?
   a. Having your team not want to stop playing, even after practice is over.
   b. Seeing one of your players finally master the skill of passing.
   c. Winning the league championship.

Look over your answers. If you most often selected "a" responses, then having fun is most important to you. A majority of "b" answers suggests that skill development is what attracts you to coaching. And if "c" was your most frequent response, winning is tops on your list of coaching priorities. If your priorities are in order, your players' well-being will take precedence over your team's win-loss record every time.

The American Sport Education Program (ASEP) has a motto that will help you keep your outlook in line with the best interests of the kids on your team. It summarizes in four words all you need to remember when establishing your coaching priorities:

Athletes First, Winning Second

This motto recognizes that striving to win is an important, even vital, part of sports. But it emphatically states that no efforts in striving to win should be made at the expense of the athletes' well-being, development, and enjoyment. Take these actions to better define your outlook:

1. Determine your priorities for the season.
2. Prepare for situations that challenge your priorities.
3. Set goals for yourself and your players that are consistent with those priorities.
4. Plan how you and your players can best attain those goals.
5. Review your goals frequently to be sure that you stay on track.

Affection

This is another vital tool you will want to have in your coaching kit: a genuine concern for the young people you coach. It involves having a love for kids, a desire to share with them your love and knowledge of lacrosse, and the patience and understanding that allow each individual playing for you to grow from his or her involvement in sport.

You can demonstrate your affection and patience in many ways:

- Make an effort to get to know each player on your team.
- Treat each player as an individual.
- Empathize with players trying to learn new and difficult skills.
- Treat players as you would like to be treated under similar circumstances.
- Be in control of your emotions.
- Show your enthusiasm for being involved with your team.
- Keep an upbeat and positive tone in all of your communications.

Character

The fact that you have decided to coach young lacrosse players probably means that you think participation in sport is important. But whether or not that participation develops character in your players depends as much on you as it does on the sport itself. How can you build character in your players?

Having good character means modeling appropriate behaviors for sport and life. That means more than just saying the right things. What you say and what you do must match. There is no place in coaching for the "Do as I say, not as I do" philosophy. Challenge, support, encourage, and reward every youngster, and your players will be more likely to accept, even celebrate, their differences. Be in control before, during, and after all practices and contests. And don't be afraid to admit that you were wrong. No one is perfect!

Consider the following steps to being a good role model:

- Take stock of your strengths and weaknesses.
- Build on your strengths.
- Set goals for yourself to improve on those areas you would not like to see copied.
- If you slip up, apologize to your team and to yourself. You'll do better next time.

Humor

Humor is an often-overlooked coaching tool. For our use it means having the ability to laugh at yourself and with your players during practices and contests. Nothing helps balance the tone of a serious skill-learning session like a chuckle or two. And a sense of humor puts in perspective the many mistakes your players will make. So don't get upset over each miscue or respond negatively to erring players. Allow your players and yourself to enjoy the ups, and don't dwell on the downs.

Here are some tips for injecting humor into your practices:

- Make practices fun by including a variety of activities.
- Keep all players involved in games and skill practices.
- Consider laughter by your players as a sign of enjoyment, not of waning discipline.
- Smile!

chapter 2

Communicating As a Coach

In chapter 1 you learned about the tools needed to COACH: Comprehension, Outlook, Affection, Character, and Humor. These are essentials for effective coaching; without them, you'd have a difficult time getting started. But none of the tools will work if you don't know how to use them with your athletes—and this requires skillful communication. This chapter examines what communication is and how you can become a more effective communicator-coach.

What's Involved in Communication?

Coaches often mistakenly believe that communication involves only instructing players to do something, but verbal commands are only a small part of the communication process. More than half of what is communicated is nonverbal. So remember when you are coaching: Actions speak louder than words.

Communication in its simplest form involves two people: a sender and a receiver. The sender transmits the message verbally, through facial expressions, and possibly through body language. Once the message is sent, the receiver must assimilate it successfully. A receiver who fails to attend or listen will miss parts, if not all, of the message.

How Can I Send More Effective Messages?

Young athletes often have little understanding of the rules and skills of lacrosse and probably even less confidence in playing it. So they need accurate, understandable, and supportive messages to help them along. That's why your verbal and nonverbal messages are so important.

Verbal Messages

"Sticks and stones may break my bones, but words will never hurt me" isn't true. Spoken words can have a strong and long-lasting effect. And coaches' words are particularly influential because youngsters place great importance on what coaches say. Perhaps you, like many former youth sport participants, have a difficult time remembering much of anything you were told by your elementary school teachers, but you can still recall several specific things your coaches at that level said to you. Such is the lasting effect of a coach's comments to a player.

Whether you are correcting misbehavior, teaching a player how to pass the ball, or praising a player for good effort, you should consider a number of things when sending a message verbally. They include the following:

- Be positive and honest.
- State it clearly and simply.
- Say it loud enough and say it again.
- Be consistent.

Be Positive and Honest

Nothing turns people off like hearing someone nag all the time, and athletes react similarly to a coach who gripes constantly. Kids particularly need encouragement because they often doubt their ability to perform in a sport. So look for and tell your players what they did well.

But don't cover up poor or incorrect play with rosy words of praise. Kids know all too well when they've erred, and no cheerfully expressed cliche can undo their mistakes. If you fail to acknowledge players' errors, your athletes will think you are a phony.

A good way to correct a performance error is to first point out what the athlete did correctly. Then explain in a positive way what he or she is doing wrong and show him or her how to correct it. Finish by encouraging the athlete and emphasizing the correct performance.

Be sure not to follow a positive statement with the word *but*. For example, don't say, "That was good location on your pass, Kelly. But if you follow through from your shoulder a little more, you'll get a little more zip on the ball." Saying it this way causes many kids to ignore the positive statement and focus on the negative one. Instead, say something like, "That was good location on your pass, Kelly. And if you follow through with your stick a little more, you'll get more zip on the ball. That was right on target. That's the way to go."

State It Clearly and Simply

Positive and honest messages are good but only if expressed directly in words your players understand. "Beating around the bush" is ineffective and inefficient. And if you do ramble, your players will miss the point of your message and probably lose interest. Here are some tips for saying things clearly:

- Organize your thoughts before speaking to your athletes.
- Explain things thoroughly, but don't bore them with long-winded monologues.
- Use language your players can understand. However, avoid trying to be hip by using their age group's slang vocabulary.

Say It Loud Enough and Say It Again

Talk to your team in a voice that all members can hear and interpret. A crisp, vigorous voice commands attention and respect; garbled and weak speech is tuned out. It's okay, in fact appropriate, to soften your voice when speaking to a player individually about a personal problem. But most of the time your messages will be for all your players to hear, so make sure they can! An enthusiastic voice also motivates players and tells them you enjoy being their coach. A word of caution, however: Don't dominate the setting with a booming voice that distracts attention from players' performances.

Sometimes what you say, even if stated loudly and clearly, won't sink in the first time. This may be particularly true when young athletes hear words they don't understand. To avoid boring repetition and yet still get your message across, say the same thing in a slightly different way. For instance, you might first tell your players, "Force your opponent to her weak side." Soon afterward, remind them to "Be in good defensive position, so you can deny the ball strong side, and if your opponent catches the ball she will be forced to use her nondominant hand." The second form of the message may get through to players who missed it the first time around.

Be Consistent

People often say things in ways that imply a different message. For example, a touch of sarcasm added to the words "Way to go!" sends an entirely different message than the words themselves suggest. Avoid sending such mixed messages. Keep the tone of your voice consistent with the words you use. And don't say something one day and contradict it the next; players will get their wires crossed.

Nonverbal Messages

Just as you should be consistent in the tone of voice and words you use, you should also keep your verbal and nonverbal messages consistent. An extreme example of failing to do this would be shaking your head, indicating disapproval, while at the same time telling a player "Nice try." Which is the player to believe, your gesture or your words?

Messages can be sent nonverbally in a number of ways. Facial expressions and body language are just two of the more obvious forms of nonverbal signals that can help you when you coach.

Facial Expressions

The look on a person's face is the quickest clue to what he or she thinks or feels. Your players know this, so they will study your face, looking for any sign that will tell them more than the words you say. Don't try to fool them by putting on a happy or blank "mask." They'll see through it, and you'll lose credibility.

Serious, stone-faced expressions are no help to kids, who need cues as to how they are performing. They will just assume you're unhappy or disinterested. Don't be afraid to smile. A smile from a coach can give a great boost to an unsure athlete. Plus, a smile lets your players know that you are happy coaching them. But don't overdo it, or your players won't be able to tell when you are genuinely pleased by something they've done or when you are just putting on a smiling face.

Body Language

What would your players think you were feeling if you came to practice slouched over, with your head down and shoulders slumped? Tired? Bored? Unhappy? What would they think you were feeling if you watched them during a contest with your hands on your hips, your jaws clenched, and your face reddened? Upset with them? Disgusted at an umpire? Mad at a fan? Probably some or all of these things would enter your players' minds. And none of these impressions are the kind you want your players to have of you. That's why you should carry yourself in a pleasant, confident, and vigorous manner. Such a posture not only projects happiness with your coaching role but also provides a good example for your young players, who may model your behavior.

Physical contact can also be a very important use of body language. A handshake, a pat on the head, an arm around the shoulder, or even a big hug are effective ways of showing approval, concern, affection, and joy to your players. Youngsters are especially in need of this type of nonverbal message. Keep within the obvious moral and legal limits, of course, but don't be reluctant to touch your players, sending a message that can only truly be expressed in that way.

How Can I Improve My Receiving Skills?

Now, let's examine the other half of the communication process—receiving messages. Too often very good senders are very poor receivers of messages. But as a coach of young athletes, you must be able to fulfill both roles effectively.

The requirements for receiving messages are simple, but receiving skills are perhaps less satisfying and therefore underdeveloped compared to sending skills. People seem to naturally enjoy hearing themselves talk more than hearing others talk. But if you read about the keys to receiving messages and make a strong effort to use them with your players, you'll be surprised by what you've been missing.

Attention!

First, you must pay attention; you must want to hear what others have to communicate to you. That's not always easy when you're busy coaching and have many things competing for your attention. But in one-on-one or team meetings with players, you must really focus on what they are telling you, both verbally and nonverbally. You'll be amazed at the little signals you pick up. Not only will such focused attention help you catch every word your players say, but also you'll notice your players' moods and physical states. In addition, you'll get an idea of your players' feelings toward you and other players on the team.

Listen CARE-FULLY

How we receive messages from others, perhaps more than anything else we do, demonstrates how much we care for the sender and what that person has to tell us. If you care little for your players or have little regard for what they have to say, it will show in how you attend and listen to them. Check yourself. Do you find your mind wandering to what you are going to do after practice while one of your players is talking to you? Do you frequently have to ask your players, "What did you say?" If so, you need to work on your receiving mechanics of attending and listening. But perhaps the most critical question you should ask yourself, if you find that you're missing the messages your players send, is this: Do I care?

Providing Feedback

So far we've discussed separately the sending and receiving of messages. But we all know that senders and receivers switch roles several times during an interaction. One person initiates a communication by sending a message to another person, who then receives the message. The receiver then switches roles and becomes the sender by responding to the person who sent the initial message. These verbal and nonverbal responses are called *feedback*.

Your players will be looking to you for feedback all the time. They will want to know how you think they are performing, what you think of their ideas, and whether their efforts please you. Obviously, you can respond in many different ways. How you respond will strongly affect your players. They will respond most favorably to positive feedback.

Praising players when they have performed or behaved well is an effective way of getting them to repeat (or try to repeat) that behavior in the future. And positive feedback for effort is an especially effective way to motivate youngsters to work on difficult skills. So rather than shouting and providing negative feedback to players who have made mistakes, try offering players positive feedback, letting them know what they did correctly and how they can improve.

Sometimes just the way you word feedback can make it more positive than negative. For example, instead of saying, "Don't drop the ball," you might say, "Cradle the ball in the pocket." Then your players will be focusing on what to do instead of what not to do.

You can give positive feedback verbally and nonverbally. Telling a player, especially in front of teammates, that he or she has performed well is a great way to boost the confidence of a youngster. And a pat on the back or a handshake can be a very tangible way of communicating your recognition of a player's performance.

Who Else Do I Need to Communicate With?

Coaching involves not only sending and receiving messages and providing proper feedback to players but also interacting with parents, fans, game umpires, and opposing coaches. If you don't communicate effectively with these groups of people, your coaching career will be unpleasant and short-lived. So try the following suggestions for communicating with these groups.

Parents

A player's parents need to be assured that their son or daughter is under the direction of a coach who is both knowledgeable about the sport and concerned about the youngster's well-being. You can put their worries to rest by holding a preseason parent orientation meeting in which you describe your background and your approach to coaching.

If parents contact you with a concern during the season, listen to them closely and try to offer positive responses. If you need to communicate with parents, catch them after a practice, give them a phone call, send a note through the mail, or send an e-mail. Messages sent to parents through players are too often lost, misinterpreted, or forgotten.

Fans

The stands probably won't be overflowing at your contests, but that only means that you'll more easily hear the few fans who criticize your coaching. When you hear something negative said about the job you're doing, don't respond. Keep calm, consider whether the message had any value, and if not, forget it. Acknowledging critical, unwarranted comments from a fan during a contest will only encourage others to voice their opinions. So put away your "rabbit ears" and communicate to fans, through your actions, that you are a confident, competent coach.

Prepare your players for fans' criticisms. Tell them it is you, not the spectators, they should listen to. If you notice that one of your players is rattled by a fan's comment, reassure the player that your evaluation is more objective and favorable—and the one that counts.

Umpires

How you communicate with umpires will have a great influence on the way your players behave toward them. Therefore, you need to set an example. Greet umpires with a handshake, an introduction, and perhaps some casual conversation about the upcoming contest. Indicate your respect for them before, during, and after the contest. Don't make nasty remarks, shout, or use disrespectful body gestures. Your players will see you do it, and they'll get the idea that such behavior is appropriate. Plus, if the umpire hears or sees you, the communication between the two of you will break down.

Opposing Coaches

Make an effort to visit with the coach of the opposing team before the game. During the game, don't get into a personal feud with the opposing coach. Remember, it's the kids, not the coaches, who are competing. And by getting along well with the opposing coach, you'll show your players that competition involves cooperation.

chapter 3

Providing for Players' Safety

One of your players appears to break free, carrying the ball down the field. But a defender catches up with and accidentally trips the goal-bound player. You notice that your player is not getting up from the ground and seems to be in pain. What do you do?

No coach wants to see players get hurt. But injury remains a reality of sport participation; consequently, you must be prepared to provide first aid when injuries occur and to protect yourself against unjustified lawsuits. Fortunately, there are many preventive measures you can institute to reduce the risk.

In this chapter we describe

- steps you can take to prevent injuries,
- first aid and emergency responses for when injuries occur, and
- your legal responsibilities as a coach.

The Game Plan for Safety

You can't prevent all injuries from happening, but you can take preventive measures that give your players the best possible chance for injury-free participation. In creating the safest possible environment for your athletes, we'll explore what you can do in these six areas:

- Preseason physical examination
- Physical conditioning
- Equipment and facilities inspection
- Player match-ups and inherent risks
- Proper supervision and record keeping
- Environmental conditions

We'll begin with what should take place *before* the season begins: the preseason physical examination.

Preseason Physical Examination

We recommend that your players have a physical examination before participating in lacrosse. The exam should address the most likely areas of medical concern and identify youngsters at high risk. We also suggest that you have players' parents or guardians sign a participation agreement form and a release form to allow their children to be treated in case of an emergency.

Physical Conditioning

Players need to be in, or get in, shape to play the game at the level expected. To do so, they'll need to have adequate cardiorespiratory fitness and muscular fitness.

Cardiorespiratory fitness involves the body's ability to store and use oxygen and fuels efficiently to power muscle contractions. As players get in better shape, their bodies are able to more efficiently deliver oxygen and fuels to muscles and carry off carbon dioxide and other wastes.

Lacrosse involves lots of running; most players will have to be able to move almost continuously (and make short bursts throughout a game).

An advantage of teaching lacrosse with the games approach is that kids are active during almost the entire practice; there is no standing around in lines, watching teammates take part in drills. Players will attain higher levels of cardiorespiratory fitness as the season progresses simply by taking part in practice. However, watch closely for signs of low levels of cardiorespiratory fitness; don't let your athletes do too much until they're fit. You might privately counsel youngsters who appear overly winded, suggesting that they train outside of practice to increase their fitness.

Muscular fitness encompasses strength, muscle endurance, power, speed, and flexibility. This type of fitness is affected by physical maturity, as well as strength training and other types of training. Your players will likely exhibit a relatively wide range of muscular fitness. Players who have greater muscular fitness will be able to run faster and shoot harder. They will also sustain fewer muscular injuries, and any injuries that do occur will tend to be more minor in nature. And, in case of injury, the recovery rate is accelerated in those with higher levels of muscular fitness.

Two other components of fitness and injury prevention are the warm-up and the cool-down. Although young bodies are generally very limber, muscles can get tight from inactivity. The warm-up should address each muscle group and get the heart rate elevated in preparation for strenuous activity. Have players warm up for 5 to 10 minutes by playing easy games and stretching.

As practice winds down, slow players' heart rates with an easy jog or walk. Then have players stretch for five minutes to help avoid stiff muscles and make them less tight before the next practice or contest.

Equipment and Facilities Inspection

Another way to prevent injuries is to check the quality and fit of all sticks and protective equipment used by your players. Inspect the equipment before you distribute it, after you have assigned it, and daily during the season. For boys' lacrosse, ensure that all players have adequate helmets, gloves, mouthguards, and arm and shoulder pads. For girls' lacrosse, ensure that all players wear their mouthguards at all times. Worn-out, damaged, or outdated equipment must be replaced immediately.

Remember also to examine regularly the field on which your players practice and play. Remove hazards, report conditions you cannot remedy, and request maintenance as necessary. If unsafe conditions exist, either make adaptations to avoid risk to your players' safety or stop the practice or game until safe conditions have been restored.

Player Match-Ups and Inherent Risks

We recommend that you group teams in two-year age ranges if possible. You'll encounter fewer mismatches in physical maturation with narrow age ranges. Even so, two 12-year-old boys might differ by 90 pounds in weight, a foot in height, and three or four years in emotional and intellectual maturity. This presents dangers for the less mature. Whenever possible, match players against opponents of similar size and physical maturity. Such an approach gives smaller, less mature youngsters a better chance to succeed and avoid injury while providing more mature players with a greater challenge. Closely supervise games so that the more mature do not put the less mature at undue risk.

Proper matching helps protect you from certain liability concerns. But you must also warn players of the inherent risks involved in playing lacrosse, because "failure to warn" is one of the most successful arguments in lawsuits against coaches. So, thoroughly explain the inherent risks of lacrosse, and make sure each player knows, understands, and appreciates those risks.

The preseason parent orientation meeting is a good opportunity to explain the risks of the sport to both parents and players. It is also a good occasion on which to have both the players and their parents sign waivers releasing you from liability should an injury occur. Such waivers do not relieve you of responsibility for your players' well-being, but they are recommended by lawyers.

Proper Supervision and Record Keeping

To ensure players' safety, you will need to provide both general supervision and specific supervision. *General supervision* is being in the area of activity so that you can see and hear what is happening. You should be

- immediately accessible to the activity and able to oversee the entire activity,
- alert to conditions that may be dangerous to players and ready to take action to protect them, and
- able to react immediately and appropriately to emergencies.

Specific supervision is direct supervision of an activity at practice. For example, you should provide specific supervision when you teach new skills and continue it until your athletes understand the requirements of the activity, the risks involved, and their own ability to perform in light of those risks. You need to also provide specific supervision when you notice either players breaking rules or a change in the condition of your athletes.

As a general rule, the more dangerous the activity, the more specific the supervision required. This suggests that more specific supervision is required with younger and less-experienced athletes.

As part of your supervision duty, you are expected to foresee potentially dangerous situations and to be positioned to help prevent them from occurring. This requires that you know lacrosse well, especially the rules that are intended to provide for safety. Prohibit dangerous horseplay, and hold practices only under safe weather conditions. These specific supervisory activities, applied consistently, will make the play environment safer for your players and will help protect you from liability if a mishap does occur.

For further protection, keep records of your season plans, practice plans, and players' injuries. Season and practice plans come in handy when you need evidence that players have been taught certain skills, whereas accurate, detailed injury report forms offer protection against unfounded lawsuits. Ask for these forms from your sponsoring organization (appendix A has a sample injury report form), and hold onto these records for several years so that an "old lacrosse injury" of a former player doesn't come back to haunt you.

Environmental Conditions

Most problems due to environmental factors are related to excessive heat or cold, though you should also consider other environmental factors such as severe weather and pollution. A little thought about the potential problems and a little effort to ensure adequate protection for your athletes will prevent most serious emergencies that are related to environmental conditions.

Heat

On hot, humid days the body has difficulty cooling itself. Because the air is already saturated with water vapor (humidity), sweat doesn't evaporate as easily. Therefore, body sweat is a less effective cooling agent, and the body retains extra heat. Hot, humid environments make athletes prone to heat exhaustion and heatstroke (see more on these in "Serious Injuries" on pages 28-29). And if *you* think it's hot or humid, it's worse on the kids—not only because they're more active but also because youngsters under the age of 12 have a more difficult time than adults regulating their body temperature. To provide for players' safety in hot or humid conditions, take the following preventive measures.

⊙ **Monitor weather conditions and adjust practices accordingly.** Figure 3.1 shows the specific air temperatures and humidity percentages that can be hazardous.

⊙ **Acclimatize players to exercising in high heat and humidity.** Athletes can make adjustments to high heat and humidity over 7 to 10 days. During this time, hold practices at low to moderate activity levels and give the players water breaks every 20 minutes.

⊙ **Switch to light clothing.** Players should wear shorts and white T-shirts.

⊙ **Identify and monitor players who are prone to heat illness.** Players who are overweight, heavily muscled, or out of shape will be more prone to heat illness, as are athletes who work excessively hard or who have suffered heat illness before. Closely monitor these athletes and give them water breaks every 15 to 20 minutes.

⊙ **Make sure athletes replace water lost through sweat.** Encourage your players to drink one liter of water each day outside of practice and contest times, to drink eight ounces of water every 20 minutes during practice or competition, and to drink four to eight ounces of water 20 minutes before practice or competition.

⊙ **Replenish electrolytes lost through sweat.** Sodium (salt) and potassium are lost through sweat. The best way to replace these nutrients is by eating a normal diet that contains fresh fruits and vegetables. Bananas are a good source of potassium. The normal American diet contains plenty of salt, so players don't need to go overboard in salting their food to replace lost sodium.

Water, Water Everywhere

Encourage players to drink plenty of water before, during, and after practice. Because water makes up 45 percent to 65 percent of a youngster's body weight and water weighs about a pound per pint, the loss of even a little water can have severe consequences for the body's systems. And it doesn't have to be hot and humid for players to become dehydrated. Nor do players have to feel thirsty; in fact, by the time they are aware of their thirst, they are long overdue for a drink.

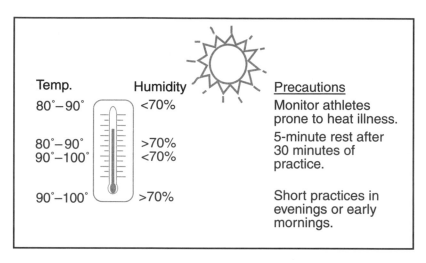

Figure 3.1 Warm-weather precautions.

Cold

When a person is exposed to cold weather, the body temperature starts to drop below normal. To counteract this, the body shivers and reduces the blood flow to gain or conserve heat. But no matter how effective the body's natural heating mechanism is, the body will better withstand cold temperatures if it is prepared to handle them. To reduce the risk of cold-related illnesses, make sure players wear appropriate protective clothing, and keep them active to maintain body heat. Also monitor the windchill (figure 3.2).

				Temperature (°F)						
		0	5	10	15	20	25	30	35	40
		Flesh may freeze within 1 minute								
	40	-55	-45	-35	-30	-20	-15	-5	0	10
	35	-50	-40	-35	-30	-20	-10	-5	5	10
Wind speed (mph)	30	-50	-40	-30	-25	-20	-10	0	5	10
	25	-45	-35	-30	-20	-15	-5	0	10	15
	20	-35	-30	-25	-15	-10	0	5	10	20
	15	-30	-25	-20	-10	-5	0	10	15	25
	10	-20	-15	-10	0	5	10	15	20	30
	5	-5	0	5	10	15	20	25	30	35
		Windchill temperature (°F)								

Figure 3.2 Windchill factor index.

Severe Weather

Severe weather refers to a host of potential dangers, including lightning storms, tornadoes, hail, and heavy rains (which can cause injuries by creating sloppy field conditions).

Lightning is of special concern because it can come up quickly and can cause great harm or even kill. For each 5-second count from the flash of lightning to the bang of thunder, lightning is one mile away. A flash-bang of 10 seconds means lightning is two miles away; a flash-bang of 15 seconds indicates lightning is three miles away. A practice or competition should be stopped for the day if lightning is three miles away or less (15 seconds or less from flash to bang).

Safe places in which to take cover when lightning strikes are fully enclosed metal vehicles with the windows up, enclosed buildings, and low ground (under cover of bushes, if possible). It's *not* safe to be near metallic objects—flag poles, fences, light poles, metal bleachers, and so on. Also avoid trees, water, and open fields.

Cancel practice when under either a tornado watch or warning. If for some reason you are practicing or competing when a tornado is nearby, you should get inside a building if possible. If not, lie in a ditch or other low-lying area or crouch near a strong building, and use your arms to protect your head and neck.

The keys to handling severe weather are caution and prudence. Don't try to get that last 10 minutes of practice in if lightning is on the horizon. Don't continue to play in heavy rains. Many storms can strike both quickly and ferociously. Respect the weather and play it safe.

Air Pollution

Poor air quality and smog can present real dangers to your players. Both short- and long-term lung damage are possible from participating in unsafe air. While it's true that participating in clean air is not possible in many areas, restricting activity is recommended when the air-quality ratings are worse than moderate or when there is a smog alert. Your local health department or air-quality control board can inform you of the air-quality ratings for your area and when restricting activities is recommended.

Responding to Players' Injuries

No matter how good and thorough your prevention program is, injuries may occur. When injury does strike, chances are you will be the one in charge. The severity and nature of the injury will determine how actively involved you'll be in treating the injury. But regardless of how seriously a player is hurt, it is your responsibility to know what steps to take. So let's look at how you should prepare to provide basic emergency care to your injured athletes and take the appropriate action when an injury does occur.

Being Prepared

Being prepared to provide basic emergency care involves three steps: being trained in cardiopulmonary resuscitation (CPR) and first aid, having an appropriately stocked first aid kit on hand at practices and games, and having an emergency plan.

CPR and First Aid Training

We recommend that all coaches receive CPR and first aid training from a nationally recognized organization (the National Safety Council, the American Heart Association, the American Red Cross, or the American Sport Education Program). You should be certified based on a practical test and a written test of knowledge. CPR training should include pediatric and adult basic life support and obstructed airway procedures.

First Aid Kit

A well-stocked first aid kit should include the following:

- List of emergency phone numbers
- Cell phone or change for a pay phone
- Face shield (for rescue breathing and CPR)
- Bandage scissors
- Plastic bags for crushed ice
- 3-inch and 4-inch elastic wraps
- Triangular bandages
- Sterile gauze pads—3-inch and 4-inch squares
- Saline solution for eyes
- Contact lens case
- Mirror
- Penlight
- Tongue depressors
- Cotton swabs
- Butterfly strips
- Bandage strips—assorted sizes

- Alcohol or peroxide
- Antibacterial soap
- First aid cream or antibacterial ointment
- Petroleum jelly
- Tape adherent and tape remover
- 1 1/2-inch white athletic tape
- Prewrap
- Sterile gauze rolls
- Insect sting kit
- Safety pins
- 1/8-inch, 1/4-inch, and 1/2-inch foam rubber
- Disposable surgical gloves
- Thermometer

Emergency Plan

An emergency plan is the final step in preparing to take appropriate action for severe or serious injuries. The plan calls for three steps:

1. **Evaluate the injured player.** Your CPR and first aid training will guide you here.

2. **Call the appropriate medical personnel.** If possible, delegate the responsibility of seeking medical help to another calm and responsible adult who is on hand for all practices and games. Write out a list of emergency phone numbers and keep it with you at practices and games. Include the following phone numbers:

- Rescue unit
- Police
- Hospital
- Fire department
- Physician

Take each athlete's emergency information to every practice and game (see appendix B). This information includes the person to contact in case of an emergency, what types of medications the athlete is using, what types of drugs he or she is allergic to, and so on.

Give an emergency response card (see appendix C) to the contact person calling for emergency assistance. This provides the information the contact person needs to convey and will help keep the person calm, knowing that everything he or she needs to communicate is on the card. Also complete an injury report form (see appendix A) and keep it on file for any injury that occurs.

3. **Provide first aid.** If medical personnel are not on hand at the time of the injury, you should provide first aid care to the extent of your qualifications. Again, while your CPR and first aid training will guide you here, the following are important guidelines:

- Do not move the injured athlete if the injury is to the head, neck, or back; if a large joint (ankle, knee, elbow, shoulder) is dislocated; or if the pelvis, a rib, or an arm or leg is fractured.
- Calm the injured athlete and keep others away from him or her as much as possible.
- Evaluate whether the athlete's breathing is stopped or irregular, and if necessary, clear the airway with your fingers.
- Administer artificial respiration if the athlete's breathing has stopped. Administer CPR if the athlete's circulation has stopped.
- Remain with the athlete until medical personnel arrive.

Emergency Steps

Your emergency plan should follow this sequence:

1. Check the athlete's level of consciousness.
2. Send a contact person to call the appropriate medical personnel and to call the athlete's parents.
3. Send someone to wait for the rescue team and direct them to the injured athlete.
4. Assess the injury.
5. Administer first aid.
6. Assist emergency medical personnel in preparing the athlete for transportation to a medical facility.
7. Appoint someone to go with the athlete if the parents are not available. This person should be responsible, calm, and familiar with the athlete. Assistant coaches or parents are best for this job.
8. Complete an injury report form while the incident is fresh in your mind (see appendix A).

Taking Appropriate Action

Proper CPR and first aid training, a well-stocked first aid kit, and an emergency plan help prepare you to take appropriate action when an injury occurs. We spoke in the previous section about the importance of providing first aid *to the extent of your qualifications.* Don't "play doctor" with injuries; sort out minor injuries that you can treat from those for which you need to call for medical assistance. Next we'll look at taking the appropriate action for minor injuries and more serious injuries.

Minor Injuries

Although no injury seems minor to the person experiencing it, most injuries are neither life-threatening nor severe enough to restrict participation. When such injuries occur, you can take an active role in their initial treatment.

Scrapes and Cuts. When one of your players has an open wound, the first thing you should do is put on a pair of disposable surgical gloves or some other effective blood barrier. Then follow these four steps:

1. *Stop the bleeding* by applying direct pressure with a clean dressing to the wound and elevating it. The player may be able to apply this pressure while you put on your gloves. Do not remove the dressing if it becomes soaked with blood. Instead, place an additional dressing on top of the one already in place. If bleeding continues, elevate the injured area above the heart and maintain pressure.

2. *Cleanse the wound* thoroughly once the bleeding is controlled. A good rinsing with a forceful stream of water, and perhaps light scrubbing with soap, will help prevent infection.

3. *Protect the wound* with sterile gauze or a bandage strip. If the player continues to participate, apply protective padding over the injured area.

4. *Remove and dispose of gloves* carefully to prevent you or anyone else from coming into contact with blood.

For bloody noses not associated with serious facial injury, have the athlete sit and lean slightly forward. Then pinch the player's nostrils shut. If the bleeding continues after several minutes, or if the athlete has a history of nosebleeds, seek medical assistance.

Treating Bloody Injuries

You shouldn't let a fear of acquired immune deficiency syndrome (AIDS) stop you from helping a player. You are only at risk if you allow contaminated blood to come in contact with an open wound, so the surgical disposable gloves that you wear will protect you from AIDS should one of your players carry this disease. Check with the director of your organization for more information about protecting yourself and your participants from AIDS.

Strains and Sprains. The physical demands of lacrosse practices and games often result in injury to the muscles or tendons (strains) or to the ligaments (sprains). When your players suffer minor strains or sprains, immediately apply the PRICE method of injury care:

P – Protect the athlete and injured body part from further danger or trauma.

R – Rest the area to avoid further damage and foster healing.

I – Ice the area to reduce swelling and pain.

C – Compress the area by securing an ice bag in place with an elastic wrap.

E – Elevate the injury above heart level to keep the blood from pooling in the area.

Bumps and Bruises. Inevitably, lacrosse players make contact with each other and with the ground. If the force applied to a body part at impact is great enough, a bump or bruise will result. Many players continue playing with such sore spots, but if the bump or bruise is large and painful, you should act appropriately. Use the PRICE method for injury care and monitor the injury. If swelling, discoloration, and pain have lessened, the player may resume participation with protective padding; if not, the player should be examined by a physician.

Serious Injuries

Head, neck, and back injuries; fractures; and injuries that cause a player to lose consciousness are among a class of injuries that you cannot and should not try to treat yourself. In these cases you should follow the emergency plan outlined on pages 25 to 26. We do want to examine more closely your role, however, in preventing and handling two heat illnesses: heat exhaustion and heatstroke.

⊙ **Heat Exhaustion.** Heat exhaustion is a shocklike condition caused by dehydration and electrolyte depletion. Symptoms include headache, nausea, dizziness, chills, fatigue, and extreme thirst. Profuse sweating is a key sign of heat exhaustion. Other signs include pale, cool, and clammy skin; rapid, weak pulse; loss of coordination; and dilated pupils.

A player suffering from heat exhaustion should rest in a cool, shaded area; drink cool water; and have ice applied to the neck, back, or abdomen to help cool the body. You may have to administer CPR if necessary or send for emergency medical assistance if the athlete doesn't recover or his or her condition worsens. Under no conditions should the athlete return to activity that day or before he or she regains all the weight lost through sweat. If the player had to see a physician, he or she shouldn't return to the team until he or she has a written release from the physician.

⊙ **Heatstroke.** Heatstroke is a life-threatening condition in which the body stops sweating and body temperature rises dangerously high. It occurs when dehydration causes a malfunction in the body's temperature control center in the brain. Symptoms include the feeling of being on fire (extremely hot), nausea, confusion, irritability, and fatigue. Signs include hot, dry, and flushed or red skin (this is a key sign); lack of sweat; rapid pulse; rapid breathing; constricted pupils; vomiting; diarrhea; and possibly seizures, unconsciousness, or respiratory or cardiac arrest.

Send for emergency medical assistance immediately and have the player rest in a cool, shaded area. Remove excess clothing and equipment from the player, and cool the player's body with cool, wet towels or by pouring cool water over him or her. Apply ice packs to the armpits, neck, back, abdomen, and between the legs. If the player is conscious, have him or her drink cool water. If the player is unconscious, place the player on his or her side to allow fluids and vomit to drain from the mouth.

An athlete who has suffered heatstroke may not return to the team until he or she has a written release from a physician.

Protecting Yourself

When one of your players is injured, naturally your first concern is his or her well-being. Your feelings for youngsters, after all, are what made you decide to coach. Unfortunately, there is something else that you must consider: Can you be held liable for the injury?

From a legal standpoint, a coach has nine duties to fulfill. We've discussed all but planning in this chapter. (See chapter 5 for developing practice plans and chapters 9 and 12 for guidance on season planning.) The following is a summary of your legal duties:

1. Provide a safe environment.
2. Properly plan the activity.
3. Provide adequate and proper equipment.

4. Match, or equate, athletes.

5. Warn of inherent risks in the sport.

6. Supervise the activity closely.

7. Evaluate athletes for injury or incapacitation.

8. Know emergency procedures and first aid.

9. Keep adequate records.

Keep records of your season plan and practice plans and of players' injuries. Season and practice plans come in handy when you need evidence that players have been taught certain skills, and injury reports offer protection against unfounded lawsuits. Hold onto these records for several years so that an "old injury" of a former player doesn't come back to haunt you.

In addition to fulfilling these nine legal duties, you should check your organization's insurance coverage and your personal insurance coverage to make sure these policies will protect you from liability.

chapter 4

The Games Approach to Coaching Lacrosse

Do you remember how as a kid you were taught by adults to play a sport, either in an organized sport program or physical education class? They probably taught you the basic skills using a series of drills that, if the truth be known, you found very boring. As you began to learn the basic skills, they eventually taught you the tactics of the game, showing you when to use these skills in various game situations. Do you remember how impatient you became during what seemed to be endless instruction and how much you just wanted to play? Well, forget the traditional approach to teaching sports.

Now can you recall learning a sport by playing with a group of your friends in the neighborhood? You didn't learn the basic skills first; no time for that. You began playing immediately. If you didn't know the basic things to do, your friends told you quickly during the game so that they could keep playing. Try to remember, because we're going to ask you to use a very similar approach to teaching lacrosse to young people; it's called the games approach, an approach we think knocks the socks off the traditional approach.

On the surface, it would seem to make sense to introduce lacrosse by first teaching the basic skills of the sport and then the tactics of the game, but we've discovered that this approach has disadvantages. First, it teaches the skills of the sport out of the context of the game. Kids may learn to throw, catch, shoot, or check, but they find it difficult to use these skills in the real game. This is because they do not yet understand the fundamental tactics of lacrosse and do not appreciate how best to use their newfound skills.

Second, learning skills by doing drills outside of the context of the game is so-o-o-o boring. The single biggest turnoff about adults teaching kids sports is that we overorganize the instruction and deprive kids of their intrinsic desire to play the game.

As a coach we're asking that you teach lacrosse the games approach way. Clear the traditional approach out of your mind. Once you fully understand the games approach, you'll quickly see its superiority in teaching lacrosse. Not only will kids learn the game better, but you and your players will have much more fun. And as a bonus, you'll have far fewer discipline problems.

With the games approach to teaching lacrosse, we begin with a game. This will be a modified and much smaller game designed to suit the age and ability of the players. As the kids play in these "mini" games, you can begin to help them understand the nature of the game and to appreciate simple concepts of positioning and tactics. When your players understand what they must do in the game, they are then eager to develop the skills to play the game. Now that players are motivated to learn the skills, you can demonstrate the skills of the game, practice using gamelike drills, and provide individual instruction by identifying players' errors and helping to correct them.

In the traditional approach to teaching sports, players do this:

Learn the skill → Learn the tactics → Play the game

In the games approach players do this:

Play the game → Learn the tactics → Learn the skill

In the past we have placed too much emphasis on the learning of skills and not enough on learning how to play skillfully—that is, how to use those skills in competition. The games approach, in contrast, emphasizes learning what to do first, then how to do it. Moreover—and this is a really important point—the games approach lets kids discover what to do in the game not by you telling them but by their experiencing it. What you do as an effective coach is help them discover what they've experienced.

In contrast to the "skill-drill-kill the enthusiasm" approach, the games approach is a guided discovery method of teaching. It empowers your kids to solve the problems that arise in the game, and that's a big part of the fun in learning a game.

Now let's look more closely at the games approach to see the four-step process for teaching lacrosse:

1. Play a modified lacrosse game.
2. Help the players discover what they need to do to play the game successfully.
3. Teach the skills of the game.
4. Practice the skills in another game.

Step 1. Play a Modified Lacrosse Game

Okay, it's the first day of practice; some of the kids are eager to get started, while others are obviously apprehensive. Some have rarely caught a ball, most don't know the rules, and none of them know the positions in lacrosse. What do you do?

If you use the traditional approach, you start with a little warm-up activity, then line the players up for a simple cradling drill and go from there. With the games approach, you begin by playing a modified game that is developmentally appropriate for the level of the players and also designed to focus on learning a specific part of the game.

Modifying the game emphasizes a limited number of situations in the game. This is one way you "guide" your players to discover certain tactics in the game.

For instance, you have your players play a 2-v-2 (two players versus two players) game in a 20- by-20-yard playing area. The objective of the game is to make four passes before attempting to score. Playing the game this way forces players to think about what they have to do to keep possession of the ball.

Step 2. Help the Players Discover What They Need to Do

As your players are playing the game, look for the right spot to "freeze" the action, step in, and hold a brief question-and-answer session to discuss problems they are having in carrying out the goals of the game.

You don't need to pop in on the first miscue, but if they repeat the same types of mental or physical mistakes a few times in a row, step in and ask them questions that relate to the aim of the game and the necessary skills required. The best time to interrupt the game is when you notice that they are having trouble carrying out the main goal, or aim, of the game. By stopping the game, freezing action, and asking questions, you'll help them understand

⊙ what the aim of the game is,

⊙ what they must do to achieve that aim, and

⊙ what skills they must use to achieve that aim.

For example, your players are playing a game in which the objective is to make four passes before attempting to score, but they are having trouble doing so. Interrupt the action and ask the following questions:

Coach: What are you supposed to do in this game?

Players: Pass the ball four times before scoring.

Coach: What does your team have to do to keep the ball for four passes in a row?

Players: Pass the ball.

Coach: Yes, and what else?

Players: You have to be able to receive the pass, too.

Coach: Okay. You have to be able to pass the ball and get the ball when it's passed. Why don't we practice passing the ball and catching the pass?

Through the modified game and skillful questioning on your part, your players realize that accurate passing and receiving skills are essential to their success in maintaining possession. Just as important, rather than *telling* them that passing and receiving skills are critical, you lead them to that discovery through a well-designed modified game and through questions. The questioning that leads to players' discovery is a crucial part of the games approach. Essentially you'll be asking your players—usually literally—"What do you need to do to succeed in this situation?"

Asking the right questions is a very important part of your teaching. At first asking questions will be difficult because your players have little or no experience with the game. And if you've learned sports through the traditional approach, you'll be tempted to tell your players how to play the game and not waste time asking them questions. Resist this powerful temptation to tell them what to do, and especially don't do so before they begin to play the game.

If your players have trouble understanding what to do, phrase your questions to let them choose between one option versus another. For example, if you ask them, "What's the fastest way to get the ball down the field?" and get answers such as "Pass it" or "Run with it," then ask, "Is it passing or running with it?"

Sometimes players simply need to have more time playing the game, or you may need to modify the game further so that it is even easier for them to discover what they are to do. It'll take more patience on your part, but it's a powerful way to learn. Don't be reluctant to change the numbers in the teams or some aspect of the structure of the game to aid this discovery. In fact, we advocate playing "lopsided" games (e.g., 3 v 1, 3 v 2) in the second game of each practice; we'll explain this concept in a moment.

Step 3. Teach the Skills of the Game

Immediately following the question-and-answer session you will begin a skill practice, which is Step 3 of the four-step process. Only when your players recognize the skills they need to be successful in the game do you want to teach the specific skills through focused drills. This is when you use a more traditional approach to teaching sport skills, the "IDEA" approach, which we will describe in chapter 5.

Step 4. Practice the Skills in Another Game

Once the players have practiced the skill, you then put them in another game situation—this time a lopsided game (e.g., 3 v 1, 3 v 2). Why use lopsided teams? It's simple: As a coach, you want your players to experience success as they're learning skills. The best way to experience success early on is to create an advantage for the players. This makes it more likely that, for instance, in a 3 v 1 game, your three offensive players will be able to make four passes before attempting to score.

A good way to practice is to use even-sided games (e.g., 3 v 3, 6 v 6) in the first game and lopsided games in the second game. The reasoning behind this is to introduce players to a situation similar to what they will experience in competition and to let them discover the challenges they face in performing the necessary skill. Then you teach them the skill, have them practice it, and put them back in another game—this time a lopsided one to give them a greater chance of experiencing success.

As players improve their skills you don't need to use lopsided games. At a certain point having a 3 v 1 or 6 v 3 advantage will be too easy for the kids and won't challenge them to hone their skills. At that point you lessen the advantage to, say, 3 v 2 or 6 v 4, or you may even decide that they're ready to practice the skill in even-sided competition. The key is to set up situations where your athletes experience success, yet are challenged in doing so. This will take careful monitoring on your part, but having kids play lopsided games as they are learning skills is a very effective way of helping them learn and improve.

And that's the games approach. Your players will get to *play* more in practice, and once they learn how the skills fit into their performance and enjoyment of the game, they'll be more motivated to work on those skills, which will help them to be successful.

chapter 5

Teaching and Shaping Skills

Coaching lacrosse is about teaching tactics, skills, fitness, values, and other useful things. It's also about "coaching" players before, during, and after contests. Teaching and coaching are closely related, but there are important differences. In this chapter we'll focus on principles of teaching, especially on teaching lacrosse skills. But many of the principles we'll discuss apply to teaching tactics, fitness concepts, and values as well. (Most of the other important teaching principles deal with communication, covered in chapter 2.) Then in chapter 6 we'll discuss the principles of coaching, which refer to your leadership activities during contests.

Teaching Lacrosse Skills

Many people believe that the only qualification needed to teach a skill is to have performed it. It's helpful to have performed it, but there is much more than that to teaching successfully. And even if you haven't performed the skill before, you can still learn to teach successfully with the useful acronym IDEA:

I – Introduce the skill.

D – Demonstrate the skill.

E – Explain the skill.

A – Attend to players practicing the skill.

These are the basic steps of good teaching. Now we'll explain each step in greater detail.

Introduce the Skill

Players, especially young and inexperienced ones, need to know what skill they are learning and why they are learning it. You should therefore take these three steps every time you introduce a skill to your players:

1. Get your players' attention.
2. Name the skill.
3. Explain the importance of the skill.

Get Your Players' Attention

Because youngsters are easily distracted, use some method to get their attention. Some coaches use interesting news items or stories. Others use jokes. And still others simply project enthusiasm to get their players to listen. Whatever method you use, speak slightly above the normal volume and look your players in the eye when you speak.

Also, position players so that they can see and hear you. Arrange the players in two or three evenly spaced rows, facing you. (Make sure they aren't looking into the sun or at some distracting activity.) Then ask if all of them can see you before you begin.

Name the Skill

Although you might mention other common names for the skill, decide which one you'll use and stick with it. This will help avoid confusion and enhance communication among your players.

Explain the Importance of the Skill

Although the importance of a skill may be apparent to you, your players may be less able to see how the skill will help them become better lacrosse players. Offer them a reason for learning the skill and describe how the skill relates to more advanced skills.

> *The most difficult aspect of coaching is this: Coaches must learn to let athletes learn. Sport skills should be taught so they have meaning to the child, not just meaning to the coach.*
> —Rainer Martens,
> founder of the American Sport Education Program

Demonstrate the Skill

The demonstration step is the most important part of teaching sport skills to players who may never have done anything closely resembling the skill. They need a picture, not just words. They need to see how the skill is performed.

If you are unable to perform the skill correctly, have an assistant coach, one of your players, or someone else more skilled perform the demonstration. These tips will help make your demonstrations more effective:

- Use correct form.
- Demonstrate the skill several times.
- Slow down the action, if possible, during one or two performances, so players can see every movement involved in the skill.
- Perform the skill at different angles, so your players can get a full perspective of it.
- Demonstrate the skill with both the right and the left hands.

Explain the Skill

Players learn more effectively when they're given a brief explanation of the skill along with the demonstration. Use simple terms and, if possible, relate the skill to previously learned skills. Ask your players whether they understand your description. A good technique is to ask the team to repeat your explanation. Ask questions like, "What are you going to do first?" and "Then what?" Watch for when players look confused or uncertain, and repeat your explanation and demonstration at those points. If possible, use different words, so your players get a chance to try to understand the skill from a different perspective.

Complex skills often are better understood when they are explained in more manageable parts. For instance, if you want to teach your players how to change direction when they cradle the ball, you might take the following steps:

1. Show them a correct performance of the entire skill, and explain its function in lacrosse.
2. Break down the skill and point out its component parts to your players.
3. Have players perform each of the component skills you have already taught them, such as cradling while dodging or switching hands while keeping their heads up.
4. After players have demonstrated their ability to perform the separate parts of the skill in sequence, reexplain the entire skill.
5. Have players practice the skill in gamelike conditions.

One caution: Young players have short attention spans, and a long demonstration or explanation of the skill will bore them. So spend no more than a few minutes altogether on the introduction, demonstration, and explanation phases. Then get the players active in a game that calls on them to perform the skill. The total IDEA should be completed in 10 minutes or less, followed by games in which players practice the skill.

Attend to Players Practicing the Skill

If the skill you selected was within your players' capabilities and you have done an effective job of introducing, demonstrating, and explaining it, your players should be ready to attempt the skill. Some players may need to be physically guided through the movements during their first few attempts. Walking unsure athletes through the skill in this way will help them gain confidence to perform the skill on their own.

Your teaching duties don't end when all your athletes have demonstrated that they understand how to perform the skill. In fact, a significant part of your teaching will involve observing closely the hit-and-miss trial performances of your players. In the next section we'll guide you in shaping players' skills, and then we'll help you learn how to detect and correct errors, using positive feedback. Keep in mind that your feedback will have a great influence on your players' motivation to practice and improve their performances.

Remember, too, that players need individual instruction. So set aside a time before, during, or after practice to give individual help.

Helping Players Improve Skills

After you have successfully taught your players the fundamentals of a skill, your focus will be on helping them improve that skill. Players will learn skills and improve on them at different rates, so don't get too frustrated. Instead, help them improve by shaping their skills and detecting and correcting errors.

Shaping Players' Skills

One of your principal teaching duties is to reward positive behavior—in terms of successful skill execution—when you see it. A player makes a good pass in practice, and you immediately say, "That's the way to pass to the target! Good follow-through!" This, plus a smile and a "thumbs-up" gesture, go a long way toward reinforcing that technique in the player.

However, sometimes you may have a long, dry spell before you have any correct technique to reinforce. It's difficult to reward players when they aren't executing skills correctly. How can you shape their skills if this is the case?

Shaping skills takes practice on your players' part and patience on your part. Expect your players to make errors. Telling the player who made the great pass that she did a good job doesn't ensure that she'll make that pass the next time. Seeing inconsistency in your players' techniques can be frustrating. It's even more challenging to stay positive when your athletes repeatedly perform a skill incorrectly or lack enthusiasm for learning. It can certainly be frustrating to see athletes who seemingly don't heed your advice and continue to make the same mistakes. And when the athletes don't seem to care, you may wonder why you should.

Please know that it is normal to get frustrated at times when teaching skills. Nevertheless, part of successful coaching is controlling this frustration. Instead of getting upset, use these six guidelines for shaping skills:

1. Think small initially. Reward the first signs of behavior that approximate what you want. Then reward closer and closer approximations of the desired behavior. In short, use your reward power to shape the behavior you seek.

2. Break skills into small steps. For instance, in learning to cradle, one of your players does well in watching for defenders around the ball, but he's careless with the ball and doesn't effectively shield the ball from defenders. He often has the crosse too far away from him as he

cradles, or he runs too fast and loses control of the ball. Reinforce the correct technique of watching for defenders, and teach him how to keep the ball and crosse close to his body. When he masters that, focus on getting him to run at a speed at which he can maintain possession of the ball.

3. Develop one component of a skill at a time. Don't try to shape two components of a skill at once. For example, in receiving a ball in the crosse, players must first "give" with the ball and then control the ball by cradling. Players should focus first on one aspect ("giving" with the ball), then on the other (controlling the ball by beginning to cradle). Athletes who have problems mastering a skill often do so because they're trying to improve two or more components at once. Help these athletes to isolate a single component.

4. As athletes become more proficient at a skill, reinforce them only occasionally and only for the best examples of the skill behavior. By focusing only on the best examples, you will help them continue to improve once they've mastered the basics.

5. When athletes are trying to master a new skill, temporarily relax your standards for how you reward them. As they focus on the new skill or attempt to integrate it with other skills, the old, well-learned skills may temporarily degenerate.

6. If, however, a well-learned skill degenerates for long, you may need to restore it by going back to the basics.

Coaches often have more skilled players provide feedback to teammates as they practice skills. This can be effective, but proceed with caution: You must tell the skilled players exactly what to look for when their teammates are performing the skills. You must also tell them the corrections for the common errors of that skill.

We've looked at how to guide your athletes as they learn skills. Now let's look at another critical teaching principle that you should employ as you're shaping skills: detecting and correcting errors.

Detecting and Correcting Errors

Good coaches recognize that athletes make two types of errors: learning errors and performance errors. *Learning errors* are ones that occur because athletes don't know how to perform a skill; that is, they have not yet developed the correct motor program in the brain to perform a particular skill. *Performance errors* are made not because athletes don't know how to do the skill but because they make a mistake in executing what they do know. There is no easy way to know whether a player is making learning or performance errors. Part of the art of coaching is being able to sort out which type of error each mistake is.

The process of helping your athletes correct errors begins with your observing and evaluating their performances to determine if the mistakes are learning or performance errors. For performance errors, you need to look for the reasons that your athletes are not performing as well as they know how. If the mistakes are learning errors, then you need to help them learn the skill, which is the focus of this section.

There is no substitute for knowing skills well in correcting learning errors. The better you understand a skill—not only how it is done correctly but also what causes learning errors—the more helpful you will be in correcting mistakes.

One of the most common coaching mistakes is to provide inaccurate feedback and advice on how to correct errors. Don't rush into error correction; wrong feedback or poor advice will hurt the learning process more than no feedback or advice. If you are uncertain about the cause of the problem or how to correct it, continue to observe and analyze until you are more sure. As a rule, you should see the error repeated several times before attempting to correct it.

Correct One Error at a Time

Suppose Jill, one of your attack players, is having trouble with her shooting. She's doing most things well, but you notice that she's releasing the ball too early, stopping her follow-through short. Consequently, she is having trouble with accuracy and power. What do you do?

First, decide which error to correct first, because athletes learn more effectively when they attempt to correct one error at a time. Determine whether one error is causing the other; if so, have the athlete correct that error first, because it may eliminate the other error. In Jill's case, correcting the follow-through will bring improvement to the shot release.

Use Positive Feedback to Correct Errors

The positive approach to correcting errors includes emphasizing what to do instead of what not to do. Use compliments, praise, rewards, and encouragement to correct errors. Acknowledge correct performance as well as efforts to improve. By using the positive approach, you can help your athletes feel good about themselves and promote a strong desire to achieve.

When you're working with one athlete at a time, the positive approach to correcting errors includes four steps:

1. Praise effort and correct performance.
2. Give simple and precise feedback to correct errors.

3. Make sure the athlete understands your feedback.

4. Provide an environment that motivates the athlete to improve.

Let's take a brief look at each step.

Step 1: Praise Effort and Correct Performance. Praise your athlete for trying to perform a skill correctly and for performing any parts of it correctly. Praise the athlete immediately after he or she performs the skill, if possible. Keep the praise simple: "Good try," "Way to hustle," or "Good form," "Good extension," "That's the way to follow through." You can also use nonverbal feedback, such as smiling, clapping your hands, or any facial or body expression that shows approval.

Make sure you're sincere with your praise. Don't indicate that an athlete's effort was good when it wasn't. Usually an athlete knows when he or she has made a sincere effort to perform the skill correctly and perceives undeserved praise for what it is—untruthful feedback to make him or her feel good. Likewise, don't indicate that a player's performance was correct when it wasn't.

Step 2: Give Simple and Precise Feedback. Don't burden a player with a long or detailed explanation of how to correct an error. Give just enough feedback so that the player can correct one error at a time. Before giving feedback, recognize that some athletes will readily accept it immediately after the error; and others will respond better if you slightly delay the correction.

For errors that are complicated to explain and difficult to correct, try the following:

- Explain and demonstrate what the athlete should have done. Do not demonstrate what the athlete did wrong.
- Explain the cause or causes of the error if this isn't obvious.
- Explain why you are recommending the correction you have selected if it's not obvious.

Step 3: Make Sure the Athlete Understands Your Feedback. If the athlete doesn't understand your feedback, he or she won't be able to correct the error. Ask him or her to repeat the feedback and to explain and demonstrate how it will be used. If the athlete can't do this, be patient and present your feedback again. Then have the athlete repeat the feedback after you're finished.

Step 4: Provide an Environment That Motivates the Athlete to Improve. Your players won't always be able to correct their errors immediately even if they do understand your feedback. Encourage them to "hang tough" and stick with it when corrections are difficult or they seem discouraged. For more difficult corrections, remind them that it will take time and the improvement will happen only if they work at it. Look to encourage players with low self-confidence. Saying something like, "You were cradling at a much better speed today; with practice, you'll be able to keep the ball and crosse closer to you and shield it from defenders," can motivate a player to continue to refine his or her cradling skills.

Some athletes need to be more motivated to improve. Others may be very self-motivated and need little help from you in this area at all; with them you can practically ignore Step 4 when correcting an error. While motivation comes from within, look to provide an environment of positive instruction and encouragement to help your athletes improve.

A final note on correcting errors: Team sports such as lacrosse provide unique challenges in this endeavor. How do you provide individual feedback in a group setting using a positive approach? Instead of yelling across the field to correct an error (and embarrassing the player), substitute for the player who erred. Then make the correction on the sidelines. This type of feedback has three advantages:

⊙ The player will be more receptive to the one-on-one feedback.

⊙ The other players are still active, still practicing skills, and unable to hear your discussion.

⊙ Because the rest of the team is still playing, you'll feel compelled to make your comments simple and concise, which, as we've said, is more helpful to the player.

This doesn't mean you can't use the team setting to give specific, positive feedback. You can do so to emphasize correct group and individual performances. Use this team feedback approach *only* for positive statements, though. Keep any negative feedback for individual discussions.

Developing Practice Plans

You will need to create practice plans for each season. Each practice plan should contain the following sections:

⊙ Purpose

⊙ Equipment

⊙ Plan

Purpose sections focus on what you want to teach your players during each practice; they outline your main theme for each practice. The purpose should be drawn from your season plan (see chapters 9 and 12). Equipment sections note what you'll need to have on hand for that practice. Plan sections outline what you will do during each practice session. Each practice consists of these elements:

⊙ Warm-up
⊙ Game
⊙ Skill practices
⊙ Game
⊙ Cool-down and wrap-up

You'll begin each session with about five minutes of warm-up activities. Then you'll have your players play a modified lacrosse game (look in chapters 8 and 11 for suggested games). You'll look for your cue to interrupt that game—your cue being when players are having problems with carrying out the basic goal or aim of the game. At this point you'll "freeze" the action, keeping the players where they are, and ask brief questions about the tactical problems the players encountered and what skills they need to solve those problems. (Review chapter 4 for more on interrupting a game and holding a question-and-answer session.)

Then you'll teach the skill the players need to acquire to successfully execute the tactic. During skill practice you'll use the IDEA approach:

⊙ Introduce the skill.
⊙ Demonstrate the skill.
⊙ Explain the skill.
⊙ Attend to players practicing the skill.

Your introduction, demonstration, and explanation of a skill should take no more than two to three minutes; then you'll attend to players and provide teaching cues or further demonstration as necessary as they practice the skill.

After the skill practices, you will usually have the athletes play another game or two to let them use the skills they have just learned and to understand them in the context of a game. During games and skill practices, emphasize the importance of every player on the field moving and being involved in every play, whether they will be directly handling the ball or backing up their teammates. No player on the field should be standing around.

The plan section continues with a cool-down and stretch. Following this you'll wrap up the practice with a few summary comments and remind them of the next practice or game day.

The games in chapters 8 and 11 include suggestions to help you modify them. These suggestions will help you keep practices fun and provide activities for players with varying skill levels.

Although practicing using the games approach should reduce the need for discipline, there will be times when you'll have to deal with players who are misbehaving in practice. In the next section we'll help you handle these situations.

Dealing With Misbehavior

Athletes will misbehave at times; it's only natural. Following are two ways you can respond to misbehavior: through extinction or discipline.

Extinction

Ignoring a misbehavior—neither rewarding nor disciplining it—is called *extinction*. This can be effective under certain circumstances. In some situations, disciplining young people's misbehavior only encourages them to act up further because of the recognition they get. Ignoring misbehavior teaches youngsters that it is not worth your attention.

Sometimes, though, you cannot wait for a behavior to fizzle out. When players cause danger to themselves or others or disrupt the activities of others, you need to take immediate action. Tell the offending player that the behavior must stop and that discipline will follow if it doesn't. If the athlete doesn't stop misbehaving after the warning, discipline.

Extinction also doesn't work well when a misbehavior is self-rewarding. For example, you may be able to keep from grimacing if a youngster kicks you in the shin, but he or she still knows you were hurt. Therein lies the reward. In these circumstances, it is also necessary to discipline the player for the undesirable behavior.

Extinction works best in situations in which players are seeking recognition through mischievous behaviors, clowning, or grandstanding. Usually, if you are patient, their failure to get your attention will cause the behavior to disappear.

However, be alert so that you don't extinguish desirable behavior. When youngsters do something well, they expect to be positively reinforced. Not rewarding them will likely cause them to discontinue the desired behavior.

Discipline

Some educators say we should never discipline young people but should only reinforce their positive behaviors. They argue that discipline does not work, creates hostility, and sometimes develops avoidance behaviors that may be more unwholesome than the original problem behavior. It is true that discipline does not always work and that it can create problems when used ineffectively, but when used appropriately, discipline is effective in eliminating undesirable behaviors without creating other undesirable consequences. You must use discipline effectively, because it is impossible to guide athletes using positive reinforcement and extinction only. Discipline is part of the positive approach when these guidelines are followed:

- Discipline in a corrective way to help athletes improve now and in the future. Don't discipline to retaliate and make yourself feel better.
- Impose discipline in an impersonal way when athletes break team rules or otherwise misbehave. Shouting at or scolding athletes indicates that your attitude is one of revenge.
- Once a good rule has been agreed on, ensure that athletes who violate it experience the unpleasant consequences of their misbehavior. Don't wave discipline threateningly over their heads. Just do it, but warn an athlete once before disciplining.
- Be consistent in administering discipline.
- Don't discipline using consequences that may cause you guilt. If you can't think of an appropriate consequence right away, tell the player you will talk with him or her after you think about it. You might consider involving the player in designing a consequence.
- Once the discipline is completed, don't make athletes feel they are "in the doghouse." Make them feel that they're valued members of the team again.
- Make sure that what you think is discipline isn't perceived by the athlete as positive reinforcement; for instance, keeping a player out of doing a certain drill or portion of the practice may be just what the athlete desires.
- Never discipline athletes for making errors when they are playing.
- Never use physical activity—running laps or doing push-ups—as discipline. To do so only causes athletes to resent physical activity, something we want them to learn to enjoy throughout their lives.
- Discipline sparingly. Constant discipline and criticism cause athletes to turn their interests elsewhere and to resent you as well.

chapter 6

Game-Day Coaching

Contests provide the opportunity for your players to show what they've learned in practice. Just as your players' focus shifts on contest days from learning and practicing to *competing*, so your focus shifts from teaching skills to coaching players as they perform those skills in contests. Of course, the contest is a teaching opportunity as well, but the focus is on performing what has been previously learned.

In the last chapter you learned how to teach your players lacrosse tactics and skills; in this chapter we'll help you coach your players as they execute those tactics and skills in contests. We'll provide important coaching principles that will guide you throughout the game day—before, during, and after the contest.

Before the Contest

Just as you need a practice plan for what you're going to do each practice, you need a game plan for what to do on the day of a game. Many inexperienced coaches focus only on how they will coach during the contest itself, but your preparations to coach should include details that begin well before the first play of the game. In fact, your preparations should begin during the practice before the contest.

Preparations at Practice

During the practice a day or two before the next contest, you should do two things (besides practicing tactics and skills) to prepare your players: Decide on any specific team tactics that you want to employ, and discuss pregame particulars such as what to eat before the game, what to wear, and when to be at the field.

Deciding Team Tactics

Some coaches see themselves as great military strategists guiding their young warriors to victory on the battlefield. These coaches burn the midnight oil as they devise a complex plan of attack. There are several things wrong with this approach, but we'll point out two errors in terms of deciding team tactics:

1. The decision on team tactics should be made with input from players.
2. Team tactics at this level don't need to be complex.

Perhaps you guessed right on the second point but were surprised by the first. Why should you include your players in deciding tactics? Isn't that the coach's role?

It's the coach's role to help youngsters grow through the sport experience. Giving your athletes input here helps them to learn the game. It gets them involved at a planning level that often is reserved solely for the coach. It gives them a feeling of ownership; they're not just "carrying out orders" of the coach. They're executing the plan of attack that was jointly decided. Youngsters who have a say in how they approach a task often respond with more enthusiasm and motivation.

Don't dampen that enthusiasm and motivation by concocting tactics that are too complex. Keep tactics simple, especially at the younger levels. Focus on providing support, moving continuously, spreading out the attack, and passing and shooting often.

As you become more familiar with your team's tendencies and abilities, help them focus on specific tactics that will help them play better. For example, if your team has a tendency to stand around and watch the action, emphasize moving more and spreading out the attack. If they are active and moving throughout the game but not in any cohesive fashion, focus them on providing support by using the triangle concept (see chapter 11).

If you're coaching 12- to 14-year-olds, you might institute certain plays that your team has practiced. These plays should take advantage of your players' strengths. Again, give the players some input into what plays might be employed in a game.

Discussing Precontest Particulars

Players need to know what to do before a contest: what they should eat on game day and when, what clothing they should wear to the game, what equipment they should bring, and what time they should arrive at the field. Discuss these particulars with them at the practice before a contest. Here are guidelines for discussing these issues:

Pregame Meal. Carbohydrates are easily digested and absorbed and are a ready source of fuel. Players should eat a high-carbohydrate meal ideally about three to four hours before a game to allow the stomach to empty completely. This won't be possible for games held in early morning; in this case, athletes should still eat food high in carbohydrates, such as an English muffin, toast, or cereal, but not so much that their stomachs are full. In addition, athletes' pregame meals shouldn't include foods that are spicy or high in fat content.

Equipment. If you have a girls' team, instruct all players to bring their mouthguards, and make sure each player has a stick and the team has several balls. You may also want to require players to wear safety equipment such as close-fitting gloves, soft headgear, and eye guards or safety goggles that meet American Society for Testing and Materials (ASTM) standards.

Goalkeepers must wear protective equipment, at least a face mask and helmet, a throat protector, and a chest protector. They should wear padded gloves and shin protection; they may also wear additional padding on hands, arms, legs, shoulders, and chest. (Padding may not be more than one inch thick.)

If you have a boys' team, instruct players to wear a protective helmet, padded gloves, arm pads, shoulder pads, a mouthguard, an athletic supporter, and a protective cup. Some players may want to wear rib pads for additional protection. Make sure each player has a stick and the team has several balls.

Time to Arrive. Your players will need to adequately warm up before a game, so instruct them to arrive 20 minutes before a game to go through a team warm-up (see "The Warm-Up" later in this chapter).

Facilities, Equipment, and Support Personnel

Although the site coordinator and officials have responsibilities regarding facilities and equipment, it's wise for you to know what to look for to make sure the contest is safe for the athletes. You should arrive at the field 25 to 30 minutes before game time so that you can check the field, check in with the site coordinator and umpires, and greet your players as they arrive to warm up. The site coordinator and umpires should be checking the facilities and preparing for the contest. If umpires aren't arriving before the game when they're supposed to, inform the site coordinator. A facilities checklist includes the following:

Field surface

✔ Sprinkler heads and openings are at grass level.

✔ The field is free of toxic substances (lime, fertilizer, and so on).

✔ The field is free of low spots or ruts.

✔ The playing surface is free of debris.

✔ No rocks or cement slabs are on the field.

✔ The field is free of protruding pipes, wires, and lines.

✔ The field is not too wet.

✔ The field lines are well marked.

Outside playing area

✔ The edge of the playing field is at least six feet from trees, walls, fences, and cars.

✔ Nearby buildings are protected (by fences, walls) from possible damage during play.

✔ Storage sheds and facilities are locked.

✔ The playground area (ground surface and equipment) is in safe condition.

✔ The fences/walls lining the area are in good repair.

✔ Sidewalks are without cracks, separations, or raised concrete.

✔ Bathroom facilities are open and operating.

Equipment

✔ Goals are held securely together.

✔ Goals are secured to the ground.

✔ Goal nets are securely attached to the posts.

Communicating With Parents

The groundwork for your communication with parents will have been laid in the parent orientation meeting, through which parents learn the best ways to support their kids'—and the whole team's—efforts on the field. As parents gather at the field before a contest, let them know what the team has been focusing on during the past week and what your goals are for the game. For instance, perhaps you've worked on a specific play in practice this week; encourage parents to watch for improvement and success in executing this play and to support the team members as they attempt all tactics and skills. Help parents to judge success not just based on the contest outcome but on how the kids are improving their performances.

If parents yell at the kids for mistakes made during the game, make disparaging remarks about the umpires or opponents, or shout instructions on what tactics to employ, ask them to refrain from making such remarks and to instead be supportive of the team in their comments and actions.

After a contest, briefly and informally assess with parents, as the opportunity arises, how the team did based not on the outcome but on meeting performance goals and playing to the best of their abilities. Help parents see the contest as a process, not solely as a test that's pass/fail or win/lose. Encourage parents to reinforce that concept at home.

Unplanned Events

Part of being prepared to coach is to expect the unexpected. What do you do if players are late? What if *you* have an emergency and can't make the game or will be late? What if the contest is rained out or otherwise postponed? Being prepared to handle out-of-the-ordinary circumstances will help you when such unplanned events happen.

If players are late, you may have to adjust your starting lineup. While this may not be a major inconvenience, do stress to your players the importance of being on time for two reasons:

- Part of being a member of a team means being committed and responsible to the other members. When players don't show up or show up late, they break that commitment.
- Players need to go through a warm-up to physically prepare for the contest. Skipping the warm-up risks injury.

Consider making a team rule stating that players need to show up 20 minutes before a game and go through the complete team warm-up, or they won't start.

An emergency might cause *you* to be late or miss a game. In such cases, notify your assistant coach, if you have one, or the league coordinator. If notified in advance, a parent of a player or another volunteer might be able to step in for the contest.

Sometimes a game will be postponed because of inclement weather or for other reasons (such as unsafe field conditions). If postponement takes place before game day, you'll need to call each member of your team to let him or her know. If it happens while the teams are on the field preparing for the game, gather your team members and tell them the news and why the game is being postponed. Make sure all your players have rides home before you leave. Be the last to leave to be sure.

The Warm-Up

Players need to both physically and mentally prepare for a game once they arrive at the field. Physical preparation involves warming up. We've suggested that players arrive 20 minutes before the game to warm up. Conduct the warm-up similar to practice warm-ups, with some brief games that focus on skill practice and stretching.

Players should prepare to perform skills they will use in the game, such as cradling, dodging, throwing, catching, shooting, and checking. This doesn't mean they spend extensive time on each skill; you can plan two or three brief practice games that encompass all these skills.

After playing a few brief games, your players should stretch. You don't need to deliver any big pep talk, but you can help your players mentally prepare as they stretch by reminding them of the following:

- The tactics and skills they've been working on in recent practices, especially focusing their attention on what they've been doing well. Focus on their strengths.
- The team tactics you decided on in your previous practice.
- Performing the tactics and skills to the best of their individual abilities and playing together as a team.
- Playing hard and smart and having fun!

During the Contest

The list you just read goes a long way toward defining your focus for coaching during the contest. Throughout the game, you'll keep the game in proper perspective and help your players do the same. You'll observe how your players execute tactics and skills and how well they play together. You'll make tactical decisions in a number of areas. You'll model appropriate behavior on the sideline, showing respect for opponents and officials, and demand the same of your athletes. You'll watch out for your athletes' physical safety and psychological welfare, in terms of building their self-esteem and helping them manage stress and anxiety.

Proper Perspective

Winning games is the short-term goal of your lacrosse program; helping your players learn the tactics, skills, and rules of lacrosse, how to become fit, and how to be good sports in lacrosse and in life are the long-term goals. Your young athletes are "winning" when they are becoming better human beings through their participation in lacrosse. Keep that perspective in mind when you coach. *You* have the privilege of setting the tone for how your team approaches the game. Keep winning and all aspects of the competition in proper perspective, and your young charges will likely follow suit.

Tactical Decisions

While you aren't called on to be a great military strategist, you are called on to make tactical decisions in several areas throughout a contest. You'll make decisions about who starts the game and when to enter substitutes; about making slight adjustments to your team's tactics; and about correcting players' performance errors or leaving the correction for the next practice.

Starting and Substituting Players

In considering playing time, make sure that everyone on the team gets to play at least half of each game. This should be your guiding principle as you consider starting and substitution patterns. We suggest you consider two options in substituting players:

⊙ **Substituting individually.** Replace one player with another. This offers you a lot of latitude in deciding who goes in when, and it gives you the greatest mix of players throughout the game, but it can be hard to keep track of playing time (this could be made easier by assigning an assistant or a parent to this task). Remember that each player is required to play one half of each game.

⊙ **Substituting by halves or quarters.** The advantage here is that you can easily track playing time, and players know how long they will be in before they might be replaced.

Adjusting Team Tactics

At the 8- to 9-year and 10- to 11-year-age levels, you probably won't adjust your team tactics too significantly during a game; rather, you'll focus on the basic tactics in general and emphasize during breaks which tactics your team needs to work on in particular. However, coaches of 12- to 14-year-olds might have cause to make tactical adjustments to improve their team's chances of performing well and winning. As games progress, assess your opponents' style of play and tactics, and make adjustments that are appropriate—that is, those your players are prepared for. Consider the following examples:

How do your opponents usually initiate their attack? Do they move the ball to get around, over, or through your defense? This can help you make defensive adjustments.

Who are the strongest players on the opposing team? The weakest players? As you identify strong players, you'll want to assign more skilled players to mark them.

Are the attack players fast and powerful? Do they come to the ball, or do they try to run behind the defense and receive passes? Their mode of attack should influence how you instruct your players to mark them.

On defense, do your opponents play a high-pressure game, or do they retreat once you've gained possession of the ball? Either type of defense could call for a different strategy from you. Knowing the answers to such questions can help you formulate a game plan and make adjustments during a game.

However, don't stress tactics too much during a game. Doing so can take the fun out of the game for the players. If you don't trust your memory, carry a pen and notepad to note which team tactics and individual skills need attention in the next practice.

Correcting Players' Errors

In chapter 5 you learned about two types of errors: learning errors and performance errors. Learning errors are ones that occur because athletes don't know how to perform a skill. Athletes make performance errors not because they don't know how to do the skill but because they make a mistake in executing what they do know.

Sometimes it's not easy to tell which type of error athletes are making. Knowing your athletes' capabilities helps you to know whether they know the skill and are simply making mistakes in executing it or whether they don't really know how to perform the skill. If they are making learning errors—that is, they don't know how to perform the skills—you'll need to make note of this and teach them at the next practice. Game time is not the time to teach skills.

If they are making performance errors, however, you can help players correct those errors during a game. Players who make performance errors often do so because they have a lapse in concentration or motivation—or they are simply demonstrating the human quality of sometimes doing things incorrectly. A word of encouragement to concentrate more may help. If you do correct a performance error during a contest, do so in a quiet, controlled, and positive tone of voice during a break or when the player is on the sideline with you.

For those making performance errors, you have to decide if it is just the occasional error anyone makes or an expected error for a youngster at that stage of development. If that is the case, then the player may appreciate your not commenting on the mistake. The player knows it was a mistake and knows how to correct it. On the other hand, perhaps an encouraging word and a "coaching cue" (such as, "Remember to follow through on your passes!") may be just what the athlete needs. Knowing the players and what to say is very much a part of the "art" of coaching.

Coach's and Players' Behavior

Another aspect of coaching on game day is managing behavior—both yours and your athletes'. The two are closely connected.

Your Conduct

You very much influence your players' behavior before, during, and after a contest. If you're up, your players are more likely to be up. If you're anxious, they'll notice and the anxiety can be contagious. If you're negative, they'll respond with worry. If you're positive, they'll play with more enjoyment. If you're constantly yelling instructions or commenting on mistakes and errors, it will be difficult for players to concentrate. Instead, let players get into the flow of the game.

The focus should be on positive competition and on having fun. A coach who overorganizes everything and dominates a game from the sideline is definitely *not* making the contest fun.

So how should you conduct yourself on the sideline? Here are a few pointers:

- Be calm, in control, and supportive of your players.
- Encourage players often, but instruct during play sparingly. Players should be focusing on their performance during a game, not on instructions shouted from the sideline.
- If you need to instruct a player, do so when you're both on the sideline, in an unobtrusive manner. Never yell at players for making a

mistake. Instead, briefly demonstrate or remind them of the correct technique and encourage them.

Remember, you're not playing for the World Cup or World Championship! In this program, lacrosse competitions are designed to help players develop their skills and themselves—and to have fun. So coach at games in a manner that helps your players do those things.

Players' Conduct

You're responsible for keeping your players under control. Do so by setting a good example and by disciplining when necessary. Set team rules of good behavior. If players attempt to cheat, fight, argue, badger, yell disparaging remarks, and the like, it is your responsibility to correct the misbehavior. Consider team rules in these areas of game conduct:

- Players' language
- Players' behavior
- Interactions with officials
- Discipline for misbehavior
- Dress code for competitions

Players' Physical Safety

We devoted all of chapter 3 to discussing how to provide for players' safety, but it's worth noting here that safety during contests can be affected by how officials are calling the rules. If they aren't calling rules correctly and this risks injury to your players, you must intervene. Voice your concern in a respectful manner and in a way that places the emphasis where it should be: on the athletes' safety. One of the officials' main responsibilities is to provide for athletes' safety; you are not adversaries here. Don't hesitate to address an issue of safety with an official when the need arises.

Players' Psychological Welfare

Athletes often attach their self-worth to winning and losing. This idea is fueled by coaches, parents, peers, and society, who place great emphasis on winning. Players become anxious when they're uncertain if they can meet the expectations of others or of themselves, when meeting these expectations is important to them.

If you place too much importance on the game or cause your athletes to doubt their abilities, they will become anxious about the outcome and their performance. If your players look uptight and anxious during a contest, find ways to reduce the uncertainties about how their performance will be evaluated and the importance they are attaching to the game. Help athletes focus on realistic personal goals—goals that are reachable and measurable and that will help them improve their performance. Another way to reduce anxiety on game day is to stay away from emotional pregame pep talks. We provided guidance earlier in what to address before the game.

When coaching during contests, remember that the most important outcome from playing lacrosse is to build or enhance players' self-worth. Keep that firmly in mind, and strive to make every coaching decision promote your athletes' self-worth.

Opponents and Umpires

Respect opponents and umpires. Without them, you wouldn't have a competition. Umpires help provide a fair and safe experience for athletes and, as appropriate, help them learn the game. Opponents provide opportunities for your team to test itself, improve, and excel.

You and your team should show respect for opponents by giving your best efforts. You owe them this. Showing respect doesn't necessarily mean being "nice" to your opponents, though it does mean being civil.

Don't allow your players to "trash talk" or taunt an opponent. Such behavior is disrespectful to the spirit of the competition and to the opponent. Immediately remove a player from a contest if he or she disobeys your orders in this area.

Remember that umpires are often teenagers—in many cases not much older than the players themselves. The level of officiating should be commensurate to the level of play. In other words, don't expect perfection from umpires any more than you do from your own players. Especially at younger levels, they *won't* make every call because to do so would stop the contest every 10 seconds.

After the Contest

When the game is over, join your team in congratulating the coaches and players of the opposing team, then be sure to thank the umpires. Check on any injuries players sustained and let players know how to care for them. Be prepared to speak with the officials about any problems that occurred during the game. Then hold a brief team circle, as explained in a moment, to ensure your players are on an even keel, whether they won or lost.

Winning With Class, Losing With Dignity

When celebrating a victory, make sure your team does so in a way that doesn't show disrespect for the opponents. It's fine and appropriate to be happy and celebrate a win, but don't allow your players to taunt the opponents or boast about their victory. Keep winning in perspective. Winning and losing are a part of life, not just a part of sports. If players can handle both equally well, they'll be successful in whatever they do.

Athletes are competitors, and competitors will be disappointed in defeat. If your team has made a winning effort, let them know that. After a loss, help them keep their chins up and maintain a positive attitude that will carry over into the next practice and contest.

Team Circle

If your players have performed well in a game, compliment them and congratulate them immediately afterward. Tell them specifically what they did well, whether they won or lost. This will reinforce their desire to repeat their good performances.

Don't criticize individual players for poor performances in front of teammates. Help players improve their skills, but do so in the next practice, not immediately after a game.

The postgame team circle isn't the time to go over tactical problems and adjustments. The players are either so happy after a win or so dejected after a loss that they won't absorb much tactical information immediately following a game. Your first concern should be your players' attitudes and mental well-being. You don't want them to be too high after a win or too low after a loss. This is the time you can be most influential in keeping the outcome in perspective and keeping them on an even keel.

Finally, make sure your players have transportation home. Be the last one to leave in order to help if transportation falls through and to ensure full supervision of players before they leave.

Differences Between Girls' and Boys' Lacrosse

The objectives of boys' and girls' lacrosse are the same: Each team tries to control the ball and score on the opponent's goal while preventing the opponent from scoring. The team with the most goals at the end of the game is the winner. Players advance the ball by running with it or throwing it to a teammate. The ball must pass the goal line to score. Given the large playing field, teams and individual players must be prepared to handle offensive, defensive, and transitional situations.

Although the boys' and girls' games share similarities, there are also some major differences. Girls' sticks have a more restricted pocket depth so that the ball is more accessible to the defense, which only may use stick-to-stick contact (the girls' game permits no stick-to-body contact). *Note:* Level C girls' youth play allows a modified, deeper pocket. Boys' sticks have a deeper pocket, which enables players to maintain possession of the ball better. Because of the differences in sticks and pockets, the techniques of throwing, catching, checking, cradling, and shooting differ somewhat between the two games.

The most significant difference between the boys' and girls' games is the amount of contact allowed, which also determines the amount of equipment a player wears. Other than limited stick-to-stick contact, the girls' game has remained a noncontact sport, with only minimal protective equipment, while the boys' game has developed to include considerable legal stick-to-body contact, requiring substantial equipment to prevent injuries.

The field markings of a lacrosse field also differ between the boys' and girls' games. The boys' game has a midfield line that restricts the number of players who may cross over to six attackers and seven defenders. The girls' field is marked with a restraining line 30 yards from the goal line and allows seven attackers and eight defenders in the scoring/defending area. The difference in the line location allows girls more midfield space and therefore more freedom in their movement up and down the field.

Additionally, one girls' rule has remained a tradition from the beginning. All players must stand when they hear the umpire whistle and may not move again until the umpire restarts play with another whistle. The umpire will instruct the necessary players to move according to the violation.

chapter 7

Girls' Lacrosse Rules and Equipment

Now we'll introduce you to some of the basic rules of girls' lacrosse. We won't try to cover all the rules of the game, but we will give you what you need to work with players who are 8 to 14 years old. We'll give you information on rule modifications, field size and markings, equipment, player positions, game play, starting and restarting the game, and fouls. The US Lacrosse *Official Rules for Girls' Youth Lacrosse* (part of *Official Rules for Girls' and Women's Lacrosse* available through US Lacrosse, www.uslacrosse.org) makes the sport more appropriate for youngsters. In a short section at the end of the chapter, we'll show you the officiating signals for lacrosse.

First, though, we'll begin by defining some terms you'll need to understand in order to teach lacrosse.

Terms to Know

Girls' lacrosse has its own vocabulary, as well as other general sport terms. Being familiar with common terms will make your job easier. All of the field markings and rule terms are further explained in the *US Lacrosse Official Rules for Girls' and Women's Lacrosse.*

arc—A pie-slice shaped area marked in front of each goal circle, at a distance of eight meters, and bound by a straight line on the sides that is at a 45-degree angle to where the goal line extended meets the goal circle. Used to define three-second violations and in the administration of major fouls. The eight-meter arc is painted on the field and fits within the fan.

attack—The offensive team.

backdoor cut—A cut in which an attacker cuts behind the defender toward the goal or ball.

channel—When a defender forces her opponent to veer in one direction and maintain that path.

crease or goal circle—Home of the goalkeeper, this circle, with an 8 1/2-foot radius, is painted on the field around the goal cage.

critical scoring area—An area on the field, not marked by any lines, with approximate boundaries of 15 yards around and 10 yards behind the goal circle. Used in the evaluation of shooting space.

cut to the ball—An offensive maneuver in which an attacker without the ball runs toward the ball carrier in an attempt to gain a position in front of her defender that enables her to more easily receive a pass.

decoy cut—A cut intended to move the defender out of a space and not necessarily to receive a pass.

defense—The team not in possession of the ball.

direct free position—The result of a major foul in which the player awarded the ball may shoot immediately, run, or pass the ball to a teammate.

drop down—A defender's move away from her player and toward the goal area to help defend a second player.

fan—A semicircular area marked on the field in front of each goal circle and bounded by a straight line extended from the goal line. Also called the 12-meter fan, this area is used in the administration of major and minor fouls.

free space—An imaginary path from the ball to the outside of either side of the goal circle.

goal line—Line painted on the field between the two goal posts over which the ball must pass entirely for a team to score a goal.

indirect free position—The result of a minor foul in which the player awarded the ball may not shoot immediately. She must pass the ball to a teammate or wait to shoot until a defender has checked her stick.

mark—To defend one particular player, within one arm and stick's length of that player.

off-ball movement—Cuts and movement by players without the ball that cause the defense to relocate.

offense—The team in possession of the ball.

open player—An offensive team member who is not marked and does not possess the ball.

passing lane—The aerial space between the ball carrier and her teammate's stick through which a pass would travel if it were made.

penalty lane—An imaginary path to the goal defined by two parallel lines that extend from each side of the goal circle to four meters on either side of the fouled player. The umpire clears the lane in some situations when the defense fouls.

player to player—A defensive strategy in which each defender closely marks one opponent and remains with that player throughout the play.

roll the crease—A move around the goal circle by an attacker with the ball, who is attempting to cut off her defender on the goal circle and taking a shot on goal from close range.

shooting space violation—Foul that occurs when a defender obstructs the free space to goal within the critical scoring area. Free space to goal is defined as an imaginary path from the ball to the outside of either side of the goal circle.

slide—A move by a defender to leave one player to mark a more dangerous opponent.

sphere—Imaginary seven-inch area surrounding a player's head. The ball carrier must keep her crosse and the ball outside of this seven-inch sphere, and the defender may not check into the sphere. She may check through it, as long as the check is going away from the head.

three-second violation—A violation by a defender who is not marking an attacker but who remains in the eight-meter arc for three seconds.

weak-side defender—A defensive teammate who is not on the ball side of the field.

Rule Modifications

The purpose of the *Official Rules for Girls' Youth Lacrosse* is to familiarize young players with the sport of women's lacrosse by introducing them to the terms, the field, the playing positions, the concept of teamwork, and the skills required to play the game safely and fairly. These rules were written by the US Lacrosse Women's Division and ratified by the US Lacrosse Youth Council in an effort to standardize youth rules for girls throughout the United States. Youth leagues may decide on age-level play that best suits their needs. The following are suggested as guidelines: 6- to 8-year-olds (Under 9), 9- to 10-year-olds (Under 11), 11- to 12-year-olds (Under 13), and 13- to 14-year-olds (Under 15).

The rules are divided by levels (A, B, and C). Teams with beginning players would be expected to use Level B or Level C rules, which do not allow checking and do allow certain stick modifications, to make throwing and catching easier. Teams would then progress to Level A rules, which allow modified checking and require the use of a regulation crosse and pocket. It is important to assess the skill level of all players to determine at which rule level the team should play.

Tournament play sponsored by US Lacrosse, such as the US Lacrosse Youth Festival, uses the following age and rule levels: Under 13 uses Level B rules and Under 15 uses Level A rules. When following an age/rule–level format at tournaments, it is important to announce to participants prior to the tournament which level(s) will be used at the event to avoid any confusion.

We strongly recommend that at least one qualified umpire be assigned to Level C games and two qualified umpires be assigned to Level A and Level B games. Youth modifications are noted throughout this and other chapters, and a complete checklist of modifications for each level is available in table 7.1. For the full list of current girls' and women's lacrosse rules, see the *Official Rules for Girls' and Women's Lacrosse*, available through US Lacrosse (www.uslacrosse.org).

Field Size and Markings

Figure 7.1 shows the markings for a lacrosse field. A regulation field is 100 yards between goals and 70 yards wide, with 10 yards playing space behind each goal. Where there are space restrictions, smaller fields can be used if both teams agree on the measurements. The *Official Rules for Girls' Youth Lacrosse* suggests the following field sizes for youth players:

Table 7.1	Official Rules for Girls' Youth Lacrosse
Level	**Specifics**
A	11 field players, one goalkeeper Field size: 100 yards × 70 yards is recommended Regular field markings, including restraining line Regular women's crosse, regulation pocket Modified checking only 25-minute halves (max) running time May shoot from direct free positions
B	11 field players, one goalkeeper Field size: 90 yards × 50 yards is recommended Regular field markings, including restraining line Regular women's crosse, regulation pocket No checking 25-minute halves (max) running time May shoot from direct free positions
C	7 field players, use of a goalkeeper is optional Field size: 50 yards × 25 yards is recommended 8-meter arc, no 12-meter fan, no restraining line, center line (no circle) Youth sticks (mesh allowed), or regular women's crosse, modified pocket No checking 20-minute halves (max) running time May not shoot from any free position

- Level A—Regulation
- Level B—Desirable field length is 90 yards between goal lines and 50 yards wide, with 10 yards behind each goal. The field should be marked according to US Lacrosse women's rules, including a restraining line.
- Level C—Desirable field length is 50 yards between goal lines and 25 yards wide, with 10 yards behind each goal. The field markings should include two goal circles (each with a two-meter radius), with a goal line in each; two eight-meter arcs around each goal circle; and a centerline.

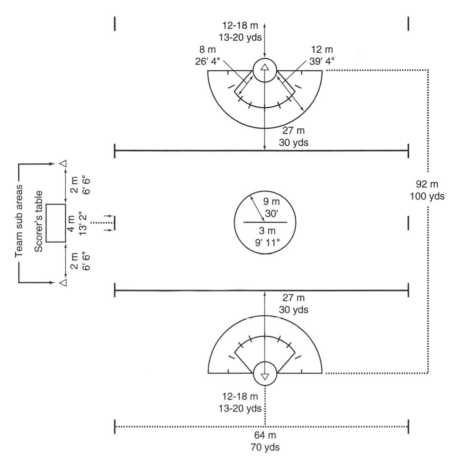

Figure 7.1 Girls' field measurements.

A unique aspect of girls' lacrosse is that the playing field has no specific measured boundaries. While the field should meet recommended minimum and maximum size standards, including distance between the goal cages and the amount of playable space behind the goal cages, each field's dimensions are defined by natural boundaries, such as benches, trees, inclines, or a surrounding track. Visible guidelines are added to each field to indicate the sidelines and are placed four meters inside the natural boundaries. These visible guidelines enable the player with the ball to see that she is approaching an unplayable area, thus allowing her to turn away, dodge, or pass the ball.

As in soccer, field hockey, and ice hockey, play starts in a center circle at the beginning of a game, after goals, and to begin the second half.

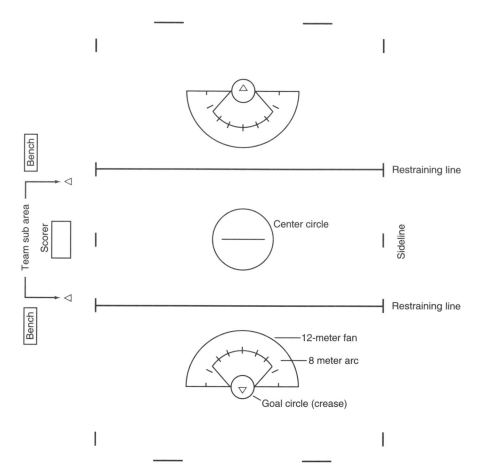

Figure 7.2 Girls' field markings.

The goal markings in front of the cage aid in the administration of fouls and penalties (figure 7.2). All players will be repositioned around the arc and fan for a free position shot depending on where the foul was committed.

Equipment

The head of a stick is made from wood or plastic and is strung with nylon or leather vertical thongs cross-woven with gut or nylon strings. The shaft may be constructed from aluminum, fiberglass, plastic, or wood (figure 7.3, a-c). In the girls' game, the goalkeeper's stick may have a mesh pocket (figure 7.3c), and girls' youth rules allow a mesh pocket for Level C players.

Regulation sticks are between 35 1/2 and 43 1/4 inches long. However, a beginning youth player may play with an even shorter stick (roughly an arm's length). Some manufacturers have developed special youth sticks for youth players. The goalkeeper's stick must also be at least 35 1/2 inches long, but it may be as long as 48 inches. It is composed of the same materials as other players' sticks and may be strung traditionally or with mesh. The head of the goalkeeper's stick is significantly larger than the heads of other sticks. It measures 13 by 16 inches.

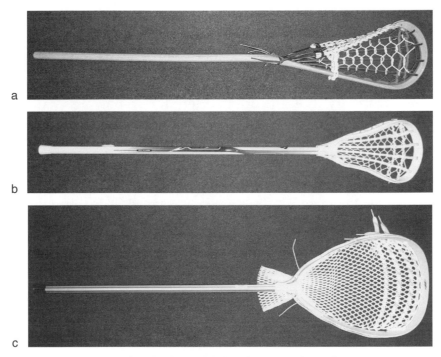

Figure 7.3   *(a)* Wood stick, *(b)* Molded stick, *(c)* Goalie stick.

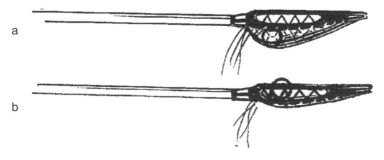

Figure 7.4   *(a)* Illegal field stick pocket, *(b)* legal field stick pocket. *Note:* The modified pocket in figure 7.4a is legal for goalies and for field sticks in Level C youth play.

The regulation pocket of a woman's lacrosse stick, used by Level B youth play and up, is legal if the ball remains even with or above the plastic or wooden walls of the head. See figure 7.4, a and b, for an illustration of a legal and an illegal pocket. At the beginning of every contest, the umpire checks that all players' stick pockets are legal. For youth Level C, a modified (deeper) pocket is allowed.

The ball for girls' lacrosse is made of solid yellow rubber, is 7 3/4 to 8 inches in circumference (a little smaller than a tennis ball), and weighs from 5 to 5 1/4 ounces. Different colored balls, including white, are available for youth games and practice purposes. Many youth programs use a "soft" ball.

Field players must wear mouthguards and sneakers or cleats. Field players may also wear close-fitting gloves, approved nose guards or eye guards, or soft head gear as long as it is close-fitting and padded where necessary. The American Society for Testing and Materials (ASTM) has established a standard for protective eyewear for girls' and women's lacrosse. Information on currently approved products is available from US Lacrosse.

Unlike field players, goalkeepers must wear protective equipment. They must wear a face mask and helmet, throat protector, chest protector, and mouth guard. Goalkeepers may wear additional padding on the arms, thighs, shins, pelvic area and hands. Protective padding can't be more than one inch thick (figure 7.5). Manufacturers have recently begun making a mouth guard and goalkeeping equipment specifically for youth of all ages and are adapting some equipment from other sports like ice hockey.

Player Positions

A regulation team comprises 11 field players and a goalkeeper. For youth Level C, there are 7 field players and a goalie is optional. The nature of the game encourages all players to play both offense and defense. Field players are usually categorized as line attack (first home, second home, and third home), line defense (point, coverpoint, and third man), and midfielders (right and left attack wings, right and left defense wings, and center) (see figure 7.6).

The common characteristics of each position for a full 12-player team are described next. Remember that these are only guidelines to help you get started.

Goalkeeper

The goalkeeper's primary job is to defend the goal cage, using her stick and her body to prevent the ball from crossing the goal line. The goal-

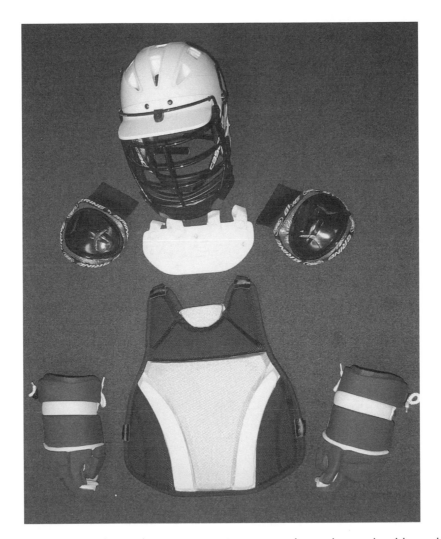

Figure 7.5 Girls' goalie equipment. (Not pictured: mouth guard, additional arm padding, pelvic protector, leg padding)

keeper should attempt to save every shot with her stick; her body is a secondary line of defense. To be successful, goalkeepers must develop good footwork, good body positioning, and the ability to cover the angles of shots. The most desirable talents for a goalkeeper are quick reflexes with hands and feet, concentration, and confidence.

For youth play, allow goalkeepers to defend the goal cage only when they are skilled and comfortable having shots fired at them. Give individual instruction to a player who desires to play goalkeeper, and make sure she's properly equipped before you allow other young players to shoot on her.

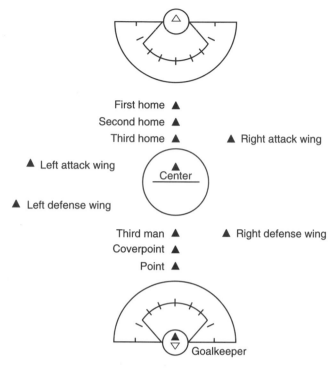

First home ▲
Second home ▲
Third home ▲   ▲ Right attack wing

▲ Left attack wing   ▲ Center

▲ Left defense wing

Third man ▲   ▲ Right defense wing
Coverpoint ▲
Point ▲

Goalkeeper

Figure 7.6 Field positions.

Point

The point, which is the defender closest to the crease, has duties similar to a sweeper in soccer or field hockey. She has the primary responsibility for individually marking the first home on the attacking team. She must be decisive in evaluating and reacting to the play of her teammates up the field from her. The point should be highly trained to defend the crease, be a reliable stick checker and shot blocker, have strong body checking positioning, and make good decisions.

Coverpoint

The coverpoint plays in front of the point and is also responsible for individually marking the second home on the attacking team. The coverpoint should be the defender who is most competent in all defensive skills, especially in one-on-one marking ability and body checking, and who, because she leads the defensive unit, is a good decision maker and communicator.

Third Man

The third man usually lines up on the circle for a draw and plays in front of the coverpoint. She is responsible for marking the third home. While still a primary defender, the third man should be assertive in disrupting midfield play by intercepting and sliding to pick up free opponents. When her team has possession of the ball, the third man is often involved in midfield transition and has occasional opportunities to score. The key traits of the third man are blocking skills, ability to anticipate a loose ball and interception opportunities, good timing, instinctive risk taking, speed to recover on defense, and versatility.

Defense Wings

The right and left defense wings mark the opposing attack wings and line up on the circle for the draw. Defense wings need to be the fastest defenders to match the speed of the attack wings and to recover back on defense to pick up a free player. Defense wings, like the third man, must possess good anticipation and marking skills. They must also be good blockers and body checkers. Valuable in transition and opportunistic on attack, defense wings should be capable of shooting from the outside.

Center

The center performs the draw. After the ball is in play, her primary responsibility is to defend her opposing center. If necessary, she fills in for her defensive teammates if they get caught out of position. She is most valuable in transition from defense to offense, and she should possess good field vision and space awareness to serve as a connector. The center must have consistent ball skills. She is a part of both the offensive and defensive units, so she must possess speed and endurance to cover both ends of the field.

Attack Wings

Off the draw, the ball frequently goes to the wings (left or right), who are lined up on the center circle. Attack wings usually are the fastest players, who must utilize the space and width of the midfield. Ideally, they use this speed to create a quick transition that leads to a fast break. While in transition, attack wings must make good decisions concerning where to pass the ball. Often involved in finishing a fast break, attack wings need to be strong passers and shooters.

Third Home

Lining up on the circle, marked by the third man, the third home is a well-rounded attack player with strong ball and shooting skills. She must be able to protect and distribute the ball while in transition to offense. An experienced player, she must be able to anticipate, recognize, and move to open spaces away from the ball to support her teammates. Finding the appropriate spaces allows her many opportunities to score. She should be quick to recognize change of possession and to switch to her defensive role of marking.

Second Home

The second home should be a dynamic attack player with great stick skills. She often is the attack's leader or playmaker. She must be able to get open and receive passes, so she can shoot or distribute the ball to her teammates.

First Home

The first home plays closest to the goal and should be able to protect the ball and feed it to her teammates. She must possess excellent cradling, dodging, and shooting skills; be able to react to the ball and her teammates' movement; and have a nose for the goal. In reaction to her opponents' movements, it is to her advantage to be able to cut in limited space and to use the goal circle to her advantage.

Game Play

Girls' lacrosse is a unique combination of individual skills and team performance. Two teams try to score by advancing the ball toward their opponent's goal with a combination of running and passing. A goal is scored for one point when the ball crosses through the imaginary plane formed by the rear edges of the goal line, the goalposts, and the top cross bar. The game allows for fast-break opportunities, as well as set offensive plays.

A team can't score if it doesn't have the ball, so keeping possession of the ball is integral to the game. The team without the ball plays defense, and team members try to gain possession by intercepting a pass, dislodging a ball from an opponent's stick, retrieving a ground ball, or blocking a pass or shot. When the team gains possession of the ball, it becomes the offensive team and creates a transition to attack the opponent's goal.

All players must develop throwing and catching skills because the ball moves faster through the air than it does when a player runs with it. The objective for the offensive team is to develop a one-on-one or an extra-player advantage (two-on-one) to make scoring easier.

The goalkeeper, who must wear specific protective equipment, defends the goal. When she gains possession of the ball, she initiates the transition to attack. The crease is defined by a circle with an 8 1/2-foot radius, and within that area the goalkeeper has special privileges. Because no one else may enter her crease area while she is in there, the goalkeeper is unguarded. She may remain in the crease with the ball for up to 10 seconds, and she is allowed to use her hands or body to play the ball. When she is out of the goal circle, the goalkeeper has no special privileges and is considered a regular field player.

Length of Game

The maximum playing time for a schoolgirls' game is 50 minutes, while collegiate play lasts 60 minutes. The clock runs continuously during play; it stops only after goals and after every whistle in the last two minutes of each half. If one team leads another by 10 or more goals, the clock keeps running even after a goal is scored. The umpire's signal for illness, accident, or injury also stops the clock.

The *Official Rules for Girls' Youth Lacrosse* suggests that Level A and Level B play 25-minute (maximum) running time halves; Level C should play 20-minute (maximum) running time. The clock may be stopped during the last two minutes of each half for youth play. Before the game begins, captains or coaches select how long the halftime break will last. It may not exceed 10 minutes.

Starting and Restarting the Game

The captains meet before the game to determine which goal each team will defend. Each half begins with a center draw administered by an umpire. The two opponents position themselves at the centerline, facing the goal they are to attack, assuming they are using the right hand at the top of the stick to draw. (The player's back is to her attacking goal if she chooses to use her left hand on top.) The players must have one foot toeing the centerline and hold their sticks back-to-back at or above waist level and parallel to the centerline. The umpire places the ball between the sticks. The players and their sticks must remain motionless until the whistle sounds. On the whistle, the players immediately lift their sticks up first, then away from their opponents to propel the ball into the air and toward the offensive end of the field (figure 7.7). Players should be taught to stand steady and firmly before the whistle sounds, then react quickly to the whistle and use their upper and lower body strength to move the ball. The ball must go above head level for play to begin legally. After a score, the umpire restarts play with a center draw. For youth players, the game can also be started with possession instead of a center draw.

If the ball goes out of bounds (boundaries are predetermined by the umpires' interpretation of natural boundaries), the umpire blows her whistle to stop play and awards the ball to the player closest to it. All players must move four meters from the boundary, maintaining the same relationship relative to each other as when the ball went out of bounds. The player awarded the ball must be given one meter of free space. Play continues with the umpire's whistle.

If two opponents are the same distance from the ball when it crosses the boundary or if players commit a double foul, the umpire restarts play with a throw. The umpire positions two players one meter apart,

Figure 7.7   Girls' center draw. Player on left has her left hand on top so her back is to the goal she attacks.

each on the side nearer the goal she is defending. On the whistle, the umpire throws the ball into the air with a short lob toward the players. The two players then sprint for the ball and play continues from this point.

If a player fouls, game play is stopped. When a foul occurs, the umpire blows her whistle and all players must stand in their current place on the field. The next section, describing players' fouls, will explain how to restart the game after a foul.

Fouls

The following section summarizes the most important and influential lacrosse rules. A more thorough review is available in the *Official Rules for Girls' and Women's Lacrosse*. Umpires impose a variety of penalties according to whether fouls are classified as major or minor. However, to some extent, the penalty imposed also depends on where the foul occurred on the field. Fouls in the critical scoring area (see "Terms to Know" on pages 63-64) carry a different penalty from fouls in the midfield, even if both are of the same magnitude.

Major Fouls

Major fouls are those that are potentially dangerous and that may have a significant effect on the game. Major fouls can be divided into three areas:

1. Fouls involving the stick
2. Fouls involving the body
3. Fouls within the critical scoring area

Fouls Involving the Stick

A player may not use the crosse in a dangerous manner nor hold her crosse around the head of the opponent. If, in an attempt to gain possession of the ball, a defender uses her stick to check roughly or recklessly, an umpire will call a penalty. A defender's stick may neither swing toward the body or head of her opponent nor hold her opponent's stick or body. A player with the ball may not hold or cradle the ball in front of her face in an attempt to protect the ball from a defender.

The *Official Rules for Girls' Youth Lacrosse* limits stick checking at various levels. No intentional stick-to-stick checking is permitted at Level B and Level C. Level A introduces modified stick checking, which allows stick-to-stick contact only when the head of the stick is below the ball carrier's shoulder and the check is away from the ball carrier's body.

Fouls Involving the Body

A second category of fouls involves misuse of a player's body. A defender may not restrain or hold a player by blocking, detaining, pushing, or tagging an opponent. A player in possession of the ball may not charge, lean into with her shoulder, or back into an opponent. A defender's body must be in position so that she does not reach around the opponent to check the stick, thus the importance of good defensive footwork.

Fouls Within the Critical Scoring Area

These three major fouls occur only within the critical scoring area:

1. **Three-second violation on a defender.** No defender may stand within the eight-meter arc for more than three seconds without marking an opponent. Each defender must have both hands on her stick and must be within a stick's reach of her opponent to be considered marking her.

2. **Obstruction of shooting space by a defender's body.** Free space to goal is defined as the cone-shaped space extending from the ball to the outside of the goal circle (see figure 7.8). No defender may stand in or cross through this free space when the ball is in the critical scoring area unless she is marking an opponent or is led by her opponent into the space. A defender may pass through the shooting space if the player with the ball is not looking to shoot, if the ball is on the ground, or if a pass is in the air.

3. **Dangerous play by an attacker shooting to goal.** A player must control the shot and her stick after releasing the ball for a shot. The umpire calls a major foul if the shooter commits a dangerous follow-through with her stick into an opponent. An umpire may also call a dangerous or uncontrolled shot on a shooter. The umpire judges this foul based on the distance, placement, and force of the shot.

When a team commits a major foul anywhere, except within the eight-

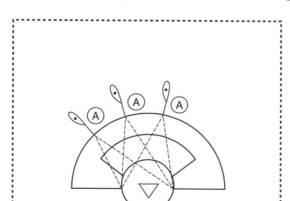

Figure 7.8 Shooting space from 3 different ball positions.

meter arc, the opposing team gets a free position at the location of the foul. The person who committed the foul stands four meters behind the fouled player. All other players must move away four meters before the official's whistle restarts play in the direction from which they approached.

If the defense fouls within the eight-meter arc, the offense gets the free position from the closest hash mark on the eight-meter arc. The player who committed the foul is placed four meters behind, on the 12-meter fan. The umpire clears the arc (and the penalty lane if necessary) of all players. The penalty lane is the area four meters, on both sides, away from the fouled player and directly toward the goal. All players must step out of the eight-meter arc toward the closest eight-meter line. This spacing maintains equity of positioning and ensures safety near the goal area. Once the umpire has restarted play with her whistle, the player with the ball on the eight-meter arc may shoot directly to goal, pass to a teammate, or run with the ball.

If the attacking team commits a major foul within the eight-meter arc, the defense gets the ball on the eight-meter arc, and the attacker who committed the foul must go four meters behind. All players must be four meters away, but players are not cleared out of the eight-meter arc, as they are on a defensive foul.

If the defensive major foul occurs in the critical scoring area but outside the eight-meter arc, the umpire awards a free position and repositions players as in a foul at midfield. However, the umpire clears only the penalty lane to goal.

Minor Fouls

Minor fouls are less severe in nature and less disruptive of the play, so the penalties are less advantageous to the team that was fouled. Minor fouls include checking an empty stick and covering or guarding a ground ball with the stick or body. A player who uses her hands or body on the ball to gain an advantage, even if the contact is incidental, commits a minor foul. If a player doesn't use a legal stick or a mouthguard, or if she wears any jewelry, she commits a minor foul. Other minor fouls include illegal substitution, delay of game, illegal draw, and intentionally putting the ball out of bounds.

The umpire awards a free position for a minor foul and moves the fouling player four meters away. For a minor foul, the fouling player moves in the same direction from which she approached; in other words, she does not need to go behind the fouled player, as she does for a major foul penalty. Again, the umpire's whistle restarts play.

Minor fouls inside the 12-meter fan are penalized with an indirect free position on the nearest spot on the 12-meter fan. The player who committed the foul moves four meters away. The penalty lane is not cleared, and the fouled player is awarded an indirect free position. Indirect free position means the player fouled may not take a shot on goal; she must pass the ball. The umpire awards a free position for minor fouls that are in the critical scoring area.

Play Around the Crease

Specific rules govern play around the crease. No player except the goalkeeper or her deputy may enter the crease or break the plane of the crease at any time. If the defensive team creates a turnover and is in clear possession of the ball and the goalkeeper is out of the crease, a deputy teammate may enter the crease to play the ball. Once the ball is loose or returns to the attacking team, the deputy must leave the crease immediately. This is to prevent an unprotected field player from defending a shot on goal.

An illegal deputy is a major foul. The umpire gives the ball to an attacker on a hash mark on the eight-meter arc and places the illegal deputy four meters behind her on the 12-meter fan. The goalkeeper cannot move into the crease until play resumes.

Like the goalie, a deputy may hold the ball for only 10 seconds while in the crease. When inside the crease, the goalie may reach with her stick outside of her crease to reach a ball, but she becomes illegally grounded if any body part touches the ground outside the goal circle. If the defensive team crosses the line or plane of the crease, it commits a minor foul, and the attack gets an indirect free position at the 12-meter fan on either side of the goal and level with the goal line. If an attacker or her stick enters the crease, the goalie gets the ball in the crease, and all the players must move four meters away before play resumes. A dangerous shot by the attack results in a major foul. The goalkeeper gets the ball and the fouling player must go four meters behind the crease.

An official may use a slow, or *held,* whistle under specific circumstances. If the defense commits a foul within the critical scoring area while the attack is on a scoring play, the umpire will hold the flag overhead and allow the attacker to continue to goal. If the player shoots, the umpire will lower the flag and allow play to continue. If the player chooses not to shoot or cannot because of the actions of the defense, the umpire will blow the whistle to stop play (refer to page 78, number 2). The foul is penalized as a major foul within the critical scoring area. The umpire does not use a held whistle for a shooting space violation (see definition on page 64) or any severe foul that endangers player safety but should stop play immediately.

Play in the Midfield

Recent rule changes for girls have had a significant effect on midfield play. A restraining line located 30 yards from each goal line has been added to limit the number of players near the goal area. If more than eight defenders or more than seven attackers are over the line at any time, the umpire will indicate a foul. The necessary players move to restore the balance at the restraining line, and play is restarted with a free position given to the team that was fouled.

Players may now enter and reenter the game while play is in progress. Substitution "on the fly" allows players to exchange places by the scorer's table any time the game is flowing. The player leaving the field must cross into the team substitution area before the new player may enter the playing field. When the umpire's whistle blows, any player running toward the team substitution area must stop running and wait for the next whistle to complete the substitution.

Officiating

Two or three umpires who are trained in lacrosse enforce the rules to ensure safety, fun, and fairness in the game. An umpire's job is easier when you have emphasized sportsmanship and discipline and have educated players and parents about the rules of the game. US Lacrosse, who certifies umpires, asks that players, coaches, and umpires observe the intent of the rules and make every effort not to take advantage of them.

Umpires on the field carry a whistle, a yellow flag, and a set of warning cards (green, yellow, and red). These cards are used to control the play and safety of the game and to penalize poor conduct by players, coaches, and fans. A green card indicates a delay of game foul, with the next delay foul indicated by showing a green and a yellow card. A third delay foul warrants a green and a red card, and the player who commits this foul must leave the game for three minutes, with a substitute allowed to enter. If a player commits a foul that is a dangerous act such as hitting another player with her stick, the umpire issues a yellow or a red card, depending on the severity of the foul. A flagrant foul warrants an immediate red card which indicates that the player is removed for the remainder of the game. A yellow card indicates that the player must leave the field for three minutes. In each instance, a substitute is allowed to enter the game. Any player receiving a second yellow card is removed for the remainder of the game. Familiarize yourself with the umpires' signals shown in figure 7.9 and teach them to the players.

a

b

c

d

Figure 7.9 Umpire signals. *(a)* Time-out, *(b)* pushing, *(c-d)* time-in.

e

f

g

h

Figure 7.9 *(continued) (e-f)* Blocking, *(g-h)* rough check.

i

j

k

l

Figure 7.9 *(continued)* *(i)* Illegal check on body, *(j)* illegal ball off body, *(k)* obstruction of free space to goal, *(l)* empty crosse check or held crosse.

m

n

o

p

Figure 7.9 *(continued)* *(m)* Free position held whistle, *(n)* goal circle foul, *(o-p)* re-draw.

chapter 8

Girls' Lacrosse Skills and Tactics

In this chapter we'll provide information for you to teach your players offensive and defensive skills, tactics, and strategies. We'll also include suggestions for identifying and correcting common errors. Remember to use the IDEA approach to teaching skills—Introduce, Demonstrate, and Explain the skill, and Attend to players as they practice the skill. For a refresher on IDEA, see chapter 5. If you aren't familiar with lacrosse skills, watch a video to see the skills performed. You may also find books on advanced skills helpful. We've provided only information about the basics of lacrosse in this book. As your players advance in their lacrosse skills, you'll need to advance in your knowledge as a coach. You can do so by learning from your experiences, by watching and talking with more experienced coaches, and by studying advanced resources.

Using Lacrosse Drills Effectively

Before we begin presenting the skills for a young player, you should know that the most effective way to learn the basic skills is to practice with partner drills. These drills use one ball and two players to optimize the number of repetitions for the time allotted to practicing one skill.

In partner drills, the players stand 10 yards apart as they execute stationary skills. Align one of the partners along a line on the field and the other partner facing her at a specified distance apart. This creates a safer formation so that balls that are not caught will not hit other players. Remind the players to wear their mouthguards.

As players develop skill and confidence, they can begin practicing these skills while on the move. Then introduce a combination of skills that have been learned, such as a ground ball pick-up followed by a pass to a partner. Make the execution of skills competitive by adding a time or completion factor. The next step is to introduce opposition from a defender. The progression from stationary partner drills, to moving to execute the skills, to adding competition provides a variety of learning experiences to keep players challenged. Only when players can safely perform all basic skills in a drill setting should small games begin. Follow a progression of easy to more challenging in teaching drills and games.

Individual Offensive Skills

Because lacrosse is essentially a giant game of keep-away, individual possession of the ball is integral to the success of the team. Teach players to become proficient at basic stick skills, such as cradling, dodging, picking up ground balls, throwing, catching, and shooting. From the very beginning, teach the use of both the right and left hands at the top of the stick for all stick skills.

Cradling

Cradling is the skill of moving the stick in a semicircular pattern to create a centrifugal force that keeps the ball in the pocket. A player with possession of the ball must cradle the ball to keep it in her stick. All other skills develop from the cradle, so your players should learn this skill first. Teach players to follow these steps when they are cradling:

1. Grasp the shaft of the stick with the right hand near the stick head. For wooden sticks this should be just below where the strings tie

through the wood and for a plastic stick, up to six inches below where the head attaches.

2. Line up the V of the right hand with the center of the pocket (the V is the space between the index finger and the thumb). See figure 8.1.

3. Position the right hand at shoulder height or above.

4. Keep the left hand at waist height and at the end of the stick.

5. Move the stick in a semicircular path between the midline of the body and the outside of the shoulder.

6. Open and close the wrists fluidly to keep the pocket facing toward the body.

After a player has learned the fundamental movement of the stick and ball with both hands on top, she can develop alternate methods of cradling to better protect the ball from an opponent. Variations include height, rhythm, and angle of the stick, and changing the position of the stick from one side of her body to the other while cradling, depending on the position of her defender (figure 8.2).

Figure 8.1   Proper hand positioning, right hand on top.

a   b

Figure 8.2   *(a)* Position of stick while cradling on right side. *(b)* Position of stick while cradling on left side with right hand on top.

Error Detection and Correction for Cradling

Young lacrosse players have difficulty cradling the ball because they do not use their arms in unison, which causes the ball to fall out of the stick.

ERROR   Dropping the ball out of the stick while cradling

CORRECTION

1. Have the player move her bottom hand up the stick shaft to within 12 inches of the top hand to develop a smoother, rocking stick motion.

2. Remind the player to continue cradling whenever she has the ball in her stick.

3. Have the player keep her elbows comfortably at her side, not sticking out and not "glued" to the sides of her body.

4. Have the player rotate her trunk and upper body with the movement of her arms.

Cradling Games

FOLLOW THE LEADER

Goal

To learn to cradle

Description

Arrange players in rows, with four to six players a stick's length apart in each row. Each player has a ball and stick and faces you. Players imitate your cradling motions. Be sure to change sides, heights, and hands.

Variation

Play Simon Says by calling out areas around the body for the players to move their stick while cradling (e.g., high right, low left, etc.).

SURVIVOR TAG

Goal

To develop confidence in controlling the ball while cradling and moving

Description

All the players are cradling a ball, except three players who are the "Its." The playing area is the center circle or an area approximately 20 yards in diameter. The "Its" chase any player and attempt to grab the stick handle or head to disrupt the cradling motion. When a player drops the ball, she must pick up the ball and exit the playing area. Once outside the playing area, she must sit and continue cradling until the winner is identified. The winner is the last player remaining in the circle with a ball in her stick. The last three players forced out are the new "Its," and play begins again.

To make the game easier

- Have fewer players be "Its."
- Allow one drop before leaving the game.

To make the game harder

- Have more players be "Its."
- Use nondominant hand only.

Dodging

Dodging is a sudden change in direction while cradling the stick and ball to move them away from a defender. A player can move her stick or body in a variety of ways to get past a defender. She can suddenly move her stick from one side to the other, from her right hand to her left hand (or vice versa), and from high to low. Her body can move from side to side, change speed, or roll. Keeping the cradle on one side of her body, she can change the height of the stick from above her head to as low as her waist. For all dodges, the attacking player must accelerate out of the dodge to gain and maintain her advantage on the defender.

Pull Dodge

The pull dodge is a quick stick movement used to change the location of the stick and the ball away from the defender. The pull dodge is the most basic and easiest of all dodges. Teach players how to do this dodge from both sides. To execute a pull dodge, players must develop these skills (figure 8.3):

1. Hold the stick in a protected position off the right shoulder.
2. Keep both hands on the stick.
3. Pull the stick across the midline of the body to the other shoulder with one strong sweeping motion.
4. Continue cradling on the left side.

a   b   c

Figure 8.3   Pull dodge. *(a)* Protected cradle off right shoulder, *(b)* halfway into pull from one side of body to the other, *(c)* continue cradle off left shoulder.

Change-of-Hands Dodge

This dodge is very similar to the pull dodge, as the stick follows the same path, but the player exchanges top hands during the dodge. It requires proficiency in cradling with both hands. For a change-of-hands dodge, players should follow this sequence (figure 8.4):

1. Hold the stick in a protected position off the right shoulder.
2. Pull the stick across the midline of the body to the other shoulder with one strong sweeping motion.
3. Replace the right hand with the left hand on top.
4. Slide the right hand down to the bottom of the stick.
5. Continue cradling off the left shoulder.

a   b   c

Figure 8.4 Change-of-hands dodge. *(a)* Protected cradle off right shoulder with right hand on top, *(b)* pull completed with left hand replacing right hand on top of stick, *(c)* protected cradle off left shoulder with left hand on top.

Roll Dodge

The roll dodge changes the direction of movement of the body and stick to get around a defender and avoid a possible stick check. Be sure to practice rolling in both directions. Players executing a roll dodge must learn the following skills (figure 8.5):

1. Hold the stick in a protected position off the right shoulder.
2. Plant the left foot out in front and opposite the right shoulder. Turn so that the ball carrier's back is passing the defender.

3. Rotate the hips in the direction in which the body is rotating, and take a large step out of the pivot to pass by the defender.

4. Protect the stick between the shoulders throughout the dodge. This is an ideal time to change the top hand on the stick.

When the fundamental dodging movements have been mastered, a player may develop combinations of dodges and add fakes to outmaneuver the opponent. Changes in stick heights may be combined with all of the dodges.

a   b   c

Figure 8.5   Progression of roll dodge. *(a)* Preparation of a roll dodge, *(b)* head rotates to lead body through roll as hands are ready to switch places, *(c)* accelerate out of dodge. Top hand switches to proper position.

Error Detection and Correction for Dodging

As they are learning to dodge, players often lose the ball as they change the stick to a new area around their body.

ERROR   Ball falls out of the stick while the player is dodging

CORRECTION

1. Have the player move both hands together.

2. Be sure the player maintains a soft top hand on the switch from right to left or from left to right.

3. Have the player continue to cradle on the new side following the strong pull.

4. Make sure that, when doing the roll dodge, the player steps around the defender and accelerates out of the roll and down the field.

Dodging Games

SLALOM

Goal

To practice various dodges on the move

Description

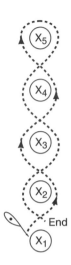

Four to six players stand facing front to back in a row five yards from the player in front of them. Only the player in front has a ball. Call out the kind of dodge you want them to execute. The first player turns and faces her line and weaves in and out of each of her teammates while running and executing the dodges toward the end of the line and back to the front. When she returns to the front of the line, she passes the ball to the next player, whom she replaces in a stationary position as the drill continues.

Figure 8.6
Slalom drill.

Variations

- *Race Around the Block.* Make the drill a race to see who can run slalom fastest without dropping the ball (figure 8.6).
- *Concentrate.* Have players execute dodges in a specific order (e.g., pull right, pull left, roll dodge, change-of-hands dodge).

GRID LOCKED

Goal

To develop the skills of dodging and passing a defender

Description

Lay out three consecutive 15-by-15-yard grids, with a goal cage at the end of the last grid (figure 8.7). Each team consists of three players. One team is on defense with one player positioned to defend in each grid without a stick. The attack team players each have a ball and line up behind the grid farthest from the goal. Each attacker tries to successfully dodge the opponent within the 15-yard space to move onto the next grid and the next defender. If the attacker does not drop the ball and gets through the grid, she scores one point for her team, and she gets an additional point if she scores a goal after the last grid. A dropped ball ends the scoring opportunity in that particular grid, but she may move on to the next grid to challenge the defender. After all attackers have had three tries through the grid to score points, the teams switch roles.

To make the game easier

- Make the grids larger

To make the game harder

- Put a time limit of five seconds on each player to get through the grid.
- The player must hit a target inside the goal for an extra point.
- Allow defenders to have sticks for defending.

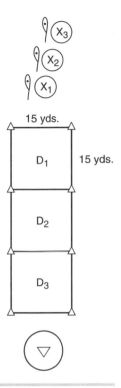

Figure 8.7 Grid Locked.

Ground Balls

Picking up a ground ball is the way a player gains possession of a ball while it's moving along the ground. The ball is rarely stationary in a game; however, it is easiest to learn ground ball pickups by practicing on a stationary ball. When players attempt to pick up a stationary ground ball, make sure they follow these instructions (figure 8.8):

1. Bend at the hips and knees.
2. Position the same foot as the top hand next to the ball (right hand, right foot; left hand, left foot).
3. Accelerate the stick head under and through the ball.
4. Push down with the bottom hand to return the stick to vertical.
5. Immediately begin to cradle the stick.

When a ball is rolling away, the player must match the speed of the ball, place the correct foot next to the ball, and execute the same movement as with a stationary ball pickup. In this case the key to success is the acceleration of the stick through the ball, so instruct the players to push their bottom hand through the ball.

Figure 8.8 Ground ball pickup. *(a)* Both hands on left side of body as it lowers at knees and hips, *(b)* align and lower stick head behind ball, *(c)* position right foot next to ball, *(d)* cradle begun as stick returns to vertical.

A ball that is rolling toward a player must be handled differently. Because the player is running toward the ball, she must give with the ball, as she does when catching. To take the momentum out of the ball, she reaches toward the ball with the top of her stick touching the ground and the stick angled upward (creating an incline plane). As the ball rolls onto the stick, she gives with the stick toward her body and begins cradling. The player continues cradling as she brings the stick to a vertical, protected position.

When a ball is approaching from either side of a player, the stick should be lowered to the bouncing ball's height and the stick placed at a right angle across the path of the ball. The player should give with this ball, as in a low catch.

When competing with an opponent for possession of the ball, a player should position her body between the ball and her opponent, creating the opportunity for her to play the ball first.

Error Detection and Correction for Picking Up Ground Balls

Beginners often struggle when trying to gain control of a ground ball because they do not position their bodies and sticks correctly. Players lose possession after the ball is in the stick because they do not cradle immediately.

ERROR   Inability to maintain control after picking up a ground ball

CORRECTION

1. Make sure players bend at the hips and knees.
2. Make sure players keep their head over the ball and the lead foot next to the ball.
3. Have players accelerate the stick through the ground ball pickup.
4. Have players begin cradling as soon as the ball is in the stick.

Ground Ball Games

SCRAMBLES

Goal

To teach body position against an opponent before picking up a ground ball

Description

Set up two lines of players five yards apart and facing the same direction. Stand in the middle of the lines with a pile of balls. As you yell the word, "Go," roll a ball out away from the players. The first player from each line goes after the ground ball, and the play continues until one of the two players has control.

Variations

- *Ground Ball Toward.* Have the players run toward you to practice a ground ball pickup as you roll the ball toward them.
- *Chance to Score.* Stand between the two lines of players and roll a ball away from the players. The player to get control of the ball is the attacker who tries to score, and the other player plays defense all the way to the goal.

GROUND BALL BASEBALL

Goal

To execute clean ground ball pickups

Description

Set up the field like a baseball diamond, using cones as bases. Each team has 5 to 10 players. The team on the "field" has players placed in positions similar to baseball (catcher, pitcher, first base, second base, third base, outfielders).

When a team is at bat, the "pitcher" rolls a ground ball to the "batter," whose goal is to pick it up and run the bases. If she misses and the catcher picks it up, it's one strike. Three strikes and the batter is out. If the batter picks the ball up, she runs while cradling the ball, and at each base she must incorporate a dodge. Meanwhile, the pitcher uses a second ball to throw a ground ball to the first baseman. She, in turn, picks it up and throws a ground ball to the second baseman, who throws a ground ball to the third baseman, who throws a ground ball to the catcher. If the fielding team gets the ground ball around the bases and back to the catcher before the batter makes it around all the bases, it is an out. If the batter makes it home first, award her team a point. After three outs or after everyone on the batting team has had an opportunity to run the bases, the teams switch roles.

To make the game easier

- Don't play "home run derby style," but instead work on "outs" at every base.
- Move the bases closer together.

To make the game harder

- Allow the batter to throw the ground ball into the field. The batter must then pick up a stationary ball on the way to first base. The fielders would then have to field the ball before throwing to first, instead of starting with a second ball from the pitcher.
- Require that all ground ball pickups be made with the nondominant hand.

Throwing

A team can't maintain possession of the ball without good throwing and catching skills. Throwing is propelling the ball with control from the stick. A player can't be a successful passer unless she learns proper throwing technique.

Two styles of overarm throwing are used in girls' lacrosse. The primary style uses the strong trunk muscles to aid the throw. In this style, the player begins the throwing motion with the stick above and behind her shoulder, as in pitching a baseball. In the second style, both hands stay in front of her body and shoulders. This style uses a strong wrist snap from both hands. The ball should be thrown and not pushed, no matter which style is used. In a proper throw the ball moves along the pocket strings and leaves the stick off of the throw strings at the top of the crosse.

Players may vary the height of the ball release to provide variety in the throw, resulting in sidearm, underhand, or reverse (backhand) passes. Players should learn to throw with both the right and left hands on top of the stick. Remember that the path of the stick dictates the direction and path of the ball.

When teaching the primary style of overhand throwing, make sure your players develop these skills (figure 8.9):

1. Pull the stick back and rotate the body toward the top-hand shoulder to prepare for a throw.
2. Slide the top hand so that the V of the hand is behind the pocket and within 6 inches of the stick head.
3. Position the stick head above and behind the shoulder.
4. Move the top hand upward first and then toward the target, with a wrist snap.
5. The bottom hand should pull the bottom of the shaft to a finishing position under the throwing arm.
6. Step onto the foot opposite the throwing hand, and rotate the shoulders and trunk.

Figure 8.9   Proper position for overhand throw. *Note:* Right hand is above and behind right shoulder.

When teaching the style of throwing in which both hands stay in front of the body and shoulders, make sure your players develop these skills (figure 8.10):

1. Pull the stick to a position above and in front of the shoulder of the top hand. The palm of the top hand will rotate to face the target and slide down the stick as much as 12 inches.

2. Cock the wrist of the top hand, which will result in the bottom hand extending away from the body.

3. Accelerate the top hand toward the target as the wrist snaps, and pull the bottom hand toward the opposite hip.

4. Step onto the foot opposite the top throwing hand.

a

b

c

Figure 8.10 Alternate throwing style. *(a)* Proper start position with top hand in front of shoulder, *(b)* mid-throw with top hand pushing as bottom hand pulls, *(c)* right wrist snaps as arm extends with left arm near left hip.

Error Detection and Correction for Throwing

A common problem for beginners is releasing the ball at the incorrect time. Many players release the ball too late or have poor throwing preparation.

ERROR   The ball is thrown directly to the ground

CORRECTION

1. Have the player start the throw with only the top hand above and behind the shoulder.

2. Have the player step onto the foot opposite the throwing hand toward the target to allow for trunk and shoulder rotation on the throw.

3. Be sure the player's bottom arm pulls the butt of the stick toward the body.

4. Be sure all throws involve a wrist snap, not a pushing motion from the top hand.

Throwing Games

SHUTTLE ACROSS

Goal

To practice accurate throwing and catching

Description

Place three or four players in a line, with a second line facing them about 15 yards away. The first player in one of the lines has a ball and passes to the first player in the other line. Have players exchange lines after each pass.

Variation

Use different passes, such as the following:

- *Coach's Call.* Call out the location of where the pass is coming from, such as from high right. Then call out where the pass is to be caught so that the thrower aims for targets around the receiver, such as high left to middle right.

○ *Ground Ball on the Move.* Have one line of players throw only bouncing or ground balls to the other line of players, who execute a ground ball pickup and then pass while on the move.

○ *Pass Away.* The second player in line throws a soft, high pass to the first player in the same line, who is cutting away from her. If the first player catches the pass, she then throws to the second player in the opposing line. If she fails to catch the pass, the ball will bounce to the opposing line, and the second player should retrieve it.

○ *Long, Short, Short.* Player 4 begins by throwing a long pass to stationary player 1. Player 1 returns pass to player 4 as she is cutting toward her. Player 4 then passes to the next player in line, player 2 (figure 8.11). Players 1 and 4 go to the end of the opposite line. Player 2 now sends a long pass to stationary player 5.

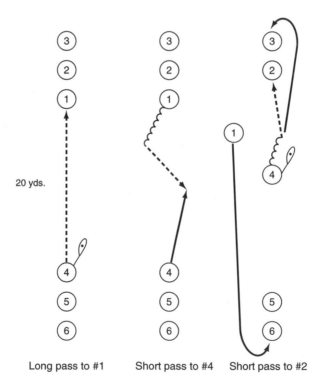

Long pass to #1   Short pass to #4   Short pass to #2

Figure 8.11 Long, short, short.

PASS THE TEAM TEST

Goal

To execute consecutive throws on the move

Description

Divide the players into two even teams and line them up facing each other about 20 yards apart. Have each line count consecutively out loud so that each player has a number. Roll two balls, one in each hand, toward a trash can goal located in the center of the two lines and at the same time call one of the numbers. The players from each team with that number run into the middle, and each player gets control of one of the balls and then returns to her line. In line she makes a pass to each team member and receives the ball back while moving down the line. After all team members have received the ball, it must be placed back in the trash can. Whoever gets the ball in the trash can first receives a point for her team.

To make the game easier

- Finish when one team completes all passes.
- Have fewer players on each team.

To make the game harder

- Require a certain type of pass.
- Use two players and four balls.

Catching

Catching is the skill of receiving a ball in the air with the stick. This is largely an eye–hand coordination skill and thus may be more difficult for some girls than others. Begin teaching with a hand-tossed ball to an underhand catch so that the give in the stick is down and with gravity. Then progress to a hand-tossed ball aimed toward the shoulder on the same side as the top hand. Eventually a player should learn to catch the ball from all angles around her body and at different heights.

Two styles of catching are used: a wrap catch and a give catch. Traditionally, girls used wood sticks and learned a wrap catch. Boys began using plastic sticks much earlier and learned a give catch. In both styles the player prepares for an incoming ball the same way, with the head extended toward the ball. In the wrap catch the first motion is rotating the wrist and wrapping the head of the stick around the ball, thus beginning the cradling motion. In the give catch, the first motion is back in line with the flight of the ball, followed by the cradling motion. Players can use either style with either a wood or plastic stick and the give catch is easier for beginning players to understand and execute.

Teach players the following steps to catching (figure 8.12):

1. Extend the top arm and stick head toward the pass before the ball arrives.
2. Watch the ball until it makes contact with the stick head.
3. Relax or soften the top hand as the ball arrives, creating a give with the ball motion.
4. Begin a cradling motion as soon as the ball has been received in the strings.
5. Protect the ball and stick with your body after the catch.

a b

Figure 8.12 Two styles of catching. *(a)* Give catch and, *(b)* wrap catch.

Error Detection and Correction for Catching

As young players are learning, they often mistime the give or wrap of the ball and they start to cradle or change direction before the ball is securely in the stick. As a consequence, the ball rebounds off some part of the stick.

ERROR   The ball bounces out of the stick

CORRECTION FOR THE WRAP CATCH

1. Be sure that the pocket of the player's stick is open to the ball before contact and that she does not begin cradling too soon.
2. Be sure that the player extends the stick head away from her body before she contacts the ball and that she does not bat at the ball.

CORRECTION FOR THE GIVE CATCH

1. Have the player maintain a soft grip on the stick to absorb the momentum of the ball.
2. Make sure that the player gives with the ball before cradling.

Catching Games

360-DEGREE CATCHING

Goal

To learn different points of release when passing and ways to catch the ball from all around the body

Description

Place six players in a circle with a diameter of 10 to 20 yards (figure 8.13). One player stands in the middle of the circle with the ball. She passes the ball to each player in the circle, without moving her feet. The players in the circle catch the ball and pass it back to the player in the middle, who catches the ball without moving her feet.

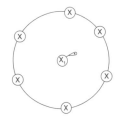

Figure 8.13
360-Degree
Catching.

Variation

- *Whirlwind*. As the players improve, have them play the game with two balls. This challenges them to concentrate and use their peripheral vision.

MULTIGOAL GAME

Goal

To increase catching and throwing skills under pressure

Description

Play 6 v 6 in a 30-by-30-yard area. Use cones to create four gates, each 5 yards wide, within the playing area. Do not set up any goals.

Players are not allowed to check the stick in this game, but they may block, intercept, and pick up ground balls. A team earns one point by passing the ball to a teammate through a gate. If a team scores, that team keeps the ball. If teammates pass and receive the ball through a gate using the nondominant hand, award their team two points. The game is nondirectional; teams can pass or score through either side of the gate. Note: Goalkeepers should participate as field players in this game.

To make the game easier

- ⊙ Give one team the advantage in numbers.
- ⊙ Add more gates.

To make the game harder

- ⊙ Require players to use their nondominant hand for catching and throwing.
- ⊙ Increase the number of defensive team players (5 v 6).
- ⊙ Do not allow players to consecutively score through the same gate.

Shooting

Shooting is propelling the ball in control toward the goal in an effort to score. Shooting uses the same techniques as throwing, except the ball is directed to a stationary target, the goal. Like passes, shots will come from a variety of release points. Tell your players to see the back of the net and to shoot to the open spaces on goal, not at the goalie. Shots taken from a distance require more force, but with all shots, placement of the ball is key. The highest percentage of successful shots are taken when players shoot from the center of the field. The player should also try to move the goalie. Once a goalie commits to a fake or moves with a shooter, the player can shoot toward the open space.

To obtain accurate placement and increased power on the shot, a player must use a wrist snap. A primary difference between a hard throw and a strong shot is that the strong shot uses an increased wrist snap to release the ball quickly, with added velocity. The wrist should use the same motion to direct the head of the crosse, as if the player were releasing a basketball shot or finishing a tennis serve. Both hands work in unison, with the top hand moving back to front and the bottom hand moving front to back. Be sure the players practice both catching a pass and shooting, as well as shooting while on the run.

When players are shooting the ball, be sure they follow these instructions:

1. Position the feet toward the goal and step onto the opposite foot from the top hand on the stick.
2. Prepare to shoot by cradling the stick into a proper throwing release point.
3. Transfer body weight from backward to forward.
4. Follow through in a controlled manner.
5. Control the wrist snap to direct the placement of the ball.

Bounce Shot

The bounce shot is intended to propel the ball down to the ground and thus requires the goalkeeper to make a difficult save. Such shots can be released anywhere, from overhead to sidearm. To perform a bounce shot, players must learn these skills:

1. Bring the stick back above the shoulder as if to throw, with the opposite foot forward and body ready to rotate.
2. Pull the stick forward, using more pull on the bottom arm, and snap the wrists down at the ground.
3. Aim for an area between the crease and the goalkeeper's feet.

Free Position Shooting

When a defender commits a major foul (for instance, pushing the ball carrier) within the eight-meter arc, the offensive player gets a free position shot. The player who was fouled goes to the hash mark closest to where the foul was committed on the eight-meter arc (figure 8.14). The player who fouled moves four meters behind the player she fouled. Those players inside the eight-meter arc must exit the arc at the closest point and stand four meters away from the fouled player. Those players on or outside the arc stand where they are but must also be four

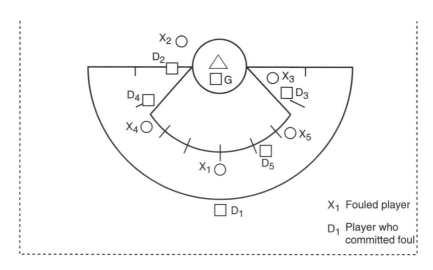

Figure 8.14　Set up for free position shot.

meters from the fouled player. Once the umpire whistles to restart play, the player with the ball may shoot, run, or pass the ball immediately. Several styles can be used to execute a free position shot. Here is the easiest method for your players to master:

1. Place the foot opposite the throwing arm on the hash mark, turn to the side, and bend slightly at the knees.
2. When the whistle sounds, take a slide step forward to gain momentum while pulling the crosse back and upward to prepare to shoot.
3. Follow through, snapping the wrists, to the area in the goal where you want the ball to go.

An attacker taking a free position shot may move and run in toward the goal on the whistle. She should analyze the defenders nearest her and have a plan in mind before the whistle because defenders will immediately move in to block the shot. If she chooses to run toward the goal cage to shoot, she will have very limited time to prepare or release a shot. The key to a successful free position shot is for players to try to move the goalie before they take a shot. An option is to make a diagonal run in front of a defender by cutting her path off and moving the goalie at the same time. The attacker must protect her stick at all times, as the defense will be trying to block or check if allowed.

Error Detection and Correction for Shooting

Players often get too excited about shooting on goal and they do not prepare properly for the shot. Often the first thing players see is the goalkeeper, and that is the target at which they shoot. Have players look at the spaces around the goalkeeper as targets and then shoot.

ERROR   Shooting at the goalkeeper's stick or directly at the goalie

CORRECTION

1. Have players look at the cage and look for shooting opportunities.

2. Have players prepare their body and stick for release of a shot.

3. Have players shoot for open spaces in the cage.

4. Have players try to shoot at a level of the goal cage different from where they are cradling the ball.

Shooting Game

POST SHOOTING

Goal

To practice catching and shooting for the far or close goal post

Description

Divide the players into four lines. The four lines form a box around the 12-meter fan. Two of these lines are feeding lines, and each player has a ball. Position the feeding lines on each side of the crease and above the goal line. The other two lines will be receiving a pass and shooting for goal. These cutting lines can start up on the 12-meter fan. Have the players rotate in a circle so that they play from all feeding and shooting lines. No goalie should be in the cage, but a shooting net or board may be used (see figure 8.15).

Reinforce the key teaching points and be sure players look at the net area inside the post that they are shooting for. Give them only one choice of where to shoot at first, then let them choose either the close or far post. Teach the players to be accurate first and then work to increase power later.

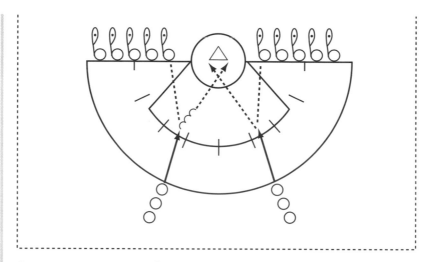

Figure 8.15 Far post shooting.

Variations

Add the challenge of hitting only the four corners of the goal cage. Call the post they are to shoot for just as they catch the pass. Have the shooters aim for high, middle, and low heights on the posts. Have them add a roll and change of hands after the catch but before the shot. Vary the feeding lines and cutting lines from all angles around the goal area.

TARGETS

Goal

To improve accuracy of shots to the goal cage

Description

Divide players into teams. You can use as many as five teams. Each team claims an eight-meter hash mark and lines up behind each other with a ball. After each player has had a chance to shoot and the balls are retrieved, the team moves to a different hash mark until each player and team have shot from each hash mark.

Prepare the goal area by attaching six markers to the goal mouth. Various shooting nets are manufactured for this purpose, or you can make a shooting board by cutting the corners and waist areas out of a piece of plywood. Other ideas include hanging pinnies, taping pieces of bright plastic, or using sticks stuck into the net. Number the markers from one to six, going around the corners of the cage, with two additional markers at waist height.

As a player steps up for her turn to shoot, call a number from one to six. She must adjust her aim to shoot toward that target. She scores a point for her team if she hits the correct target and if the ball has the speed of a shot, not a soft pass. Teams add up their individual scores after a full round of shots have been taken.

To make the game easier

- ⊙ Use big, numbered targets.
- ⊙ Allow the player to be closer to the goal or to run in toward the goal before a shot.

To make the game harder

- ⊙ Players must move on a diagonal.
- ⊙ Players catch a pass on the move before a shot.
- ⊙ Players fake to one target and shoot to another.

Individual Defensive Skills

Defenders guard offensive players to prevent them from scoring. Defenders should try to mark, or guard, the player to whom they are assigned, staying near that offensive player and between the ball and the goal.

When an opponent has possession of the ball, the defender tries to dictate the path the attacker takes. The defender does this by occupying a space on the side of the offensive player. Only when the defender has her body and stick in proper position may she consider a stick check if her level of rules allows. The US Lacrosse Rules Committee has adapted some specific modifications for younger and less experienced players, which address the issue of safety for stick-to-stick checking.

Defensive Body Positioning

The defender's goal is to position her body in a space that limits the ball carrier's options and to control the ball carrier's path to the goal. The defender may choose to force the attacker to her weaker cradling side; into a double-team; or away from the center of the field, where the attacker has fewer shooting or passing options.

Teach players to follow these steps when they body check:

1. Keep the feet facing the same direction as the ball carrier's feet, not running backwards.
2. Remain in a hip-to-hip body position while running with the ball carrier. Keep the body next to and not directly in front of the ball carrier.
3. Strive to control the ball carrier's path by getting into a space before the attacker can get there.
4. Carry the stick in an upright position between the shoulders, ready to block or stick check if allowed.

Because so many players rely on a strong or dominant hand for accurate passing and shooting, the defender, by positioning her body as an obstacle on the strong side of the ball carrier, can effectively slow the attacker or force a bad pass (figure 8.16). If a defender gets caught on the wrong side of her opponent, she should try to cross the path of the ball carrier to the strong side, forcing the opponent to use her weaker hand. This is called *turning*, or *crossing*, a player.

Figure 8.16 Proper body checking position forcing to opponent's right side.

Error Detection and Correction for Body Checking

Too often, defensive players commit to play the ball for a block or possibly a stick check and lose proper body position.

ERROR   Defender loses body position on the ball carrier

CORRECTION

1. Make sure that the defender stays hip to hip and does not get ahead of or in front of the attacker.

2. If the defender loses the correct body position, recover to the proper hip-to-hip position on the attacker's chosen side.

3. Teach defenders how to block a pass or shot from the proper defensive body position.

Defensive Body Positioning Game

CROSSING THE ENGLISH CHANNEL

Goal

To practice defensive body positioning and footwork

Description

Mark off a space 10 yards by 20 yards with cones or lines. Pair players and give one player a ball. The other player is the defender and has no stick. The player with the ball runs through the 20-yard channel, while the defender tries to maintain proper body position and footwork while moving with the ball carrier. The defender should try to remain on only one side of the ball carrier for the length of the channel.

Use cue words such as "hip to hip," "feet facing forward," or "force her to the sideline." Defenders should not let attackers get more than two steps ahead. Maintain a safe distance (about one to two feet) between players so that there is enough space and time to react.

Variation

⊙ *Meet Me Halfway.* The defender starts halfway across the channel. On the word "Go," the defender tries to close the gap between herself and the ball while trying to get to a side of the channel to force the oncoming ball carrier to her weak side, or to the sideline of the grid. The defender's footwork and timing are critical.

Stick Checking

Stick checking is the repeated tapping motion a defender uses to dislodge the ball from her opponent's stick. All checks must be controlled. US Lacrosse is attempting to send a consistent message regarding stick checking for youth players. As noted in the *Official Rules for Girls' Youth Lacrosse*, players below the seventh-grade level should not use stick checking, which is introduced only in Level B and A rules. The Rules Committee hopes that mandating no checking will allow the beginning player to work on the fundamentals of the game—passing, catching, footwork, proper positioning, and marking—before she is introduced to the more advanced skill of stick checking.

Introduce stick checking after players have mastered the fundamentals. Players on seventh- and eighth-grade teams are allowed to use modified checking as an intermediate step toward full checking. *Modified checking* is defined as checking the stick if it is below shoulder level, using a downward motion away from the other player's body (figure 8.17). Use of modified checking allows the older youth player to learn proper checking skills, while at the same time encouraging good cradling and stick-handling skills for the attack player. Umpires and coaches should strictly enforce this rule, never allowing checks near a player's head or face.

Note that stick-to-stick contact is not necessarily a violation of the no-checking/modified-checking rule. A defender who is holding her stick in good defensive position may force the attack player to cradle into her stick, causing contact. This is not considered a stick check, as the attack player initiated the contact, not the defender. A similar situation would exist when the defender puts her stick up in an attempt to block or intercept a pass and the attacker makes contact while in the act of throwing or catching the ball.

When teaching stick checking, make sure your players have learned the following:

1. Correctly position the body before attempting to stick check.
2. Establish a rhythm and make contact when the opponent's stick is most available during the cradling motion. Only stick-to-stick contact is allowed.
3. Keep the body in balance for multiple checks.
4. Repeat quick taps on the opponent's stick.
5. Keep the feet moving and anticipate a ground ball.

Young lacrosse players can become overzealous with stick checks. You must emphasize the importance of body positioning! Injuries occur when players are out of position or are out of control with their stick checks. Immediately penalize illegal stick checks.

Figure 8.17 Proper execution of modified stick checking. *(a)* Defender in white in correct body position for check, *(b)* proper stick to stick contct, *(c)* release of stick check by defenders as ball drops to ground.

Error Detection and Correction for Stick Checking

A defensive player attempts a large swing to check the ball and, if unsuccessful, gets beaten by the ball carrier.

ERROR   Defensive player commits to one big swing with her stick

CORRECTION

1. Have the player maintain hip-to-hip body positioning while checking.
2. Maintain a space between defender and attacker. Do not allow her to step toward the ball to check.
3. Have the player keep her feet moving at all times to position for a check.
4. Make certain the player's checks are small taps.
5. Make sure the player times the stick check with the cradling motion to allow repeated stick-to-stick contact.

Stick Checking Game

WOODPECKER

Goal

To teach the motion and control of stick checking

Description

Pair players. One player holds her stick out from waist level and horizontal to the ground while the second player performs a series of tapping motions with the side or wall of her stick, making firm, rapid, and repeated contact like a woodpecker. Be sure the motion of the checking stick is downward on contact to the ball carrier's stick. Players switch roles and repeat the exercise.

Encourage players to maintain control in their checks. They should use a firm wrist, snap down, and release, which will help them learn to check without a large windup. Repeat the series with a ball, and discuss the success of dislodging the ball based on where the stick contact is made. Encourage players to practice with both hands on the top of the stick.

Variations

Require a certain number of stick-to-stick contacts or taps before trying to dislodge the ball. Have the checker run in place to simulate checking on the move. Allow the standing player to pivot on one foot and move the stick around her but still at waist level.

Blocking

Blocking is a skill that requires eye tracking and visual coordination; it can be taught. To execute a block, a defensive player positions her stick to block a pass or shot as it leaves the offensive player's stick. Stick position and timing are essential elements of this skill.

Teach your players the following steps for blocking (figure 8.18):

1. Extend the stick vertically toward the sky. Don't reach toward the opponent's stick.

2. Loosen the grip of the top hand and slide the stick through to extend the reach into the path of the ball.

3. Let the ball carrier begin the throwing motion before extending the stick into the passing lane. Timing is critical.

4. Watch the ball out of the offensive player's stick and into the defender's stick.

a

b

Figure 8.18 Blocking a pass. *(a)* Proper body and stick position to prepare for block, *(b)* proper extension of stick and tracking ball visually into blocker's stick.

Blocking Game

MONKEY IN THE MIDDLE

Goal

To practice blocking

Description

Players 1 and 2 stand facing each other 10 yards apart. As player 1 passes the ball to player 2, a defender (the monkey) stands one step in front of player 1 and attempts to block the pass. If the monkey is successful, she gets possession and carries the ball to the other end to give to player 2. If she is unsuccessful, she must circle player 1 and sprint to the other end, where she tries to block player 2's pass to player 1. Alternate the roles of passers and monkeys. Reinforce the key points. Be sure players do not jump to try to block the pass.

Variation

⊙ *Heighten the Challenge.* Allow passers to fake and move them farther apart. Let them pivot on one foot only and protect the ball before the pass. Or use two monkeys—one on either end.

Intercepting

Intercepting is catching a pass that was intended for the opponent. Interceptions are a matter of timing, anticipation, and patience. Intercepting is one of the hardest skills to master, but it is a very valuable defensive skill.

Have your players follow these instructions to execute an interception (figure 8.19):

1. Extend the stick by loosening the grip of the top hand and pushing through with the bottom hand.
2. Reach up in front and beyond the opponent's stick.
3. Time the acceleration of the stick and body once the pass is in the air.
4. Be sure to step in front of the opponent and accelerate away.
5. Be ready to beat your opponent to the loose ball.

Figure 8.19   Executing an interception.

Error Detection and Correction for Blocking and Intercepting

Blocking and intercepting both rely on patience, timing, and good visual tracking. When the defender senses the ball is about to be released, she should visually track the ball into her stick for the block or interception. Defensive players, in their eagerness to get the ball, often commit with their sticks and bodies too soon.

ERROR   Missing the ball in flight

CORRECTION

1. Have players keep their sticks in ready position and extend them at the proper time. Do not let them swing the sticks in the air in an attempt to bat the ball.

2. Have players extend their sticks straight up for the block. Do not allow them to step or reach forward toward the opponent.

3. Have players keep their eyes on the ball, track it, and see it into their sticks.

4. Have players extend their sticks beyond the opponent's for an interception and accelerate through the catch.

Intercepting Games

COUGARS ON THE CHASE

Goal

To teach tracking, timing, and anticipation on interceptions

Description

Players 1 and 2 stand 15 yards apart and pass the ball back and forth. A line of three or four players stand 5 yards to the side and at right angles to players 1 and 2. As the ball leaves player 1's stick, a player standing to the side of player 2 accelerates in front and tries to intercept the pass. If she is successful, she returns the ball to player 2 and runs to the end of player 1's line. If she is unsuccessful, she returns to the end of her line.

Encourage the "cougars" to sprint and reach for the ball with a fully extended stick, stepping toward the ball as they go to catch it. Change the side and angle of approach to start from behind the passers.

ULTIMATE LACROSSE

Goal

To encourage defenders to go for interceptions and blocks

Description

Play 6 v 6 in a playing area of 30 by 60 yards, with goal lines marked at the ends. The team with the ball tries to complete a pass to a player beyond the goal line for a point. No player may run with the ball (so the game resembles Ultimate Frisbee). The defensive team only may get a turnover by recovering a ground ball first or by intercepting or blocking a pass from the opponent for an additional point. Play for a designated time to see which team can accumulate the most points.

To make the game easier

- Eliminate points for blocking.
- Allow five steps after a reception.

To make the game harder

- Give the team that scores a goal three points and allow the defending team a point for each block or interception.
- Allow the team with the ball to have an extra (neutral) player.

Defensive Positioning

Individual defensive positioning refers to the defensive player's position in relation to the ball and to an opponent without the ball. In the instructions on body checking, you learned about the importance of the defender's body position in relation to the ball carrier. If a defender's opponent does not have possession of the ball, she must adjust her position in relation to her opponent and the location of the ball. The closer the ball carrier is to her teammate, the tighter the defender should mark her player. If the ball carrier is far away, she can take a step or two away from her player (without the ball) so that she can see her player and the ball carrier, with enough space and time to make an interception. At this point all players must understand about the shooting lane and three-second violations (figure 8.20).

Figure 8.20   Rope outlines the shooting lane. *Note:* The player on the right is standing illegally in the shooting lane.

These are the key points in teaching defensive positioning in front of the goal (figure 8.21):

1. Position the body so that it is both closer to the goal and closer to the ball than the opponent.
2. Keep the stick up to show coverage of the passing lane and readiness to intercept.
3. Stand so one foot is pointing toward the opponent and the other foot is open to the center of the field.
4. Position the head and eyes so that both the ball and the opposing player can be seen at all times.
5. Constantly reposition as the ball is passed or carried to a new location.

When defending within the arc, a defender always wants to be prepared to deny a pass to her opponent and be positioned to intercept any pass. If she is unable to intercept a pass to her opponent, she should immediately adjust her feet to get into proper body checking position. She must also know where the ball is so that she is ready to help a teammate.

At this level, when a defender's opponent goes behind the goal cage to receive a pass, we recommend that the defender stay on the front side of the goal. The defender must know where the ball is in front of the goal, especially now. She must be reminded of several very important rules that are written to protect her safety.

Figure 8.21 Player in black in front of goal is in proper defensive position.

Error Detection and Correction for Defensive Positioning

A defender off the ball often makes two common mistakes: She watches the ball as she moves and loses track of her player, or she watches only her player and is not aware of where the ball is going.

ERROR   Allowing the opposing player to get away or losing sight of the ball

CORRECTION

1. Teach players to always see and know where both their marked player and the ball are located.

2. Teach players to anticipate opponents' cuts, not only react to them. A player should always maintain a ball-side and goal-side position with her marked player.

3. Teach players to anticipate an overthrow or loose-ball situation, and encourage them to get to the loose ball first.

Defensive Positioning Games

FREEZE PASS

Goal

To teach defensive positioning in relation to the ball and a goal

Description

Four to six players scatter around the 12-meter line. Half of the players are designated as defense by wearing pinnies. Offensive players may not move from their spots as they pass the ball among each other. Offensive players should hold a caught pass until you have a chance to check visually the defensive position of each defender. Then blow your whistle so that the attacker may make another pass. Defenders may not intercept or block the passes. They should concentrate on moving their feet and sticks into the proper area in relation to the ball and their opponents.

Review the position of each defender as each pass is made. The player on the ball should adjust her feet to force the attacker in one direction only. Check that the defenders next to the ball and one pass away have proper stick positioning. Check to see that the proper goal-side and ball-side position is maintained at all times.

DEFEND YOUR EIGHT-METER ARC

Goal

To reinforce proper defensive positioning within the critical scoring area

Description

Six or more players are in the critical scoring area, with a goalie or a shooting net in goal (figure 8.22). One offensive player in the eight-meter area is moving to get open as she is marked by one defensive player. The other four players around the 12-meter fan pass the ball among them. (They need an extra supply of balls near their feet.) When the offensive player is free inside the eight-meter arc, she should receive a pass and look to shoot. If the player scores on the shot, start another ball on the outside. If a goalie or the shooting net rebounds the shot, the ball is in play for the attacker and defender. Have the two players inside the eight-meter arc stay in for a designated number of balls, and award points for taking a shot and making a goal, as well as for the defender gaining possession and carrying the ball outside the 12-meter fan.

To make the game easier

⊙ Limit the defenders to just attempting to block the shot.

⊙ Allow the attacker to go out to the 12-meter fan to receive the ball.

To make the game harder

⊙ Limit the defender to just intercepting the entry pass.

⊙ Add an additional defender.

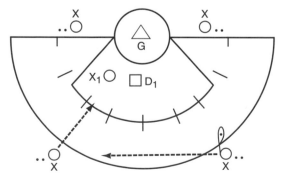

Figure 8.22 Defend Your Eight-Meter Arc.

Crease Defense

The crease defender is a player who defends an opponent with or without the ball who is behind the goal line extended. (We recommend that defenders at the youth level not follow their offensive player behind the goal.) When she is in position in front of the goal, she must make sure that she is in a legal and safe playing position. The goal circle defender may not be in the shooting lane, commit a three-second violation, or enter the crease. The defender's mission is to take the space ahead of the opponent and move out to guard the player and prevent her from catching a pass. When she is defending a player with the ball who is challenging from behind the cage, she should meet the player just behind the goal line extended and then force her up the side of the eight-meter arc. She always tries to keep her opponent moving away from the cage and to continually decrease her angle for shooting. This situation is often a good time for a double-team.

Error Detection and Correction for Crease Defense

Far too often, a ball carrier who challenges a defender from behind the goal circle is able to outrun the defender and turn toward the middle of the field to take a high-percentage shot.

ERROR The offensive player is able to shoot from the middle of the field after challenging from behind the goal circle.

CORRECTION

1. Remind defenders that their job is to limit or dictate where the offensive player may go with the ball.

2. Review and encourage defenders to concentrate on proper body checking and footwork and then, if in position, to consider a stick check or a block.

3. Encourage the defender to lead the attacker where she wants her to go instead of following her.

4. Practice the timing of a defender getting to the goal line extended, planting a foot to push off, and changing directions before the ball carrier arrives.

Crease Defense Game

QUEEN OF THE CREASE

Goal

To have crease defenders learn how to play a ball carrier challenging from behind the goal.

Description

Divide the players into groups of five to seven and send them to a goal area with a goalkeeper. Each player in the group plays defense against the others for one time. After one player has had a turn defending everyone in the group, the defender changes. Points are given as follows: one point for defense if a shot is taken but does not score and two points for defense if they gain control of the ball before or after the shot. Attackers can only score one point if they score a goal. Add up each player's points at the end, both offensive and defensive to crown the queen of the crease.

To make the game easier

- Allow the goalie to join the defender for a double-team.
- Allow the attacker to only challenge from one side of the crease.

To make the game harder

- Increase the numbers to 2 v 2 or 3 v 3.
- Limit the attacker to just five seconds to get a shot off.

Movement Without the Ball

As in all games involving a ball, it is faster to move the ball in the air than to run with it. Moving the ball through the air requires you to teach skills like passing and catching, as well as player and ball movement principles. Teaching young girls the concepts of movement without the ball is much more difficult than teaching them what to do with the ball. Such tactics as supporting the ball, moving to get the ball, and cutting are now presented.

Supporting the Ball

Knowing when and where to cut is one of the most important and challenging decisions for each player on the field. The player with the ball should have three passing options: She should be able to pass the ball forward, laterally, or backward (a back pass). Passing the ball forward toward the goal advances the ball most directly and is most threatening to the defense. A lateral pass across the field is appropriate to get the ball to a part of the field that has more open space and to a player who may not be so closely marked. A back pass allows a team time to reposition itself, to create and use space, and also possibly to change sides of the field. To support the ball after each pass, players off the ball need to constantly move to reposition themselves so that the player with the ball has all three options available. Back passes are often made to the goalkeeper because she is an unmarked player who can use her crease for protection.

Error Detection and Correction for Supporting the Ball

Most young girls at first will not understand cutting or supporting the ball. Instead, they are likely to run parallel to the ball and toward the goal. Look for opportunities to show how a cut into another area would be a better option to help the ball carrier.

ERROR   The passer does not have a teammate available to pass to

CORRECTION

1. Teach players with the ball to look and listen for teammates in all directions around them for an opportunity to pass.

2. Make sure the player with the ball is ready to release a pass in an instant when she locates a free teammate.

3. Encourage attackers to give several options to the ball carrier by cutting into several different spaces around her.

4. Encourage attackers to be aware of their teammates and not just the ball, so they do not all cut into the same space at the same time.

5. Encourage the ball carrier to pass only to teammates who are moving or cutting, not to those who are standing.

Supporting Game

SUPPORT WITH TWO BALLS

Goal

To improve off-the-ball movement and support around the ball

Description

Play a game of 6 v 6 using two balls at the same time on a short field. Use a trash can at each end as a goal. Each team starts with one ball, but as play progresses, one team could end up with both balls. Players need to react to the closest ball and therefore must focus on support. Require that a minimum number of passes be made before a goal can be attempted, and award a team one point for every goal scored. After a goal is scored, the closest defender restarts play with a clear. The clearing defender may run or pass the ball.

To make the game easier

⊙ Assign players to work within groups on their team. For instance, player A would always be supported by player B or C.

⊙ Limit the number of steps a player may take with the ball to five. This will encourage more passing.

To make the game harder

⊙ Add a third ball and more players.

⊙ Require the player with the ball to have support on two of her four sides at all times. If she does not, it is a turnover.

Moving to Get the Ball

In the game of lacrosse, a player is guarded or marked closely by an opposing player. The first thing an offensive player must do is to move in some direction to get away from her defender so that she has room to make a catch and receive a pass from her teammate. This is best accomplished by making a move or several small steps in the wrong direction. The player is trying to turn or get her defender off balance for just a second so that she can accelerate away from the defender. Such individual maneuvers are similar to basketball moves, with common names like jab step, stutter step, crossover, roll, or change of direction. When the defender has been outmaneuvered, the attack player accelerates, or cuts, into a space to receive a possible pass.

Players may cut in all directions in relation to the ball. The most difficult to defend is a cut directly to the ball, where the attack player has gained a step on the defender and positions her body in front of the defender to protect her catch. However, space and a defender's position may require a cut in a different direction, such as away from the ball, which is called a flat (90-degree) cut. For instance, it's a flat cut if you run straight across the width of the field when the ball is coming straight down the length of the field. Often a player cuts for the ball and runs out of space on the field or gets too close to the ball carrier. You also must teach players how to make space on the field for themselves or their teammates. Making space refers to the act of clearing an area for another player to cut into to receive a pass.

Error Detection and Correction for Moving to Get the Ball

Often the attacker simply attempts to outrun the defender and is not free to receive a pass. When she continues the cut too long, she gets too close to the ball carrier.

ERROR   Cutter is not free to receive the pass from her teammate in time to use the existing available space

CORRECTION

1. Encourage the attacker to learn many different moves to cause the defender to misstep and then just accelerate to the ball once the misstep occurs.

2. Teach the attacker to make an adequate space to cut into before she accelerates toward the ball.

3. Teach the attacker to get a step ahead of the defender, then to step across the defender's path to use her own body to protect the catch.

Moving Player Game

PASS TO A MOVING PLAYER FOR POINTS

Goal

To encourage players to move to a space to catch a ball

Description

Play 3 v 3 in a 25-by-25-yard area with no goals. The team with the ball may only score points for passing to a teammate who is running to receive the pass. Each completed pass is one point. The defenders may only intercept the ball in the air. A team plays for a designated time (for instance, two minutes) and then switches from attack to defense. Attack is awarded a point for every pass caught on the move. Defense is awarded a point for every interception or knocking the ball to the ground.

To make the game easier

⊙ Play 4 v 3 or 5 v 4.

⊙ Award a point for every time a teammate touches rather than catches a ball.

To make the game harder

⊙ Only award points for cuts directly to the ball.

⊙ Allow the defenders to block the pass from their player as well.

Spacing and Timing of Cuts

When a player masters the skill of freeing herself to receive a pass from a teammate, you can begin to develop the concept of teamwork—consecutive passes among teammates to maintain possession while advancing the ball down the field. While player 1 is cutting to receive a pass from player 2, player 3 is preparing to cut to receive a pass from player 1. Teach all beginning lacrosse players the concepts of making space to cut into and knowing the proper timing of a cut.

All young athletes find the skills of making space and knowing when to use this space challenging. Most young athletes move into the space where they want to catch the pass, and then they stand and call for the ball. They have used up the space in which they want to catch the ball too soon and they stop, which often results in an opportunity for a defender to intercept the pass. A player must first decide if there is enough room around the ball to cut into and then decide when to cut. Players learn how to make these decisions through trial and error in practice.

If a pass is incomplete, the failure could lie with either the passer or the cutter. Often, a ball carrier has tunnel vision toward the goal and is unlikely to look for options to her side or behind her. A passer must keep her stick in a ready position to pass the ball at any moment and in any direction. A cutter may fail to provide support to the passer at the right time; she may move into a space either too early or too late. All teammates should try to be aware of each other so that two cutters do not cut into the same space at the same time.

Passing Game

PASS ALONG

Goal

To develop the concept of creating space and cutting at the right time

Description

Arrange four to six players in a 30-by-30-yard space. Assign each player a consecutive number.

Part I—to develop space awareness, have them try to pass to consecutive numbers in order (1 to 2, 2 to 3, etc.) while using all the space given to them. All passes must be at least 10 yards long. Emphasize moving to catch the ball.

Part II—To develop the idea of timing players cutting movement, spread the ordered passing over a larger distance. Have two or more teams start at one sideline of a field and spread evenly across the width. Start the race among teams to move the ball to the opposite sideline using the numbered sequence they have practiced from Part I.

Part III—To develop both spacing and timing, start all team members on one sideline. Each player must play the ball only once. See which team can create the most efficient and fastest way to move the ball across the field.

To make the game easier

⊙ Add more players.

⊙ Allow the players to run five steps with the ball.

To make the game harder

- Do not allow any steps between catches.
- Have the players repeat the number sequence two times in 50 yards.
- Have the players use 100 yards.

Spreading the Field

All team games that use a ball make using space properly a challenge. Offensive players must keep reasonable distances between each other and the ball to create space for teammates to pass into, run through, and move the ball efficiently in. When attackers bunch up, the defenders are brought too close together, which makes it easy for them to defend, possibly with a check, double-team, block, or interception of the ball. When two attack players stand very near each other, one defender can guard both.

Although the restraining line limits the number of players near the goal area, there is no offside rule, as in soccer, to prevent players from positioning themselves closer to the goal than the ball. Therefore, it is sound attacking strategy to position some attack players close to the goal, so they may cut to the ball and then sprint downfield to get in a position (lower) between the goal and the ball carrier. The cut, replacement below the ball, and recut process allows players to use, create, and reuse the space in front of the goal.

Spacing Game

CENTER CIRCLE BULL'S-EYE

Goal

To develop a sense of timing and distance between cutters and teammates

Description

Using the center circle of a lacrosse field (20 yards in diameter), make an inner bull's-eye circle of 6 to 8 yards (figure 8.23). The area inside the bull's-eye is very hot, and a player can survive only if she runs through the area within three seconds. Only one player may be in the

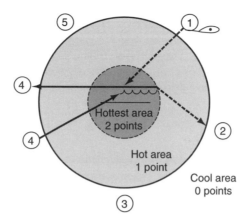

Figure 8.23   Center Circle Bull's-Eye.

center circle at any one time, and her teammates must be at least 10 yards from each other on the outside of the circle.

The object of the game is for a team of 5 to 7 players to score as many points as possible in a given time. A team scores two points if they successfully pass and catch a ball to a moving cutter and the catch is made within the bull's-eye (the hottest area). The team scores one point if the pass is caught within the large circle (the hot area) but outside the center circle. The player who has caught the ball may run or pass the ball to the circle edge. A point is taken away if more than two players are in the bull's-eye at the same time or if any two team-mates are caught standing closer than 10 yards to each other on the outside of the circle. Players may pass to each other outside the circle (the cool area) for no points.

To make the game easier

- Allow more time for the cutters to cross the bull's eye.
- Have the attackers follow a sequence of assigned numbers as to the order of who cuts to the middle.

To make the game harder

- Add one or two defenders who stay in the center circle to inter-cept.
- Allow no more than two players to cut through the center circle at once.

Extra-Player Concepts

Like most other games involving a ball, the attacking team should try to create a situation where there are more attackers on the move to their goal than defenders. This is often referred to as a fast-break opportunity for the offense. Many such opportunities will occur in a game of lacrosse, and the fundamental skills of player and ball movement should be taught and practiced.

Running a Fast Break

The object of any team on defense is to create a turnover from the opponent and then to counterattack with an extra player. When the ball changes possession, the new attacking team must react very quickly to gain an advantage. To gain this advantage each attack player must use a burst of speed to outrun her opponent and get goal side of her. Such a quick transition should create an extra player for the new attacking team.

Principles for a fast-break situation are common for all ball games. In lacrosse, it is important to keep distance between teammates, or spread the field. Also, leave the path to the goal open for the ball carrier as she runs toward the goal, which is the most threatening for the defense. Once the ball carrier has drawn a new defender, she must locate and pass the ball to the unguarded player. Remember to teach players to look for and prepare to pass to the new free teammate.

Fast-Break Game—Offensive

EXTRA ATTACKER FAST BREAK

Goal

To score on the fast-break opportunity

Description

Set up the field in a 30-by-20-yard area, with a goal at each end (figure 8.24). Divide players into two even teams, with one goalie at each goal. One team starts on defense, the other on attack. They remain that way for a designated time (such as five minutes) and then switch roles. The attacking team forms two lines outside of each goal cage at

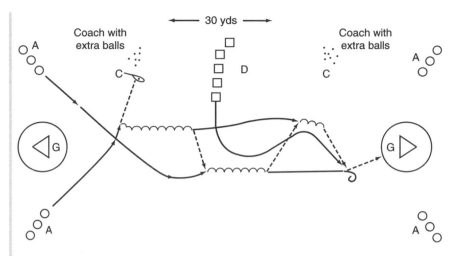

Figure 8.24   Extra Attacker Fast Break.

each end of the field (a total of four attack lines). The defensive team forms one line on the sideline at the midfield.

Start by passing the ball to one of the two players from the attacking team. (Alternate the end of the field from which you start the ball.) A defender from the side comes to the middle. These three players play 2 v 1. If the defender comes up with the ball, she has two choices. First, she can clear the ball to a defensive player on the sideline for one point. Second, she can try to beat the opposing two players and go to the goal. If she gets a shot, award one point; if she scores, award two points. If the goalie saves the ball and clears successfully to the defender, award the defenders one point. If the attackers get a shot on goal, award one point. If the attackers score, award two points.

To make the game easier

⊙ Add a second defender after a certain amount of time.
⊙ Make the field smaller.

To make the game harder

⊙ Add a third attacker after a certain amount of time.
⊙ Make the field wider so that the single defender has more ground to cover.

Defending a Fast Break

If the attacking team gains a numerical player advantage when coming through the midfield, the defensive unit downfield must prepare to meet the challenge of being outnumbered and to prevent a high-percentage or an unguarded shot. The defense should pressure the ball as soon as possible to slow the attacker's progress down the field, while the weak-side and other defenders recover below the ball and evaluate how to best prepare for defensive coverage. With the objective of stalling the ball carrier as much time as possible to allow more teammates to recover downfield, defenders attempt to slow the ball's movement by constantly reacting to the ball movement and communicating with each other about who is pressuring the ball and who is covering. Introduce the terms "ball" (call for defending the ball carrier), "help" (defender being beaten by opponent), and "I've got two" (defender recognizing she is covering two opponents). The goalkeeper should think of herself as the last defender, and she should come out of her crease to intercept passes as necessary rather than letting a free attack player catch a pass and shoot on her.

Fast-Break Game—Defensive

INTRODUCTION TO TRANSITION

Goal

To defend the fast break

Description

The playing area is 50 by 30 yards, with a goal at each end (figure 8.25). Divide players so that they form three lines on one endline, and start with two defenders positioned at the far end. Have a goalie in each goal.

To start, the game is played 3 v 2. One of the three attack players receives a pass from the goalkeeper (or coach) with the ball, and these players move toward the opposite goal to face the first two defenders. The job of the defense is to delay the fast break and look for an interception. If the team of three gets a shot or scores, the defending team becomes the offense. The player who shot becomes the defender, so now the game turns to a 2 v 1 and goes the opposite way down the field. (The attack players who did not shoot stay back on that end of

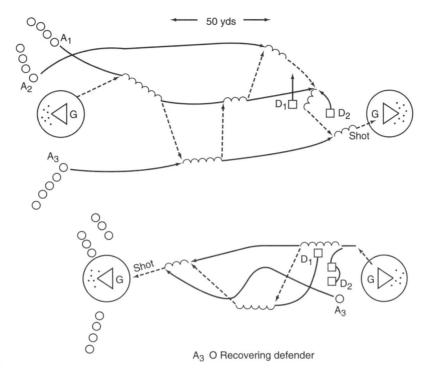

Figure 8.25   Introduction to Transition.

the field.) Once these two players take a shot or score, a new attack group of three immediately comes onto the field and starts with a goalie clear. The two attack players who stayed behind now play defense. Award one point for each goal. Switch goalkeepers after a designated number of possessions, as in 15 offensive starts of 3 v 2.

To make the game easier

⊙ Shorten the length and width of the field.

⊙ Do not start each progression with a goalie clear, but instead allow the field player to start with the ball.

To make the game harder

⊙ Put a time limit on the amount of time the attacking team has to get a shot off.

⊙ Allow any one of the three players to become the lone defender rather than just the person who took the shot. This decision is based on field positioning of the attacking team.

Offensive Team Strategies

Every time a player catches the ball, she needs to turn to goal and challenge the defender to make herself a scoring threat. A team with possession of the ball has two objectives: First, to move the ball down the field and score; second, to maintain possession of the ball so that the opponents cannot score. When a team first gains possession of the ball, the players should try to fast break down the field and look for a good scoring opportunity. If the fast break is well defended and no scoring chance can be identified, then a team should try to organize into some sort of team offensive movement or pattern. With the recent addition of the restraining line, a team's offense is set with seven players who have crossed over the line to play attack. Any player on the field, except the goalkeeper, may score a goal; hence, all field players should know the team's offenses. During play inside the restraining line, any attack player may run out across the restraining line and allow a teammate to enter the attack area in her place.

Playing Behind the Goal Circle

A unique aspect of girls' lacrosse is that the ball and any of the players are allowed within the space behind the goal circle. Space behind the goal circle provides a great area in which to feed the ball to a teammate. A direct feed from behind the goal for an immediate shot, like you might see in ice hockey, is the most challenging play for goalkeepers to defend. It is also very difficult for the goalkeeper and the defenders to cover the ball behind the goal circle while paying attention to movement and cutters in front of the goal. As the offense changes the point of attack by moving the ball behind the cage, defenders will have to reposition. During this adjustment, an alert attacker can cut free to the cage.

Teach young players how to feed a pass from behind the cage to a teammate in good scoring position. A player with the ball behind the cage has almost unlimited space and time to look for a feed to a teammate; however, her pass will have to avoid the goal cage, goalkeeper, and her defender. She must pass the ball accurately and time the pass correctly. Encourage the feeders to pass the ball in a direct line and not use a lob-type feed. To make this easier for the feeders, have them prepare to pass by raising the top hand and head of the stick to a position well above shoulder height.

Playing Offense Within the Restraining Line

With the addition to the rules of the restraining line, a team can build offenses based on up to seven attack players being allowed in the 30-yard area leading to the goal. (Note: Level C of the youth rules has no restraining line, and players should use a shortened field of 50 by 25 yards.) If a team has not been able to create either an extra-player advantage in midfield or a fast-break opportunity to score, players should organize into a team offense. Most often a team will begin the organized portion of the offense with the ball behind the goal, where there is likely to be less pressure on the ball carrier. At this point, a team offense can be identified verbally to all players in the attack area by you or a player. This may also be a pause during which players can switch back over the restraining line with another teammate.

Instruct your players on where to stand around the goal area before beginning an organized offense. The addition of a three-second rule for defenders makes it clear that defenders may not stand inside the eight-meter arc unless they are marking one player within stick's length. To best open up the space in front of the goal, have the attackers move away from the goal circle at least 10 meters so that the defenders must exit the eight-meter arc. As there is a 12-meter fan lined on the field, it may be easiest to instruct the players to start on this line.

Offensive Game

RESTRAINING LINE TRANSITION

Goal

To teach players to evaluate the exchange of players over the restraining line during transition

Description

Players are divided into two teams of six players each, one team with pinnies (figure 8.26). The game is played similar to half-court lacrosse with four attackers and four defenders within the attacking area trying to score. The two remaining players from each team are positioned over the restraining line. Play is continuous for a designated time, so there is no break in play. Have extra balls behind the goal cage to keep the play moving on missed shots. Any missed shot is a turnover

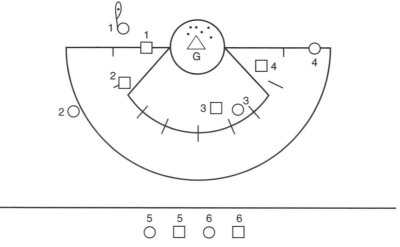

Figure 8.26   Restraining Line Transition.

for the defense. The ball must be cleared after a turnover by a defender or the goalkeeper to a specific area or over the restraining line. Award points for shots, goals, and defensive takeaways.

Each of the following conditions sets up an advantage to one team. The aim is to have the players figure out what advantage can be gained and then to use the possible advantage to their team's benefit.

Variations

- The ball must be passed over the restraining line to complete the transition.
- The ball must be run over the restraining line to complete the transition.
- The new attacking team must have at least one player switch over the restraining line on a change of possession.
- The new defending team must have at least one player switch over the restraining line on a change of possession.
- Both teams must switch a player over the restraining line on each change of possession.
- All players have a number and must switch out in numerical order.
- Both teams must switch two players over the restraining line on every change of possession.
- The ball only has to clear the 12-meter fan for transition to be complete.

Using Movement Patterns and Set Offenses

Deciding how many patterns to use and how complex the team's offense should be is directly dependent on the age and learning level of the players. You should give the players some idea of how the seven players inside the restraining line are going to proceed in an attempt to score a goal, but players at this age do not need a massive playbook.

First, you must convince the players that an organized movement pattern or set play will help them score more goals. Then you must select a pattern or play that is appropriate for their level. Avoid using plays that are set up so that only one or two of the strongest players handle the ball. Encourage movement that involves all players or is set based on the ball's position rather than player positions.

Many plays and offensive patterns may be created or borrowed from other team sports like basketball, ice hockey, water polo, or soccer. Some examples appropriate for young girls follow, and they are all adaptable to any number of attack players.

⊙ **Pass and cutaway.** After a pass to a teammate who is around the 12-meter line, the passer cuts backdoor to catch her defense watching the ball, not the player. The cutaway also leaves space for the player with the ball to challenge to goal. A second option for this movement is for the original player cutting away to finish her cut on the opposite side of the eight-meter arc and for a teammate on the opposite side to cut toward the ball.

⊙ **Priority cuts toward the ball and in front of the goal cage.** With every perimeter pass, a player from the opposite side of the 12-meter fan should cut directly to the ball through the primary scoring area in front of goal, asking for the ball. The feeder should first look to pass to these cutters. If a pass to them would be unsuccessful, she should look next to pass around the perimeter.

⊙ **Use two passes to move the defense, and then look to the opposite side of the field for an opening.** Make at least two consecutive permeter passes in the same direction (to the right or to the left), which will cause the defense to shift in that direction. While the ball is being passed in one direction, two players on the opposite side of the 12-meter fan prepare to cut through the eight-meter arc.

⊙ **Clearing a space for the ball.** This movement pattern involves clearing a space ahead of the ball. After a pass to the right along the perimeter, the player next to the receiver cuts backdoor to the goal, looking for a pass, and makes a space for the ball carrier. The cutter should exit the eight-meter arc opposite from where she started. The ball continues in the same direction to the right, and, with the next pass, the player ahead of the ball cuts away, creating a space. After at least three passes and cutting movements, a large area will open up for a player to challenge to the goal. This movement creates an overload of players in one area and a natural large space in which to challenge one on one.

⊙ **Double two-player stack at the 12-meter fan.** Set up with two feeders behind the goal, one on each side, and place two stacks of two people on the 12-meter fan. Have the seventh attacker out wide to one side as an outlet. As the ball is passed to one of the feeders behind the goal, the two players in the stack opposite from the feeder work as a first and second cutter and cut toward the feeder. Reset at the 12-meter fan and run again.

Special Offensive Situations

Defensive fouls within the critical scoring area can create special offensive situations. Play is stopped to set up most special situations. Teach your players the specific advantages and disadvantages of these situations.

Free Position on the Eight-Meter Arc

After a major foul in the eight-meter arc, the umpire designates the fouled player or another player to take a position with the ball on a hash mark on the eight-meter arc. All other players must clear the eight-meter arc to the closest point and be four meters away from the fouled player. The defender who fouled must go four meters behind the fouled player. The player with the ball may shoot, pass, or run with the ball when the whistle sounds. Many players run into the eight-meter arc to try to get closer for a shot, but this often leads to a successful block or stick check by a defender and a loss of possession for the attacker. A better option is to pass to a teammate who is in better position to shoot or who is behind the goal and can challenge or reset a play. Although a player may shoot at the sound of the whistle, youth players often lack strength and physical development to shoot successfully from that distance. However, shooters may use a bounce shot, which is more difficult for a goalkeeper to handle.

Free Position on the 12-Meter Fan

After a minor foul by the defense in the 12-meter fan, the umpire awards the offense an indirect free position on the 12-meter fan. The player with the ball may not shoot on goal, so she should pass the ball to a teammate who may be free to shoot right away. If moving the ball closer to the goal is not a good option, then she should create space by cradling or running the ball away from the goal and then passing to a teammate.

Defensive Team Strategies

The best team defense is a pressuring player-to-player marking system in which players are also taught to help each other. The best way to defend as a unit is to be interdependent and interacting. Teammates help each other by constantly communicating about the location of the ball and the position of players in an attempt to create a turnover by surprising and pressuring the player with the ball. The most effective way to pressure the ball carrier is to double-team her.

The best way to develop a team defensive concept is to assign a role to each player according to her location on the field and to the ball's position. One defender is assigned to mark the ball carrier and keep pressure on her to force a pass. The defender can accomplish this in several ways, such as forcing the ball to the outside of the field or to the attacker's weaker hand to pass. She may also have an occasion where a good stick check is possible, and she can always try to block the pass with her stick. If the ball is in the air, all teammates at least have an equal chance of intercepting and gaining possession.

The second role to define for a defender is playing next to the ball carrier. This is a key position, as this defender may have the best chance to intercept. She also must be aware of possible opportunities to help her teammate and double-team the ball. The key is for the second defender to time her move toward her teammate in order to double team so as not to leave her player unmarked for too long.

The third role is that of a defender positioned at least two passes away from the ball. This defender is to prepare to cover for her teammate if her teammate does lose her player or to free up that teammate to double-team. The third defender should try to anticipate the move to a new player and intercept if possible. Other defenders farther away from the ball should also be looking for unmarked opponents who may be scoring threats.

Double-Team

A double-team occurs when two defenders simultaneously commit to pressure the ball carrier for the purpose of gaining possession of the ball. This skill is especially useful in containing a ball carrier running toward the goal. Similar to a trap in basketball, two defenders are gambling that their pressure on the ball will create an opportunity for a turnover or force the ball carrier to give up possession.

Coordination of the timing and body positions of the two defenders is critical. The defender on the ball should have established a solid body checking position to one side of the ball, forcing the ball carrier to cradle away from her. At the proper moment, the second defender should slide toward the ball carrier and position her body on the side opposite her teammate (figure 8.27). With two sides of the ball surrounded, the defenders have a better opportunity to stick check or block a pass. When a defender leaves her assigned opponent to come to double, she should keep her stick up and in the passing lane from her player. This added pressure usually causes the ball carrier to panic and not execute a good pass. The ball carrier may back away from the double-team, and then the defenders must decide whether to stay with the added pressure or to return to playing their players individually.

When a defender prepares to leave her opponent to double-team, she calls, "Double," so that her teammates know she has left a player open. When her teammates hear she is leaving to double-team, they act as a unit to cover for her and prepare to mark the player who is now open. This is called a defensive slide, or sliding to the open player.

A double-team can be used successfully anywhere on the field. However, if the ball carrier outmaneuvers the two committed defenders or passes to the free player, the defensive team risks chasing the ball down the field. This may result in an offensive fast-break or extra-player opportunity. Double-teams must be well executed and well timed, or the call to double may turn into a call for trouble.

Figure 8.27 Proper double-team positioning.

Defensive Games

CHANNEL ESCORT

Goal

To teach defenders to move together and to communicate while forming a double-team

Description

Mark a 10-by-20 yard channel with cones. Arrange players in groups of three with one ball per group. Player 1 has the ball and stands at the short end of the channel. Player 2, without a stick, stands next to her in a good defensive body checking position. Player 3, with a stick, stands five yards down the channel. When player 1 begins to move the ball, player 3 tells player 2 she is in position and will add on to double-team player 1. Switch defender's roles to come back up the channel. A different player becomes the ball carrier after each round trip.

Encourage loud, crisp verbal signals. Stop the play to correct the defenders if they are out of position. Show players how to recover if the ball carrier gets to the outside of either defender.

DOUBLES IN TRANSITION

Goal

To successfully execute double-teams

Description

The area of play is 15 by 30 yards with a goal at each end. There are two teams of equal numbers of players, and each team lines up on a separate sideline 15 yards apart. Players should line up with a few yards between each of them. A goalie is in each goal.

To start play, roll a ball to the middle of the playing area. The first player in each line fights for possession. Whichever team does not get possession of the ball adds a second player, so they can try to execute a double-team on the ball (1 v 2). The player who gains possession tries to score. Award one point for each goal.

With each change of possession, teammates that are waiting on the sideline join so that defense is always one person up. For example, on the first ball, player A gains possession. Player B is on defense, and a teammate C joins her. Player B steals the ball, so now she and her teammate C are on the attack. At this point, two more players from player A's team join to make it 2 v 3. The number of players in the game can build up to 6 v 7, depending on the number of changes of possession. A goalie save is counted as a change of possession. Play stops when a goal is scored. Once a goal is scored, the field is cleared and a new ball starts a 1-v-2 game.

To make the game easier

⊙ Make the field smaller.

⊙ Designate who will start on attack and who on defense, eliminating the fight for possession.

To make the game harder

⊙ Increase the number of starting players to two per team, and the team without possession adds a third.

⊙ Allow attackers to use players on the sideline as passing options.

Defensive Transition From Goalkeeper Clear

After the defensive team has gained possession of the ball, it must have a strategy for clearing the ball out of the defensive end of the field. It is often helpful to pass the ball to the goalkeeper when organizing a transition because she may hold the ball in the crease for 10 seconds. The organization for transition begins with creating space on the field, so players often cut away from the goal circle and back to the ball. The goalkeeper should clear to one side, not directly in front of her, because a turnover in the center provides your opponent with the best opportunity to score. Additionally, after the ball has been cleared to one side, a weak-side defender recovers to a position in the center of the field to act as a safety valve in case of a turnover farther up field. The transition to offense should support the ball with three options at all times, with players in position to receive a backward, lateral, or forward pass.

Transition Games

EXTRA GOALIE CLEARS FOR TEAM POINTS

Goal

To execute and reward successful goalkeeper clears

Description

Play with teams up to 12 v 12 on a regulation-size field; have a goalie in each goal (figure 8.28). Play can be as in a regulation game, or you can call for a clear each time the offensive team successfully crosses the restraining line in possession. Use cones to divide the field into three segments: goal line to 12-meter fan extended, 12-meter fan extended to restraining line, and restraining line to outside of center circle. Each time a player takes a shot (even if it scores), the goalie clears the ball to a member of her defending team. Award the most points (three) if the goalie and her teammates successfully clear to the farthest segment before a turnover. Award only one point if the defensive team makes a turnover before the level of the 12-meter fan. A turnover can be converted into a quick scoring opportunity for the attacking team.

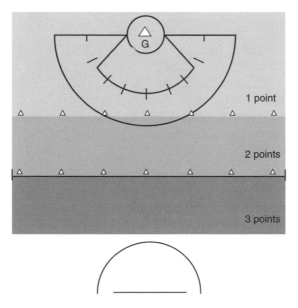

Figure 8.28   Extra Goalie Clears.

(continued)

Extra Goalie Clears *(continued)*

To make the game easier

⊙ Take away pressure from the defenders trying to get free for a clear.

⊙ Award greater point values for closer areas (for example, a player who clears to the 12-meter fan area gets three points).

⊙ Focus on clearing to only one specific area.

To make the game harder

⊙ Allow an extra attack player to pressure the goalie around her crease during the goalie clear.

⊙ Place a time limit of 10 seconds on the goalie and her teammates to clear the first or second segment.

⊙ Don't allow the goalie to clear to the same place twice in a row.

HALF-FIELD TEAM PLAY

Goal

To teach the offense and defense how to take advantage of an extra-player, fast-break situation

Description

Set up four attackers, four defenders, a goalkeeper, and one ball. Any number of players up to seven per side may be used, as long as the numbers are even per team. The ball starts on the outside midfield. Start play and continue until there is a turnover or a shot on a goal. Reset the players back in the midfield with a new ball.

Freeze the play to illustrate both good and bad decisions. Watch for defenders who make decisions too early or too late in relation to the ball movement, and note those who make no commitment or don't communicate when they make a move.

The most successful way to practice team defense is to play in a half-field situation, where players may have to defend a fast break or be matched evenly with their opponents. Defenders should always be encouraged to intercept a pass in the air as the first line of team defense. Various opportunities to play all the defensive roles will occur as the ball moves downfield.

chapter 9

Girls' Lacrosse Season Plans

Up to now you've been introduced to the basic skills of coaching: what your responsibilities are as a coach, how to communicate well and provide for safety, how to use the games approach to teach and shape skills, and how to coach on game days. But game days make up only a small portion of your season. You and your players will spend much more time in practice than in competition. How well you conduct practices and prepare your players for competition will greatly affect both your and your players' enjoyment and success throughout the season.

In this chapter, we present three levels of season plans: one for Level C, one for Level B, and one for Level A. Use these plans as guidelines for conducting your practices. These plans are not the only way to approach your season, but they do present an appropriate teaching progression. For safety reasons, be sure the basic skills have been taught, drilled, and practiced under competitive practice situations before introducing a game. Remember to incorporate the games approach as you use these plans, to put your players in a gamelike situation that introduces them to the main tactic or skill that you want them to learn that day. Then guide your players through a short question-and-answer session that leads to the skill practice.

Some coaches may face the added challenge of very limited practice meetings and times. Take what information you can and adapt it to your situation. Each practice, regardless of your daily purpose and practice length, should include

1. a warm-up and stretching;
2. stick work, both stationary and on the move;
3. conditioning;
4. small-game situations (1 v 1, 2 v 2, 3 v 3, with and without goalie);
5. large-game situations (7 v 7 and larger);
6. time for discussion, question and answers, and reinforcement of successes; and
7. fun.

Refer to chapter 5 (pages 45-47) for how to run a practice. In chapter 8 you will find descriptions of all the skills and tactics and games you can use to practice them. Throughout the season plans, we refer you to the appropriate pages for those skills and tactics and games.

Remember to keep the introductions, demonstrations, and explanations of the skills and tactics brief. As the players practice, attend to individual players, guiding them with tips or with further demonstration. Good luck and good coaching!

Season Plan—Level C

This season plan is for players who have had little or no exposure to lacrosse. Do not assume they have any knowledge of the game. Help them explore the basic skills and tactics of the sport, as suggested in the following season plan.

Practice 1

- **Purpose:** Team introduction—To learn the basics of catching, throwing, and cradling
- **Games:** Survivor Tag (p. 90), Pass the Team Test (p. 103)
- **Skill development:** Catching technique, throwing technique, and cradling

Practice 2

- **Purpose:** To learn the basics of ground ball pickups and dodges
- **Games:** Ground Ball Baseball (p. 98), Grid Locked (p. 94)
- **Skill development:** Ground ball pickups and left- and right-side dodges

Practice 3

- **Purpose:** To review and combine previous skills and introduce shooting
- **Games:** Multigoal Game (p. 106), Post Shooting (p. 109)
- **Skill development:** Shooting skills

Practice 4

- **Purpose:** To learn to move without the ball and support around the ball
- **Game:** Support With Two Balls (p. 128)
- **Skill development:** Ball support and passing options

Practice 5

- **Purpose:** To understand possession and balance on attack
- **Games:** Pass Along (p. 131), Center Circle Bull's Eye (p. 132)
- **Skill development:** Possession and balance

Practice 6

- **Purpose:** To focus on individual defensive skills of blocking and intercepting
- **Game:** Ultimate Lacrosse (p. 120)
- **Skill development:** Blocking and intercepting

Practice 7

- ⊙ **Purpose:** To focus on individual defense and defensive positioning
- ⊙ **Games:** Queen of the Crease (p. 126), Defend Your Eight-Meter Arc (p. 124)
- ⊙ **Skill development:** Defensive forcing and crease defense

Practice 8

- ⊙ **Purpose:** To introduce modified checking (when appropriate) and extra-player concepts
- ⊙ **Game:** Extra Attacker Fast Break (p. 134)
- ⊙ **Skill development:** Modified stick checking and extra-player advantage

Practice 9

- ⊙ **Purpose:** To introduce transition, review defense within the scoring area, and teach three-second and shooting lane violations
- ⊙ **Games:** Defend Your Eight-Meter Arc (p. 124), Introduction to Transition (p. 136)
- ⊙ **Skill development:** Forcing defense in scoring area

Practice 10

- ⊙ **Purpose:** To teach double-teams
- ⊙ **Game:** Doubles in Transition (p. 145)
- ⊙ **Skill development:** Double-team positioning

Practice 11

- ⊙ **Purpose:** To understand and execute specialty situations, including restraining line and eight-meter penalties
- ⊙ **Game:** Restraining Line Transition (p. 139)
- ⊙ **Skill development:** Eight-meter free positions and use of restraining line

Practice 12

- ⊙ **Purpose:** To teach transition from a goalkeeper clear and review restraining line rules during play
- ⊙ **Game:** Extra Goalie Clears for Team Points (p. 147)
- ⊙ **Skill development:** Goalkeeper clears

Practice 13

- **Purpose:** To review movement off the ball and improve shooting
- **Games:** Multigoal Game (may add second ball) (p. 106), Post Shooting (with variations) (p. 109)
- **Skill development:** Improvement of general field awareness and accuracy on shots

Practice 14

- **Purpose:** To review offensive and defensive unit interdependence and transition
- **Game:** Half-Field Team Play (p. 148), with conditions
- **Skill development:** Improvement of general field awareness

Season Plan—Level B

This season plan builds on the previous one, as players practice the fundamental skills and tactics and add a few new tactics, including fakes with the stick and defensive pressure.

Practice 1

- **Purpose:** Team introduction—To learn the basics of catching, throwing, cradling, and fakes
- **Games:** Survivor Tag (p. 90) , Pass the Team Test (p. 103) (emphasize both hands)
- **Skill development:** Catching technique, throwing technique, cradling, and faking

Practice 2

- **Purpose:** To learn the basics of ground ball pickups and dodges
- **Games:** Ground Ball Baseball (p. 98), Grid Locked (p. 94)
- **Skill development:** Ground ball pickups and left- and right-side dodges

Practice 3

- **Purpose:** To introduce shooting and review and combine previous skills
- **Games:** Post Shooting (p. 109), Multigoal Game (p. 106)
- **Skill development:** Shooting (with variations) and combining skills in a game

Practice 4

- ⊚ **Purpose:** To learn to move and support around the ball
- ⊚ **Game:** Support With Two Balls (p. 128)
- ⊚ **Skill development:** Ball support and passing options

Practice 5

- ⊚ **Purpose:** To understand possession and balance on attack
- ⊚ **Games:** Pass Along (p. 131), Center Circle Bull's Eye (p. 132)
- ⊚ **Skill development:** Possession and balance

Practice 6

- ⊚ **Purpose:** To develop individual defensive skills
- ⊚ **Game:** Ultimate Lacrosse (p. 120)
- ⊚ **Skill development:** Defensive positioning, intercepting, and blocking

Practice 7

- ⊚ **Purpose:** To review defensive positioning and teach crease defense and modified stick checking (when appropriate)
- ⊚ **Games:** Queen of the Crease (p. 126), Ultimate Lacrosse, with modified stick checking (p. 120)
- ⊚ **Skill development:** Crease defense and stick checking

Practice 8

- ⊚ **Purpose:** To teach double-teams and defensive positioning
- ⊚ **Games:** Doubles in Transition (p. 145), Defend Your Eight-Meter Arc (p. 124)
- ⊚ **Skill development:** Double-teams and defensive positioning

Practice 9

- ⊚ **Purpose:** To work on individual denial defensive positioning and double-teams when available and to teach three-second and shooting lane rules
- ⊚ **Game:** Defend Your Eight-Meter Arc, with 2 v 2 in the eight-meter area (p. 124)
- ⊚ **Skill development:** Individual defense and use of double-teams within eight-meter area

Practice 10

- **Purpose:** To introduce extra-player concepts
- **Game:** Extra Attacker Fast Break (p. 134)
- **Skill development:** Use of an extra attacker

Practice 11

- **Purpose:** To teach defending a fast break and importance of transition
- **Games:** Introduction to Transition (p. 136), Doubles in Transition (p. 145)
- **Skill development:** Extra-player concepts and transition

Practice 12

- **Purpose:** To understand and execute specialty situations, including restraining line and eight-meter penalties
- **Game:** Restraining Line Transition (p. 139)
- **Skill development:** Eight-meter free positions and use of restraining line

Practice 13

- **Purpose:** To introduce play behind the goal cage and offensive movement
- **Game:** Half-Field Team Play, with emphasis on conditions for offense (p. 148)
- **Skill development:** Ball control to settled offense around the goal area

Practice 14

- **Purpose:** To teach defensive team transition from goalie clear
- **Game:** Extra Goalie Clears for Team Points (p. 147)
- **Skill development:** Full field possession

Season Plan—Level A

At this stage players are refining the skills they have learned from past years. This season plan builds on the previous one and leaves you more time for real gamelike play. To be creative, you should add conditions to the games and create new variations.

Practice 1

- ⊙ **Purpose:** To review the basics of catching, throwing, cradling, and fakes
- ⊙ **Games:** Pass the Team Test (emphasize both hands) (p. 103), Multigoal Game (p. 106)
- ⊙ **Skill development:** Catching technique, throwing technique, cradling, and faking

Practice 2

- ⊙ **Purpose:** To review the basics of ground ball pickups, dodges, and shooting
- ⊙ **Games:** Grid Locked, with shot (p. 94), Post Shooting, with variations (p. 109)
- ⊙ **Skill development:** Ground ball pickups and left- and right-side dodges

Practice 3

- ⊙ **Purpose:** To learn to time movements and support around the ball
- ⊙ **Games:** Support With Two Balls (p. 128), Pass Along (p. 131)
- ⊙ **Skill development:** Ball support and timing of cuts

Practice 4

- ⊙ **Purpose:** To understand possession and balance on attack
- ⊙ **Games:** Pass to a Moving Player for Points (p. 130), Center Circle Bull's Eye, from within the 12-meter fan (p. 132)
- ⊙ **Skill development:** Possession, balance, and timing of cuts

Practice 5

- ⊙ **Purpose:** To review individual defensive skills—blocking, intercepting, and modified stick checking (when appropriate)

- **Game:** Ultimate Lacrosse, with modified stick checking (p. 120)
- **Skill development:** Blocking, intercepting, and stick checking

Practice 6

- **Purpose:** To review defensive positioning and double-team positioning
- **Games:** Crossing the English Channel, to goal (p. 113), Doubles in Transition (p. 145)
- **Skill development:** Individual defensive positioning and double-teams

Practice 7

- **Purpose:** To review crease defense and individual denial defensive positioning plus double-teams when available, teach three-second and shooting lane rules
- **Game:** Defend Your Eight-Meter Arc, with 2 v 2 in the eight-meter area (p. 124)
- **Skill development:** Crease and denial defense and use of double-teams within eight-meter area

Practice 8

- **Purpose:** To review extra-player concepts
- **Game:** Extra Attacker Fast Break, add more players (p. 134)
- **Skill development:** Use of an extra attacker

Practice 9

- **Purpose:** To review defending a fast break and importance of transition
- **Games:** Introduction to Transition (p. 136), Doubles in Transition (p. 145)
- **Skill development:** Extra-player concepts and transition

Practice 10

- **Purpose:** To understand and execute specialty situations, including restraining line and eight-meter penalties
- **Game:** Restraining Line Transition (p. 139)
- **Skill development:** Eight-meter free positions and use of restraining line

Practice 11

- ⊙ **Purpose:** To introduce play behind the goal cage and offensive movement
- ⊙ **Game:** Half-Field Team Play, with emphasis on conditions for offense (p. 148)
- ⊙ **Skill development:** Ball control to settled offense around the goal area

Practice 12

- ⊙ **Purpose:** To teach defensive team transition from goalie clear
- ⊙ **Game:** Extra Goalie Clears for Team Points (p. 147)
- ⊙ **Skill development:** Full field possession from goalie clear

Practice 13

- ⊙ **Purpose:** To work on extra-player offense and defense
- ⊙ **Game:** Half-Field Team Play, starting with one less defender (p. 148)
- ⊙ **Skill development:** Half-field fast break

Practice 14

- ⊙ **Purpose:** To develop full field transition from goalie clear to scoring opportunity
- ⊙ **Game:** Extra Goalie Clears for Team Points, add scoring points (p. 147)
- ⊙ **Skill development:** Full field possession from goalie clear to shot

chapter 10

Boys' Lacrosse Rules and Equipment

In this chapter we'll introduce you to some of the basic rules of boys' lacrosse. We won't try to cover all the rules of the game, but rather we will give you what you need to work with players who are 8 to 14 years old. We'll give you information on rules modifications, ball and field dimensions, equipment, length of game, player positions, game procedures, rules, and scoring. The *US Lacrosse Rules for Boys' Youth Lacrosse*, (part of the *Boys' Lacrosse Rules Book* available through US Lacrosse, www.uslacrosse.org) makes the sport more appropriate for youngsters. In a short section at the end of the chapter, we'll show you the officiating signals for lacrosse.

First, though, we'll begin by defining some terms you'll need to understand to teach lacrosse.

Terms to Know

Boys' lacrosse has its own vocabulary. Being familiar with common terms will make your job easier.

backup—An attacker's move into a position to regain possession after a shot. Also refers to an off-ball defender who positions himself so that he can support a teammate guarding the ball carrier.

checking—Attempting to dislodge the ball from the opponent's stick by stick or body contact.

clear—A pass or run to advance the ball from the defensive to the offensive half of the field.

close defense—The three defensive players who play immediately behind and in front of their goal, and who are responsible for covering the three opposing attackers player for player. Close defenders often use a stick with a longer handle than midfielders or attackers use.

cradling—Moving the arms and wrists to keep the ball in the stick pocket and ready for passing or shooting.

crease—The circle, with a nine-foot radius, around each goal.

cut—Movement of an offensive player without the ball to free himself to receive a pass or shot.

dodge—The ball carrier's move to elude an opponent.

extra-man offense—The offensive unit's numerical advantage that results from at least one member of the opposite team serving time in the penalty box.

fast break—An offensive transition play resulting from a numerical advantage over the defense, traditionally a four-on-three advantage.

feed—A pass to a teammate in scoring position.

goal line extended—An imaginary line that runs parallel to the end line from the goalposts to the sideline.

ground ball—A loose ball.

hold—A legal technique used by defensive team members to push their opponent away from the goal. A defender can apply legal holds with his hands, arms, and body to the side or front of the attacker.

holding—Illegally impeding an opponent from moving forward or dodging. A holding violation usually occurs when a defender impedes the progress of the ball carrier with his stick.

hole—The area immediately outside of the crease in front of the goal.

invert—To carry the ball in front of the goal (for an attacker) or behind the goal (for a midfielder) to isolate the ball carrier.

isolation (iso)—The space created for the ball carrier to dodge an opponent in a one-on-one situation. The ball carrier and his teammates work together to create the space.

man-ball—Tactic of one man's scooping a loose ball while a teammate body checks the opponent closest to the ball but within the legal five-yard distance.

man-down defense—The defensive unit that is outnumbered by at least one player as the result of one or more of its players serving time in the penalty box.

on the fly—How substitutions are made while the clock is running. One player runs off the field through the legal substitution area, and another runs on after the first player is completely off the field.

pick—An offensive tactic in which an off-ball player stands motionless to block the path of a player defending the ball carrier or a cutter.

pinch—Position of off-ball defenders who move into the hole to support the defender covering the ball carrier.

riding—Preventing the defenders from advancing the ball from their defensive end of the field to their own offensive end of the field.

scoop—Technique of picking up a loose ground ball.

screen—An offensive tactic in which a player stands in front of the goalie to obscure his vision when another offensive teammate is dodging to shoot from the midfield area.

slide—A move by an off-ball defender leaving his assigned attacker to block (stop) a ball carrier moving unobstructed to the goal.

square-up—Body-on-body, stick-on-stick defensive position.

unsettled situation—A situation in which the defense has not had an opportunity to set up.

ward off—The illegal movement of the ball carrier's free arm to deflect the stick check of his opponent.

X—The area directly behind the goal.

Rule Modifications

As stated in the bylaws of the US Lacrosse Youth Council (USLYC), eligibility for participation in boys' Under 15 events sanctioned by US Lacrosse and its Youth Council will be based on the following criteria (note: these rules also serve as recommendations for youth leagues in organizing their teams):

1. Youth players will be boys age 15 and under and must further qualify as follows to participate in USLYC-sanctioned youth lacrosse activities: (a) player has not attained 15 years of age as of December 31 in the year preceding a USLYC sanctioned event, and (b) the player has not participated in any high school program as a member of a high school freshman, junior varsity, or varsity team.

2. Leagues may be organized by age or grades. Physical maturity should be considered when grouping players. If your program has enough players, the age/grade groups should play separately. The following is an example, with ages determined as of December 31 in the year preceding the USLYC–sanctioned event:

- Senior Division: Under 15/eighth grade. May have competitive divisions grouped by ability.
- Junior Division: Under 13/sixth and seventh grades. May have competitive divisions grouped by ability. Note: Players 12 years old or in sixth grade may have difficulty playing with 14-year-old or eighth-grade boys.
- Lightning Division: Under 11/fourth and fifth grades. Noncompetitive. Ages and grades may play together. Multiple teams within a program should be balanced.
- Bantam Division: Under 9/second and third grades. Noncompetitive. Ages and grades may play together. Multiple teams within a program should be balanced.

Modifications for each level are noted throughout this book. For the complete list of youth and high school rules, see the *Boys Lacrosse Rules Book*, written by the National Federation of State High School Associations and endorsed by US Lacrosse (available through US Lacrosse at www.uslacrosse.org).

Young players may enjoy playing on a modified field size with fewer players (7 v 7 on a 30-by-60-yard field, for example). Also, youth teams may play without the offside rules, permitting all players to move freely from the offensive end to the defensive end without the offside regulations. Reducing the number of players and allowing them to move freely between the offensive and defensive ends of the smaller field give young players the opportunity to handle the ball more often and to participate in both the offensive and defensive tactics of the game.

Ball and Field Dimensions

The solid rubber ball used in boys' lacrosse is between 7 3/4 and 8 inches around and weighs between 5 and 5 1/4 ounces. The ball is usually completely white, but a yellow or orange ball may be used for improved visibility.

Boys' lacrosse is played on a field similar in size to soccer and football fields. An official lacrosse field is 110 yards long and 53 1/2 to 60 yards wide. The field is marked with a centerline, which is used during the face-off and when play is resumed after an offside penalty. On both sides of the centerline is an area designated as a restraining box. The goal cages are surrounded by an 18-foot-diameter crease circle (figure 10.1). As stated earlier, the rules for boys' lacrosse allow for playing with a reduced field size.

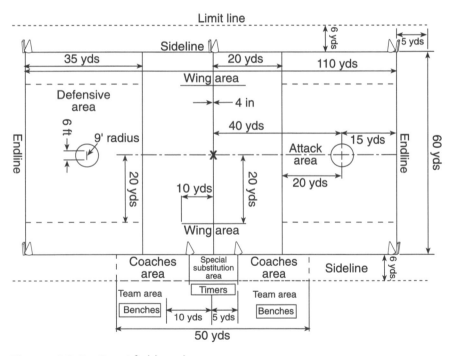

Figure 10.1 Boys' field markings.

Equipment

All boys' lacrosse field players must wear a protective helmet, throat protector, padded gloves, arm pads, shoulder pads, and mouthguard. An athletic supporter, cup, cleats, and—especially for younger players–rib pads are recommended (figure 10.2). Goalies should wear the same equipment, although the arm and shoulder pads are optional. Boys' goalies may also wear leg pads and shin guards.

Figure 10.2　Boys' lacrosse equipment.

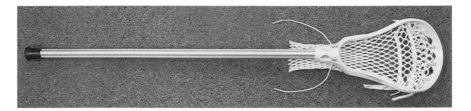

Figure 10.3   Stick used in boy's lacrosse.

Keep two factors in mind when selecting sticks for the beginning player: stick length and pocket type. Young players should begin with a stick with a shaft as long as their arm, or between 30 and 40 inches (figure 10.3). Beginning players and coaches should not be restricted by the minimum length rule of 40 inches required in the boys' high school and college game. Instead, take into consideration the size of the participant, and select a stick length that is comfortable for each player. Move players toward a 40-inch stick as they get older and bigger. When defenders have developed good fundamentals, they can increase the length of the stick to 48 to 60 inches. The soft mesh pocket is a good choice for beginning players at each position. It makes catching and throwing easier and helps with overall skill development. The traditional strung pocket is more difficult to break in and initially makes catching more difficult, and it also results in a stiffer pocket that requires more maintenance.

Players may not alter their sticks to gain an unfair advantage against their opponents. The pockets on boys' sticks can be deeper than in the girls' game, but too deep a pocket often results in the ball catching on the strings and hooking down toward the ground during a pass. It also is illegal and results in up to a three-minute, nonreleasable penalty (for all levels except Bantam) for a pocket to be so deep that the top of the ball is visible below the bottom edge of the sidewall when a player holds the stick parallel to the ground at eye level. (In a nonreleasable penalty, a player must serve the full penalty, even if the man-up team scores a goal.) This rule does not apply to the goalie's stick.

Length of Game

A boys' lacrosse game consists of four quarters with short breaks after the first and third quarters and a 10- to 15-minute halftime break between the second and third quarters. The USLYC boys' rules for 15 and under suggest the following periods:

- Senior and Junior Divisions—Four quarters, 10-minute stop clock, and sudden victory 4-minute overtime periods
- Lightning and Bantam Divisions—Four quarters, 12-minute running clock, and one overtime running clock period of 5 minutes, no sudden victory

A running clock never stops. A start/stop clock starts and stops, as it would in a regulation game.

Player Positions

Each of the four basic positions in boys' lacrosse has primary responsibilities, but a successful lacrosse team is one in which all players work together and blend positional duties with team play.

Attack

The three attackers are traditionally the primary ball handlers, passers, scorers, and feeders. They are finesse players who play directly in front of and behind the goal. Attack players need to have excellent stick skills and accuracy.

Midfield

The three midfielders are the all-purpose players. They must have great speed and stamina because they play on both the offensive and defensive ends of the field. The midfielders are involved in a lot of transitional play, and teams often have two to three groups of midfielders. Midfielders are a team's workhorses.

Defense

The defenders match up defensively on the opposition's attackers. They are involved in the clearing game (getting the ball out of their defensive half) and often begin the transition from defense to offense after receiving an outlet pass from the goalie or scooping a ground ball. Defense players need excellent stick skills and good agility.

Goalie

The goalie is the last line of defense and also the leader in the defensive unit. He is responsible for stopping the ball from entering the goal and for initiating the transition to offense by outletting (passing) the ball to a teammate. Goalies need to be fearless and to have above-average stick skills.

Offensive Formations

The positioning of the six offensive players who have the ball on their opponent's end of the field depends on the skills and experience of the players and on your personal preferences. Place players where they can use their athletic and lacrosse skills best.

Offensive team formations are described this way:

1. By the number of players positioned in the midfield (positioned at the top of the restraining box). These players are usually midfielders.

2. By the number of players positioned on the crease (directly in front of the goal mouth) and extending out to the wing area. These players can be attackers or midfielders.

3. By the number of players positioned behind the goal. The players in these positions are usually attackers.

A few traditional formations include the 3-1-2, 2-2-2, 2-3-1, and 1-4-1 (figure 10.4, a-d).

Teams play two kinds of defense in lacrosse: man-to-man and zone. Man-to-man defense in lacrosse is very similar to man-to-man defense in basketball. Each player guards one assigned opponent, and all other teammates help out if the ball carrier beats his defender. These concepts give beginning players the tactical knowledge they need to understand the game better.

In zone defense, players defend specific areas and the players who enter them. This can be effective, but young players should learn man-to-man skills and tactics first and then assimilate them later into zone defense strategies.

Game Play

Ten players comprise a boys' lacrosse team: three attackers, three midfielders, three defenders, and a goalkeeper. The transitional component of lacrosse provides each player with the opportunity to initiate and participate in both the offensive and defensive parts of the game. Lacrosse shares the principal objectives of soccer and hockey, which are to pass or run the ball into the offense area and shoot it past the opponent's goal line.

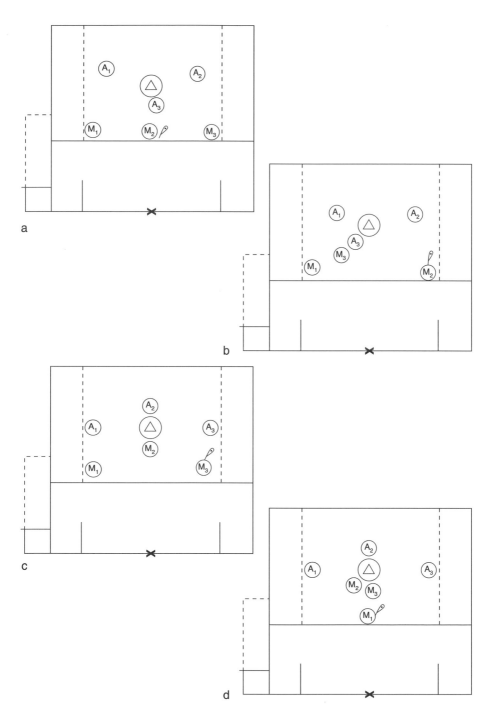

Figure 10.4 Offensive formations— *(a)* 3-1-2, *(b)* 2-2-2, *(c)* 2-3-1, *(d)* 1-4-1.

The rules of the game require each team to keep three players on their opponents' side of the field when the ball is on their own side. Four players (usually the three defenders and the goalie) are required to stay in their end when their offense has possession of the ball. This rule provides a six-player-versus-six-player situation (really six offense against seven defense when the goalie is counted) that results in the "even" play of the game. Six offensive players pass, dodge, cut, and shoot as six defensive players, with their goalie, to protect their goal.

The three attackers designated primarily as offensive players combine with the three midfielders to play settled offense (six-on-six) when they possess the ball on their opponents' half of the field. The midfielders are truly transitional players who play on both ends of the field, offense and defense. The three midfielders combine with three defenders and the goalie to defend their goal when the ball is in their end.

The six-on-six aspect (see the "Six-on-Six" Settled Game section in Chapter 11) is only one component of the game, and the transitional component provides many fast-break and unsettled situations where the offense may outnumber the defense by a six-to-five, five-to-four, or four-to-three margin. These unsettled situations arise frequently throughout the game and provide many exciting scoring opportunities.

A goal scores one point when the ball crosses through the imaginary plane formed by the rear edges of the goal line, the goalposts, and the top cross bar. Most goals are shot, but goals also count when a player kicks the ball in or when the ball rolls in after hitting an offensive or defensive player.

Starting and Restarting the Game

At the beginning of each quarter and after each goal, a player from each team faces off. The two face-off players crouch at the center of the field facing their opponent's half of the field. Their sticks are one inch apart on the ground and parallel to the midline (figure 10.5). The umpire places the ball between the heads of their sticks, steps away, and blows the whistle. The two face-off players and their remaining midfield teammates attempt to gain possession of the ball. The attack and defensive players must stay in their respective restraining boxes until the umpire signals that one team has gained possession.

If team A passes or carries the ball across the sideline or endline, the umpire awards the ball to team B, with one exception. When the ball goes out of bounds on a shot to goal, the umpire awards the ball to the team whose player is closest to it. A shot on goal gives either team an

Figure 10.5   Boys face-off.

opportunity to gain possession of the ball. Remember: The umpire awards the ball to the player closest to the spot where the ball goes out of bounds, which means offensive players should back up their teammates' shots on goal. Defenders and goalies also have the opportunity to gain possession of the ball.

When the ball goes out of bounds on the sideline or endline, you can request that the scorer sound the horn for the purpose of substitution. The official's whistle stops the clock, and either team can substitute at this point. The clock also stops on any personal or technical foul.

Substitutions

In lacrosse, substitutions can take place at any point in the game if they are done "on the fly," as in hockey. Players (usually midfielders) can run off the field through the designated substitution area (see figure 10.1 on page 163). As one player exits the field, another steps on. With youth players, however, you should try to substitute players in a settled situation, so they can see their position on the field.

Be aware of the offside rule in all substitutions on the fly that involve attackers or defenders. Have players exit and enter on their respective defensive or offensive sides of the midline. For example, if a defender is subbing on the fly, he should exit the field on the defensive end, and the player entering should enter the game on the defensive end after his teammate has exited.

Rules

Lacrosse rules allow safe, continuous, free-flowing games. Even though lacrosse rules allow body and stick checking, limitations provide for a safe game. The *Rule's for Boys' Youth Lacrosse* has different body checking rules for each age group, ranging from no body checking to limited body checking.

A player may body check any opponent within five yards of a loose ball, including the ball carrier, by contacting him from the front or side, above the knees and below the shoulders. Spearing—leading with the head to make direct contact with another player—is illegal and dangerous to both players. *Reinforce this to your players.* (*Note:* Body checking is not allowed in the Lightning and Bantam Divisions.) Stick checking is legal; however, a player must direct his check at his opponent's stick in an attempt to dislodge the ball. The ball carrier's glove is considered part of the stick and can be checked (although pounding on the gloves is illegal), but stick checks are not allowed to any other part of an opposing player. Infractions result in a one-minute slashing penalty.

Personal Fouls

Boys' lacrosse categorizes two varieties of fouls: personal fouls and technical fouls. Personal fouls are the more serious of the two and often result in the offending player serving a one-minute penalty in a sideline area designated as the penalty box. In severe cases, personal fouls can result in two- or three-minute penalties or in expulsion from the game. These rare situations usually result from excessive slashing, fighting, or other poor behavior. Here are the specific personal fouls called in a game:

cross checking—Using the portion of the stick handle that is between the hands to check or push an opponent.

illegal body checking—Hitting an opponent from the rear, at or below the knees, or above the shoulders, or hitting an opponent when he does not possess the ball or is not within five yards of the ball.

slashing—Striking an opponent anywhere except on his stick or on the gloved hand holding the stick. Any poke check not making contact with the gloved hand while holding the stick will be considered a slash for the Lightning and Bantam Divisions. Any one-handed check will be a foul for the Bantam Division.

tripping—Obstructing an opponent at or below the knees with the stick, hands, arms, feet, or legs.

unsportsmanlike behavior—Any conduct an umpire considers unsportsmanlike. No profanity, on the field or on the bench, is permitted in youth lacrosse.

Note: No body checking is allowed in the Bantam Division. There are no time-serving penalties in this division: instead, the committing player must be substituted and the ball awarded to the other team.

Technical Fouls

Penalties for technical fouls are less severe than for personal fouls, and they depend on which team has possession of the ball when the penalty occurs. If the team who commits the technical foul has the ball or if neither team has possession of the ball, the fouled team gets the ball and the fouling team serves no penalty time. If the fouled team has possession of the ball at the time of the technical foul, the umpire administers a 30-second penalty to the offending player or team (except for Bantam Division—see previous section). The technical foul of offensive stalling is not enforced in the Lightning and Bantam Divisions.

Other Infractions

These other infractions can be called during a game:

crease violation—Contact with the goalkeeper or his crosse while the goalkeeper and the ball are within the goal crease area, whether or not the goalkeeper has the ball in his possession. Any interference with the goalie results in the umpire indicating a "play on" situation or awarding the ball to the goalkeeper's team at the center of the field.

holding—Impeding the movement of an opponent by holding him with the head of the crosse or by using a portion of the stick handle.

interference—A player's impeding, in any manner, the free movement of an opponent, except in these circumstances: that opponent has possession of the ball, the ball is in flight and is within five yards of the player, or both players are within five yards of the ball.

offside—A team fails to keep three players in the offensive half of the field or four players in the defensive half.

pushing—Pushing an opponent from any direction. "Equal pressure" is allowed. A push is exerting pressure after contact is made; it is not a violent blow.

An attacking player may never go into the opponent's goal crease. Any offensive player who touches the crease circle or lands inside the circle causes his team to lose possession of the ball. If the defense has gained possession when the crease violation occurs, the ball is awarded to the offended team at the center of the field.

Officiating

One or two people with knowledge of lacrosse rules officiate each game. Umpires enforce the rules to ensure a safe, fair, and fun contest. Umpires also require good behavior from players and coaches. You can be a big help to umpires by behaving appropriately and emphasizing disciplined play. Familiarize yourself with the officiating signals shown in figure 10.6 and teach them to the players.

a

b

c

d

Figure 10.6 Official signals. *(a-b)* Illegal body check, *(c-d)* crosse checking.

e

f

g

h

Figure 10.6 *(continued) (e)* Tripping, *(f)* holding, *(g-h)* warding off.

i

j

k

l

Figure 10.6 *(continued)* *(i)* Stalling, *(j)* offside, *(k)* score, *(l)* play on.

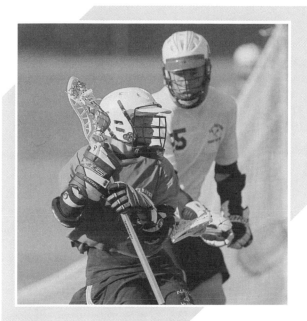

chapter 11

Boys' Lacrosse Skills and Tactics

In this chapter we'll provide information for you to teach your players general lacrosse skills, as well as specific offensive and defensive skills. As your players are mastering the fundamental and specific skills, you can begin to introduce them to offensive and defensive tactics. We have included many competitive drills and games that combine skills, tactics, and fitness in gamelike situations. We also included suggestions for identifying and correcting common errors. Remember to use the IDEA approach to teaching skills—Introduce, Demonstrate, and Explain the skill, and Attend to players as they practice the skill. For a refresher on IDEA, see chapter 5.

We've provided information only about the basics of lacrosse in this book. As your players advance in their lacrosse skills, you'll need to advance in your knowledge as a coach. You can do so by learning from your experiences, by watching and talking with more experienced coaches, and by studying advanced resources.

Using Lacrosse Drills Effectively

Before we begin the discussion of offensive and defensive lacrosse skills, let us say a word about how to use drills effectively in your practices. The methods of organizing drills for lacrosse depend on the skill level and experience of the players. Introduce beginner players to skill practice with partner drills. These drills use pairs of players with one ball for each pair. Players stand facing each other about 10 yards apart as they execute single skills with little movement. As players develop skill and confidence, they can practice skills while moving. Remind players to wear all equipment during every aspect of practice, including during drills.

Organize your group drills so that players move and execute basic fundamentals or combinations of fundamentals, such as scooping and passing. The final progression to facilitate skill development involves adding opposition and competition. At this stage, moving players must execute a variety of skills and tactics, with resistance from opposing players. These drills (games) are fun for players, as well as an efficient method of teaching the game of lacrosse. A balanced combination of drills that include partner, movement, and competitive work provides a variety of learning experiences and helps keep the players' attention. Make skill development fun for players. Keep instruction concise, and change drills frequently to keep players focused.

Individual General Skills

The basic skills needed to play lacrosse include the following:

- Ready position
- Cradling (bottom-handed, upright, top-handed)
- Throwing
- Catching (on the stick side, off-stick side, over the shoulder)
- Scooping
- Dodging (inside and out, roll, face, and split)
- Shooting
- Defense
- Face-offs

Ready Position

Develop the basic ready position for catching and throwing by having a player hold the stick with his arms at his sides and the stick parallel to the ground. His hands are hip-width apart; the palm of his top hand faces forward; and his bottom hand covers the butt of the stick, with that palm facing his body (figure 11.1). The player then raises the head of his stick to the off-ear position on the same side as his dominant hand.

Cradling

Cradling is often the first skill that the beginning player learns. By coordinated and rhythmic motion of the arms and hands, the player positions the ball in the center of the pocket and develops a "feel" for the ball (figure 11.2).

Figure 11.1 Ready position.

Figure 11.2 Cradling.

Bottom-Handed Upright Cradle

The bottom-handed upright cradle allows the player to carry the ball in the ready position where he can pass, shoot, and dodge. In this cradle, the bottom hand cradles the stick, and the stationary top hand is the guide hand. The bottom-handed cradle is best used in open space where the ball carrier is not under immediate pressure from a defender.

Teach players to follow these steps for the bottom-handed upright cradle:

1. Initiate the cradling motion by holding the stick diagonally across the body with the head of the stick in the ready position.
2. Bend the top arm to form a 90-degree angle at the elbow. The thumb and index finger encircle the shaft of the stick.
3. Use the bottom hand to cradle the stick: Begin with the palm facing the body and rhythmically rotate the bottom wrist out and in.

Top-Handed Cradle

The top-handed cradle is best in situations where the ball carrier is pressured by a defender and needs to shield the ball and his stick. The top hand initiates the cradling motion, and the stationary bottom hand is the guide hand.

Teach your players to perform the top-handed cradle this way:

1. Begin in the ready position with the stick diagonally across your body (figure 11.3a).
2. Begin the cradle with the palm of the top hand facing the body. Rotate the wrist out and back rhythmically (figure 11.3b).
3. Feel the ball in the center of the pocket (figure 11.3c).

One-Handed Cradle

More advanced offensive players use the one-handed cradling technique to shield and carry the ball when they are under direct pressure from a defensive player.

Teach players to follow these steps to cradle with one hand (figure 11.4):

1. Grasp the stick handle with the top hand about five inches down from the head. Position the thumb of the top hand in front of the handle and pointing up.
2. Position the head of the stick behind the head and shoulders, with the shaft perpendicular to the ground.

a   b   c

Figure 11.3   Top-handed cradle. *(a)* Ready position, *(b)* begin cradle, *(c)* ball is in center of pocket.

3. Rotate the shoulders to the side of the body to create a wide body surface for shielding the stick.

4. Use the arm's natural motion to facilitate the cradle while running. Hold the off-stick hand out from the hip to help protect the stick.

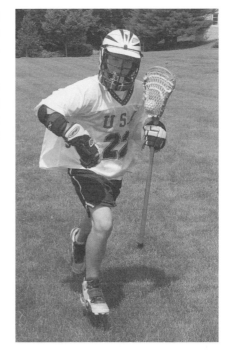

Figure 11.4   One-handed cradle.

Cradling Games

CRADLING GAME

Goal

To work on cradling skills

Description

Play 1 v 1 in a 15-by-15-yard square. Several squares can be set up within the penalty box to enable four groups to work at the same time (figure 11.5). Start the game by tossing the ball to one of the players. He is to protect the ball by running and cradling. He must work to keep his stick to the outside, with his body between the defender and the ball. Award one point if the player is able to cradle the ball for 10 seconds without dropping it.

To make the game easier

- Increase the size of the playing area.
- Have the defender play without his stick.

To make the game harder

- Reduce the size of the square.
- Have the ball carrier cradle in his nondominant hand.
- Play two defenders against one ball carrier.

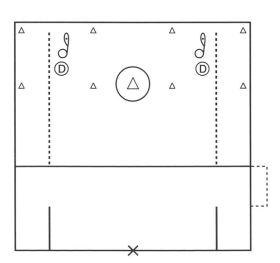

Figure 11.5
Cradling Game.

CREATIVE CRADLING

Goal

To develop cradling skills while moving

Description

Have each player inside the defensive box with a ball in his stick. Players should be spread out evenly in the box. On your whistle, players move throughout the box while cradling and keeping their heads up. Players cannot run through the crease with the ball. Players stop and start on your whistle (10 to 15 seconds of cradling and moving, with a 5- to 10-second rest between repetitions). Players can use a variety of cradling techniques, and dodges can be added as players become better skilled. Encourage players to change direction and speed as they become more proficient at cradling (see figure 11.6).

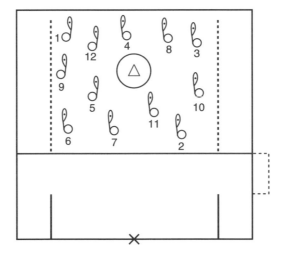

Figure 11.6 Creative Cradling.

Throwing

Many of the principles of throwing the ball in lacrosse are similar to those in baseball. Teach new players the throwing motion by demonstrating a one-handed throw.

To throw correctly, the player must develop these skills:

1. Hold the stick in the ready position with the head of the stick to the side and above the ear (figure 11.7a).
2. Turn so that the shoulders are perpendicular to the target, pointing the off-stick shoulder at the target.
3. To initiate the throwing motion, throw with the top hand, pull with the bottom hand, and step with the front foot toward the target (figure 11.7b).

a   b

Figure 11.7 Throwing.

4. Throw the ball to the receiver's stick side and to the head of his stick as he holds it in the ready position.

5. Follow through and carry the stick to a position with the head pointing at the target and the stick parallel to the ground.

Catching

Players must know how to catch the ball consistently while running or standing still. Catching involves proper stick positioning, eye–hand coordination, and a soft touch.

Catching on the Stick Side

Teach players to catch on the stick side first. The receiver pulls the head of the stick back slightly to decelerate the ball as it reaches the pocket.

To catch on the stick side, players should follow these instructions:

1. Be in the ready position to catch a ball coming toward the head of the stick (figure 11.8a).

2. Focus on the ball and watch it enter the pocket (figure 11.8b).

3. Cushion the ball into the pocket by gently relaxing the top hand of the stick as the ball arrives (figure 11.8c).

4. Keep the ball slightly in front of the body.

a   b   c

Figure 11.8   Catching on the stick side.

Catching on the Off-Stick Side

To catch the ball on the off-stick side, the receiver pushes the stick across his face, similar to the motion of a car's windshield wiper.

Teach players to follow these steps to catch on the off-stick side:

1. Watch the ball into the pocket of the stick and cushion the ball into the pocket (figure 11.9a).
2. Catch the ball with the pocket facing the passer and bring the stick back across the face to the ready position (figure 11.9b).
3. Continue to rotate the stick back to the ready position so that the stick, pocket, and ball are in position to pass (figure 11.9c).

Catching Over the Shoulder

A lacrosse player catching the ball while moving away from the passer is similar to a football receiver breaking upfield to receive a pass from his quarterback.

To catch over the shoulder, players must develop these skills:

1. Look back over the shoulder that's on the same side as the head of the stick. (Look over the right shoulder to receive a pass on the

a   b   c

Figure 11.9 Catching over the shoulder.

right side; turn the head and body to the left to receive a pass on the left side.)

2. "Look" the ball into the pocket of the stick, and keep the top hand and elbow away from the body (figure 11.9, a-c).

Error Detection and Correction for Catching

A soft mesh pocket helps beginning players develop catching skills. Proper technique includes decelerating the ball (cushioning it) and catching the ball in the ready position.

ERROR Reaching out in front of the body to catch the ball

CORRECTION

1. As the ball approaches, begin to move the head of the stick back and in the direction the pass is traveling.

2. Cushion the ball into the pocket.

3. Watch the ball from the passer into the pocket of the stick.

4. Practice catching with the backside of the pocket. Because there is little or no pocket on this side, the ball must be cushioned.

Throwing and Catching Games

PARTNER PASSING—DOMINANT HAND

Goal

To develop throwing and catching skills with the dominant hand

Description

Players line up in pairs 10 yards apart and pass the ball back and forth, concentrating on the basic throwing and catching mechanics: stand perpendicular to the receiver, point the stick shoulder at the receiver, hold the stick above the head, position the hands away from the body, step and throw, and follow through. Players cushion the ball when receiving it.

Variation

Catch with the nondominant hand or catch with the dominant hand and switch hands to throw with the nondominant hand.

RIGHT-ON-RIGHT PASSING AND CATCHING

Goal

To develop passing and catching skills while moving

Description

Two lines of three to four players each stand 20 yards apart facing each other. Start the game with all players holding their sticks in their right hand. The first player in one line carries a ball a few steps and throws it with his right hand to the first player in the other line, who is moving toward him. The thrower follows the pass, then goes to the end of the opposite line.

The receiver and passer move toward each other, and the receiver calls, "Help!" The passer throws the ball overhand to the ready position of the receiver. Be sure players hold their sticks to the inside and in the ready position when passing and receiving.

Variation

- *Left-on-Left Passing and Catching.* All players throw and catch with their left hands. Start by catching with the dominant hand then switch to the nondominant hand when passing.

FOUR CORNER PASSING

Goal

To practice throwing and catching on the run

Description

Lines of three or four players stand in each corner of the attack box. The first player in line 1 carries the ball and runs toward the first player in line 2, who acts as the receiver. When the ball carrier is midway between the lines, he yells, "Break!" and the receiver breaks toward line 3. When the receiver in line 2 catches the ball and is midway between lines 2 and 3, he yells, "Break!" and the first person in line 3 becomes the receiver. This process continues around the square until each person has caught and received the ball two or three times.

Make sure all play is right handed, with sticks to the outside. Don't let the receiver break until the ball carrier is in position to make a pass and yells for a break. Instruct the receiver to call, "Help!" and to give the passer a target in front so that he can make a lead pass.

Variations

⊙ For advanced practice, have players catch the ball over their shoulder (sticks to the inside) and then change hands (sticks to the outside).

⊙ The receiver can move directly toward the ball carrier to receive the pass, then circle away to pass to the next receiver. The receiver must move through the pass and circle away, keeping his stick to the outside. This variation provides excellent practice of clearing skills.

DIAMOND PASSING

Goal

To practice advanced offensive stick handling

Description

Four lines of players stand in a diamond formation, each line 12 yards from a marker in the center of the diamond. Player 1 has the ball and passes it right handed to player 2, who has executed a V-cut by moving in toward the marker and then breaking to the outside. Player 2 plays left handed, with his stick to the outside. When player 2 catches the ball, his stick changes hands, and he passes to player 3 with his right hand. Each player follows his pass and goes to the end of that line (see figure 11.10).

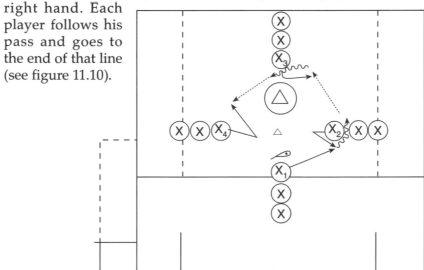

Figure 11.10 Diamond Passing.

Variation

Add four defenders to introduce pressure. The defenders move out to cover each receiver. When a defender moves out to play the receiver, he should arrive as the ball reaches the receiver and be positioned in the defensive ready position, stick down and parallel to the ground, knees bent, and partially sitting. Each off-ball defender moves to the center and keeps his head moving to watch both his man and the ball.

OVER THE SHOULDER

Goal

To practice throwing and catching over the shoulder

Description

Two lines of three or four players stand 20 yards apart facing each other. Player 2 in line 1 begins with the ball and moves to his right. When he yells, "Break!" player 1 in his line breaks with his stick in the right-handed, over-the-shoulder position. As player 1 receives the ball, he looks to line 2. Player 2 in line 2 calls, "Help!" and receives the pass. Player 2 in line 2 now moves laterally to his right and yells, "Break!" as player 1 in line 2 breaks with his stick in the right-handed, over-the-shoulder position. After passing, each player goes to the end of the opposite line.

To receive a pass, players should keep their stick at helmet level. The receiver should look over his shoulder and follow the ball with his eyes into the pocket of the stick.

HOT ROCK

Goal

To improve throwing skills

Description

Position three offensive players against two defensive players in a square 20 yards by 20 yards (small cones can be used to identify boundaries). The three offensive players pass and move within the square, trying to maintain possession. The defense works together, with one player covering the ball and the other defender splitting the remaining two offensive players. Several squares can be set up to allow more players to play. All players should have an opportunity to play offense and defense (see figure 11.11).

Variations

- Award a goal for four consecutive passes by the offense.
- Award a goal for an interception or for the defense gaining possession.
- See how many passes can be made in a 30-second period.

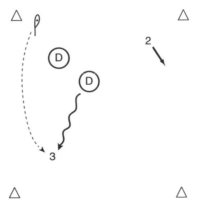

Figure 11.11   Hot Rock.

Scooping

The ability of individual players to scoop up loose balls contributes to the success of team play. The team that can "swarm" the ground ball and gain possession controls the tempo of the game.

To scoop properly, players should follow these instructions:

1. Move the stick out to the side and almost parallel to the ground.
2. Bend at the knees and waist while approaching the ball.
3. Lower the head of the stick and the butt hand, and accelerate through the ball.
4. Hit the ground approximately six inches in front of the ball with the stick. The scooping motion should carry the stick several inches in front of the ball.
5. Concentrate totally on the ball with your head down.
6. Plant the left foot to the side and close to the ball when scooping.
7. Bring the head of the stick to the ready position and continue to run to an open area.
8. Look up the field and be ready to pass or dodge.

The scooper moves through the ball and continues to move away from pressure by keeping his body between the defender and the ball.

Man, Ball, Release, Help

Verbal communication enables teammates to work together to win ground balls. These words cue teammates.

"Man"—A teammate within five yards of a loose ball may choose to body check or shield an opponent from a loose ball. He calls, "Man," and clears the way for a teammate to scoop the ball. He may make body contact only from the front or side and within five yards of the ball.

"Ball"—The player going for the loose ball calls, "Ball," to alert his teammates that he has an opportunity to scoop the ball.

"Release"—After a player has scooped the ball, he yells, "Release," to alert teammates that he has the ball. A technical foul of interference results if a player makes body contact with an opponent after a teammate secures possession.

"Help"—Players off the ball move to receive a pass from the scooper. An open player alerts the scooper of his position by calling, "Help."

Error Detection and Correction for Scooping

Team success depends on the individual players' scooping skills.

ERROR   Missed scoops

CORRECTION

1. Approach the ground ball at full speed and get low by bending at the knees and waist.

2. Keep the stick out to the side, with the back hand lowered to a position between the knees and hips.

3. Put the head of the stick down six inches in front of the ball.

4. Bring the head of the stick and ball up to the ready position while completing the scoop.

5. Be ready to pass the ball to an open teammate.

Scooping Games

1 V 1 SCOOPING WITH OUTLET

Goal

To develop scooping and passing skills under pressure

Description

Three lines of players stand five yards apart. One line is the outlet "help" line, and the other two lines compete for possession of the loose ball. Stand in between the two lines and roll out a ground ball. The player that scoops the ball passes to the outlet, while the opponent plays defense. Each player goes to the end of his line.

Instruct players to scoop through the ball and run away from pressure. They should protect their stick after scooping the ball by keeping their body between the defender and the stick.

PARTNER SCOOPING AND CRADLING

Goal

To develop scooping skills

Description

Players line up in pairs 10 yards apart facing each other. One player has the ball at his feet. On your command, he scoops up the ball and passes it to his partner. Be sure the scooper drops his leg on his off-stick side and bends his knees. The scooper must yell, "Ball," and, "Release," and the receiver yells, "Help." After scooping the ball, the ball carrier runs several steps and passes to his partner. For a variation, have players scoop with their nondominant hand.

SCOOPING AND PASSING

Goal

To develop scooping and passing skills

Description

Two lines of players stand 20 yards apart. Player 2 in line 1 rolls the ball forward to player 1 in line 1, who runs after it and scoops. The scooper goes through the ball, scoops it, and passes it to player 2 in line 2. Player 2 in line 2 then rolls the ball forward for player 1 in line 2 to scoop. Player 2 in each line moves up to become player 1. Each player goes to the end of the line he passed to. Require players to use appropriate communication.

2 V 1 GROUND BALL

Goal

To develop skill and teamwork on ground balls

Description

Three lines of players stand five yards apart. Roll out a ball between the middle player and either of the end lines. The players in two of the lines are teammates, and the players in the third line are their opponents. The players in the teammates' line work together against a single opponent to win a ground ball. The player closest to the ball goes to scoop the ground ball, and the other player goes between the ball and the opponent's body to body check him from the front or side and above the knees. Make sure teammates communicate clearly and correctly.

Dodging

All players in possession of the ball have the opportunity to advance the ball upfield and toward their opponent's goal by passing, running, and dodging. All players should learn several basic dodges. Players in any position can use the inside-and-out dodge, face dodge, roll dodge, and bull dodge.

Inside-and-Out Dodge

The inside-and-out dodge is the easiest of dodges to execute. It is used at every level of play and is highly effective. As the dodger approaches his defender, carrying the ball in his right hand, he steps aggressively to the inside (away from his stick side) and then plants off this foot and drives to his stick side. This quick step away from his intended direction is often enough to create separation between the dodger and the defender. The fake left and go right or fake right and go left is similar to moves in football, basketball and soccer. The player just steps hard away and goes!

Face Dodge

When a defender rushes at the ball carrier with his stick up, a face dodge is appropriate. The face dodge requires a good setup for effective execution. A ball carrier sets up a face dodge by placing his stick up in the ready position for a pass or shot.

Teach players to follow these steps to execute a face dodge:

1. As the defender tries to check the stick, bring the stick across the body from the ready position on the stick side to the opposite side of the body (figure 11.12a).
2. While bringing the stick across the body, dip the head and shoulders slightly, then drive forward off the left foot (for right-handed players), cross the right foot over the left, and keep the eyes looking straight ahead (figure 11.12b).
3. Keep two hands on the stick and continue to move away from the rushing defender.
4. Bring the stick back to the ready position on the stick side.

a   b

Figure 11.12   Face dodge. *(a)* Bring stick across body, *(b)* cross right foot over left with eyes looking straight ahead.

Roll Dodge

The roll dodge is most effective when a defender overcommits and tries to poke or check the ball carrier's stick.

Players executing a roll dodge must learn the following skills:

1. Plant the foot on the off-stick side, with the toe pointing straight ahead (a right-handed player would plant the left foot). Pivot 180 degrees to the off-stick side while bending the knees so that the back is toward the defender (figure 11.13a).

2. Step out with the right foot, plant it, and swing the body around to follow it (figure 11.13b).

3. Continue to run past the defender (figure 11.13c).

Bull Dodge

Use the bull dodge against a defender who is standing still. The dodger simply fakes to his off-stick side and then runs by, or through, the defender's stick.

Teach players the following bull dodging steps:

1. Roll the shoulders from parallel to the defender's stick to perpendicular to it.

2. Move past the defender and use the shoulders and head to protect the stick. The beaten defender may try a desperation stick check.

a   b   c

Figure 11.13   Roll dodge.

Dodging Games

LINE DODGING

Goal

To develop face, roll, and bull dodging skills

Description

Two lines of three or four players each stand 20 yards apart, face-to-face. Player 1 in line 1 moves forward with the ball as player 1 in line 2 moves out to the middle to offer passive defensive resistance. The ball carrier dodges the defender and passes to player 2 in line 2. The former ball carrier then becomes the defender. Instruct the defensive player to set up the offensive dodger in one of three ways: by charging him with his stick low and at the dodger's stick (dodger roll dodges), by charging him with his stick high and at the dodger's stick (dodger face dodges), or by having the defender stand still (dodger bull dodges). Initially, work on one dodge at a time.

Cradling and Dodging Game

SHOW TIME

Goal

To develop ball-handling and dodging skills without a defender

Description

Position all players in the penalty area, giving each player a ball (see figure 11.14). As players cradle and move throughout the penalty area, they execute one or more dodges indicated by the coach. Players must keep their heads up and not look at the ball in their sticks. The coach awards one point to each player who successfully cradles the ball and executes the dodge indicated.

To make the game easier

- ○ Have fewer players in the penalty box to create more space.
- ○ Have players execute only one dodge at a time.

To make the game harder

- ○ Have players combine two dodges.
- ○ Have players use their off hand.

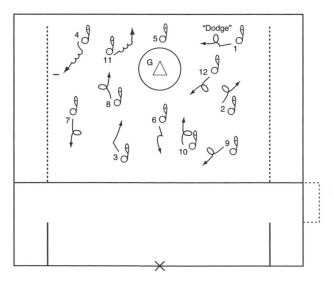

Figure 11.14   Show Time.

GO FOR IT

Goal

To develop dodging and defending skills

Description

Play 3 v 3 with a goalie in the goal (figure 11.15). Offensive players work the ball to set up an opportunity to execute the dodge specified by the coach. Award one point to the offense for successfully creating dodging space (off-ball players) and executing the dodge (ball carrier) specified by the coach. Award the defense one point for stopping the dodger.

To make the game easier

⊙ Play 1 v 1.

To make the gamer harder

⊙ Play 4 v 4.

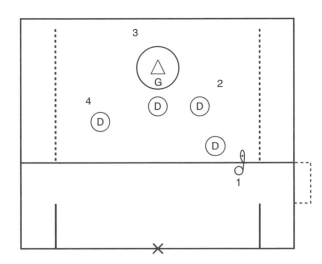

Figure 11.15
Go For It.

Individual Offensive Skills

Midfielders and attackers must develop skills to maximize offensive opportunities. These skills include ball handling—inside roll, split dodge, one-handed cradling, and changing direction—as well as off-ball play—cutting and picking.

Inside Roll

When an attacker drives with the ball from behind the goal, he often finds himself playing directly against a defender on the side of the goal. The area above the goal line extended and at the top of the circle is a good spot for the inside roll. When the ball carrier feels the pressure from the defender on his upfield shoulder, he can perform an inside roll.

To perform an inside roll, a player must follow these steps:

1. Pivot off the front foot (figure 11.16a). For a right-handed player, this is the left foot.
2. Drop the center of gravity by bending at the knees and "sitting down."
3. Keep the stick protected behind the head and body.
4. Drop the right foot toward the goal and pivot off the left foot, around the defender (figure 11.16b).
5. Keep the stick parallel to the body and close to the chest during the pivot. Do not switch hands.

After the inside roll, the player will be in a great position to shoot on goal (figure 11.16c).

a   b   c

Figure 11.16 Inside Roll.

Split Dodge

The ability to handle and shoot the ball with both hands enhances players' effectiveness. All players can use the split dodge to create a shooting opportunity.

Teach players to follow these steps to do a split dodge:

1. Run across the field while cradling the ball in the right hand forcing the defender to run parallel and in a hip-to-hip position (figure 11.17a).
2. Plant the stick-side foot and redirect the body diagonally switching the hands by sliding the left hand to the top of the shaft and placing the right hand at the end of the shaft (figure 11.17b).
3. Bring the stick quickly across the face (figure 11.17b-c).
4. Accelerate toward the goal (figure 11.17d).

A young player can start with the ball in his nondominant hand and set up a shot with his preferred (dominant) hand by using the split dodge. The right-handed player starts with the ball in his left hand and splits back to the right.

Error Detection and Correction for the Split Dodge

The dodger's ability to bring the stick across his body by switching and sliding his hands allows him to move in either direction. This skill is very similar to a crossover dribble in basketball.

ERROR   Dropping the head of the stick out of the ready area when switching hands

CORRECTION

1. Execute the dodge quickly, or else the stick is exposed while dodging a defender. Make sure to bring the stick across the body.
2. Plant the stick-side foot (outside foot) and push off this foot toward the inside foot. Then step with the inside foot at a 45-degree angle in the original line of direction.
3. Drive upfield at a 45-degree angle to the defender.
4. Move the stick from hand to hand (ready position to ready position) when dodging. Keep the stick within the frame of the body.

Figure 11.17
Split dodge. *(a)* Force defender to hip-to-hip position, *(b)* plant stick-side foot, *(c)* bring stick quickly across face, *(d)* accelerate to goal.

Change of Direction

The ball carrier uses a change of direction to shield the ball from his opponent. This advanced move requires the ball carrier to stop and reverse his direction. The ball carrier concentrates first on protecting his stick; he can work on speed as he becomes more skilled.

To change directions, players should follow these instructions:

1. Drive diagonally across the field, plant the foot opposite the stick, and bend the knees. These steps should be executed when a defender slows down the ball carrier or the ball carrier exhausts field space.
2. Pivot away from the defender, keeping the stick protected by the upper body. Keep the body between the defender and the stick.
3. With the back to the defender and as the shoulders and head start to move away from the original line of direction, pull the stick back with the top hand and switch hands.
4. Keep the stick completely shielded from the defender.

Error Detection and Correction for Change of Direction

Players must be able to protect the ball when changing direction against a defender who is applying heavy defensive pressure.

ERROR   Exposing the ball when executing a change of direction

CORRECTION

1. Keep the head and upper body between the defender and the stick.

2. Switch hands on the stick as the shoulders come around.

3. Keep the stick behind the body so that it is completely shielded from the defender. Don't drag the stick behind after coming out of the dodge.

4. Accelerate after completing the change of direction.

Shooting

A team can't win if it can't score goals. Shots fall into two categories, each with its own techniques and strategies: inside (within 10 yards of the goal) and outside (from 10 to 18 yards away from the goal). Help your players practice and develop both types.

Inside Shooting

Many inside shots result from a feed behind the goal to the shooter cutting toward the goal from the front. In this situation, the shooter takes one cradle as he catches the ball, and then he shoots the ball overhand, low and to the far goal pipe. For example, if the shooter catches the ball on the right side of the goal (facing the goal from in front of the cage), he cradles it to gain control and then shoots low and toward the left goalpost. Imagine a triangle in each of the four corners of the goal, measuring one foot by one foot along the posts. These are called the "scoring triangles," and your players should shoot to these areas. Depending on the goalie's position, players can also shoot for open net.

Teach your players how to change the plane of the ball when they take a shot. Changing the plane refers to catching the ball up high and changing the direction of the ball by shooting low. Most goalies keep their body and stick up high when the ball is close to the goal, which makes them vulnerable to a low shot.

The basic concepts of shooting include the following:

1. Shoot overhand and follow through (figure 11.18a-b).

2. Always look for the open space in the goal, shooting low and away from the goalie. A common mistake is to look at the goalie, his stick, or the goal pipes.

3. Bounce outside shots.

4. Change the plane of inside shots. For example, catch the ball high and shoot it low.

a   b

Figure 11.18 Shooting. *(a)* Ready position for overhand shot, *(b)* follow through.

Outside Shooting

A ball carrier dodging and moving toward the goal or a player who receives a pass and has time to wind up has the opportunity to take an outside shot. Outside shots that bounce in front of the goalie have a better chance of being successful than direct shots do. A prepared shooter tests the ground during the pregame warm-up to study how the ball will bounce. He locates a spot far enough out from the goal mouth to prevent the goalie from catching the ball in the air but close enough to allow the ball to bounce into, but not over, the goal. Aiming for a spot about one foot in front of the crease circle usually brings success.

Shooting on the Run

When shooting on the run, the player drives diagonally toward the cage. Teach these skills, which are similar to inside shooting skills, to players learning to shoot on the run:

1. Shoot the ball overhand and follow through to the target. Shoot right handed when driving right and left handed when driving left.

2. Shoot the ball low and to the far post to the scoring triangle.

3. Use a screen when shooting bounce shots from the outside. The shooter watches for a teammate to position himself in front of the goalie to obscure the goalie's vision while the shooter dodges from the front of the goal. The screener positions himself one foot off the crease circle and directly in front of the goalie. As the shot goes past, he turns to look for any rebounds.

Room and Time Shooting

Sometimes the shooter might have time to wind up and shoot the ball after catching a pass. The basic shooting principles apply:

1. Look for a screen and use his feet as a target.

2. Point the off-stick shoulder and foot toward the target.

3. Step with the front foot, cross over with the back foot, and step again with the front foot—a movement similar to throwing a ball for distance. Get the body into the shot!

4. Keeping the head of the stick up high, shoot the ball toward the unguarded post (probably the outside post), and follow through to the goal.

Error Detection and Correction for Shooting

Players often miss the goal because they use poor technique, and they don't follow the basic shooting principles.

ERROR Missing the goal when shooting

CORRECTION

1. Carry the basic techniques of passing over into shooting.
2. Shoot the ball overhand and on the ground when dodging from the midfield. Bounce the ball in front of a screen.
3. When in the restraining box and moving away from the center of the goal, shoot with the stick to the outside of the field.
4. Shoot the ball to the unguarded post and to the scoring triangle.
5. Change the plane of the shot when shooting inside. For example, catch the ball up high and redirect it low and to the unguarded post. Always shoot for the scoring triangle.

Shooting Games

SAME-SIDE SHOOTING

Goal

To develop catching and inside shooting skills with both hands

Description

Two lines of feeders stand behind the cage, and two lines of cutters and shooters stand at the top of the restraining box—one line of cutters and one line of feeders on each side of the goal, drilling together. Each of the feeders has a ball. The first cutter cuts to the side of the crease, with his stick to the outside; and the first feeder, also with his stick to the outside, moves laterally and up the field to feed the ball to the cutter, who takes an inside shot. Feeders go to the end of the cutters' line and cutters go to the end of the feeders' line, but all players stay on their original side of the cage. After a designated time they switch sides.

Require the feeders to move laterally and up the field to create a feeding lane. The shooter should catch the ball and shoot it to the scoring triangle at the far post.

Variation

Switch roles so that the players behind the cage are cutters and the players at the top of the restraining box are feeders. The feeders feed the cutters coming up the field for a shot.

DRIVE FROM THE CENTER AND SHOOT

Goal

To practice shooting accurately while on the run

Description

One line of players faces the goal at the top and in the center of the attack box. Each player in turn runs left or right and shoots the ball with his stick to the outside. Give each player a ball to keep the game moving quickly.

Have players execute a bull or split dodge while shooting the ball on the ground toward the far scoring triangle. Instruct players to shoot while running. Do not let them slow down to wind up.

SHOOT AWAY

Goal

To work on shooting skills

Description

Play 3 v 2 with a goalie in the goal (figure 11.19). The offense works the ball around to create a clear shooting opportunity. Award two points for every goal scored using a bounce shot and one point for every goal scored with a different shot. Award the defense two points for gaining possession.

To make the game easier

- Play 3 v 1.
- Award a point for all shots on goal.

To make the game harder

- Have players shoot with their off hand.
- Subtract one point from the offense if they miss the goal.

(continued)

Shoot Away *(continued)*

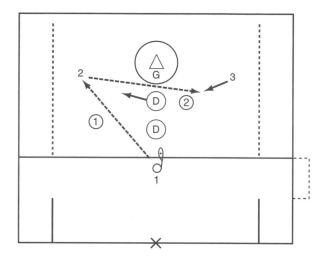

Figure 11.19 Shoot Away.

Playing Without the Ball

Even when an offensive player does not have the ball, he must keep moving to make it more difficult for the defense to cover him. The art of playing without the ball requires learning where and when to move.

The V-Cut

The V-cut enables a potential receiver to create a passing lane on the perimeter of the defense. The receiver moves four or five steps in toward the goal, then quickly breaks away toward the passer. Timing is important, and both the passer and the receiver move toward each other so that the pass is short. Both players have their sticks to the outside of the defender.

Cutting

A cutting opportunity exists whenever an off-ball defender watches the ball carrier instead of the man he is covering. Each off-ball offensive player must watch his teammate with the ball and his own defender to spot a cutting opportunity.

Cutters must learn these skills:

1. Cut to the ball carrier at full speed with the stick in the ready position. The best time to cut is when the defender is ball watching.
2. Call, "Help," to get the feeder's attention.
3. Time the cut. Make eye contact with the feeder, and cut when he is ready to pass the ball.
4. Discontinue the cut and round back to the original position if a pass isn't received in front of the goal. Do not crowd the feeder's space by moving into the feeder's area with the defender.
5. Move laterally to get the stick clear of the defender's stick.

Cutting Game

PLAYING THE CUTTER

Goal

To develop offensive and defensive cutting skills

Description

Two lines of midfielders, one offensive and one defensive, stand at the top of the attack box. One midfielder from the defensive line steps forward to defend the cutting offensive midfielder. Two attackers, each with a ball, stand behind the goal, with the goalie in position. On your signal, the cutter runs at the defender, fakes, and cuts to an attacker. That attacker feeds him.

Be sure the cutter head fakes as he moves toward the feeder and that he angles to the edge of the crease to avoid running into it. Teach the defender to watch the cutter's hips—not his head, shoulders, or eyes—as the defender shuffles back and cushions the cutter on his approach.

Picking

Picks are used to free a teammate for a shot or for a cut to the feeder. The ball carrier, pick man, and cutter work together to create a scoring opportunity. The pick man stands motionless to allow his teammate to run his defender into the pick. The pick man must prepare for and protect against contact because his teammate's defender might run into him.

Face-Offs

The face-off at the center of the field begins play at each quarter and after a goal. The team that consistently gets possession of the ball on the face-off controls the tempo of the game.

During a face-off, two opponents stand at the center of the field, each facing his offensive goal. The two wing midfielders stand ready on the wing lines with their opponents. The attackers and defenders must stay in their areas until the official signals that one team has possession of the ball or until a loose ball enters the box area. The umpire places the ball at the center of the field on the ground and instructs both face-off players to assume the face-off position (all face-offs are taken right handed).

Teach your players the following steps for facing off:

1. Assume a low, crouched position with the feet shoulder-width apart and weight evenly distributed.
2. Place the right hand at the top of the shaft of the stick, with the palm facing forward and the left hand shoulder-width from the top hand. Rest both hands on the ground, with the handle of the stick parallel to the midfield line.
3. Keep the stick one inch from the ball on the ground, being sure to match the back of the pocket with the opponent's.
4. Keep both hands and both feet to the left of the throat of the crosse.

The clamp-and-step is a basic face-off technique that enables the face-off man to gain possession of the ball himself or to direct the ball to one of his wing players.

When the umpire sounds the whistle, the face-off man proceeds this way:

1. Stay low and step to the head of the stick. Clamp down over the ball with the top hand, and drive into the opponent with the right shoulder. At the same time, pull back with the left hand toward the left knee. Coordinate all movements to occur simultaneously.
2. Try to get the head and upper body over the ball and pivot the hips into the opponent, positioning the body between the ball and the opponent.
3. Direct the ball out to an area or to a wing player.

Individual Defensive Skills

When a team loses possession of the ball, it becomes the defensive team; therefore, all players must develop basic defensive skills.

Defensive Stance

The basic defensive stance in lacrosse is similar to the ready position of a linebacker in football. The defender stands with his feet apart and establishes a low center of gravity so that he can move quickly in any direction.

Teach players the following aspects of defensive positioning (figure 11.20):

1. Keep the feet shoulder-width apart.
2. Bend the knees and lower the center of gravity.
3. Bend forward slightly at the waist. The weight of the head and shoulders stays over the feet.
4. Hold the stick parallel to the ground directly in front of the body.

Defensive players stay between the ball carrier and the goal, best accomplished by using good footwork with the proper body position.

Figure 11.20 Defensive stance.

Footwork

To build the foundation for effective defensive play, instruct your players how to correctly move their feet and position their bodies in response to the movement of the ball carrier. Basic defensive footwork consists of shuffle steps and hip-to-hip running.

When the ball carrier moves slowly, the defender shuffles his feet and keeps his shoulders square to the ball carrier. When the ball carrier begins to run faster, the defender turns and runs hip to hip with him (figure 11.21). The defender establishes the hip-to-hip position with a crossover step. He pushes off the foot closest to the ball carrier, brings his back foot across the front of his body, turns his hips, and runs.

When the ball carrier runs at the defender, the defender uses a drop step. He steps back with the leg closest to the ball carrier and "opens his hips" in that direction. The defender then shuffles or runs hip to hip with the ball carrier, depending on the ball carrier's speed. Some keys to correct footwork include adapting to the movement of the ball carrier. In other words, if the ball carrier

- ◉ is moving slowly, shuffle;
- ◉ is running, run hip to hip; or
- ◉ runs directly at the defender, drop-step and open the hips in that direction.

Figure 11.21 Establishing the hip-to-hip position.

Error Detection and Correction for Footwork

Correct footwork is the most important component of playing good defense. Reinforce the importance of footwork as the foundation for playing effective defense.

ERROR Changing from a shuffle to a hip-to-hip run in the wrong situation

CORRECTION

1. Remind defenders to follow the motion pattern of the ball carrier. When the ball carrier moves slowly, the defender shuffles his feet. When the ball carrier runs, the defender crosses over and runs hip to hip with him.

2. Teach players to create a cushion between them and the ball carrier by shuffling back as the ball carrier approaches. When the ball carrier drives straight at a player, the player drop-steps and opens his hips in that direction.

Footwork Game

AGILITIES

Goal

To develop footwork fundamentals

Description

Four lines of players are positioned side by side, 10 yards apart, facing you. The first player steps out and reacts to your stick movement and verbal signals that include the following:

- Shuffle right and left.
- Shuffle right and left, then drop and run.
- Run hip to hip laterally.
- Shuffle back at a 45-degree angle.
- Spring back at a 45-degree angle.
- Drop-step, open hips, and run straight backward.
- Run at me, and then on my signal break down to the defensive ready position.

After players go through the series of commands or various combinations of the commands, they go to the end of the line. Keep movements short and at high intensity.

Stick Position

Teach beginning players to play "preferred-hand defense." The defensive player keeps the stick in his dominant hand and moves the head of the stick to keep it in front of the ball carrier. The defender carries his stick at the height of the number on the ball carrier's jersey.

The defender combines good footwork and stick position to keep the ball carrier at least one stick's length away from him. This space, or cushion, between the ball carrier and the defender makes it easier for the defender to react to the ball carrier's dodges and changes of direction.

Checking

Stick checks won't be effective unless they're preceded by good footwork that puts the defender in good body position. Emphasize that good defensive play requires correct body position combined with correct stick position. Teach players to make their stick checks short, vigorous, aimed at the opponent's stick, and under control. *Note:* Any one-handed check is considered a slash in the Bantam Division.

Poke Check

The poke check is the most basic and most commonly used check. It effectively disrupts the ball carrier, without extending the defender into a vulnerable, off-balance position. *Note:* A check not making contact with the gloved hand is considered a slash in the Lightning and Bantam Divisions.

To poke check, players should follow these instructions:

1. Assume the basic defensive stance and stick position.
2. With the back hand, push the stick through the thumb and forefinger of the top hand (figure 11.22a). (This motion is like the motion used to shoot pool.)
3. Keep the body a stick's length away from the ball carrier to create a cushion between the ball carrier and the defender.
4. Aim the poke at the ball carrier's bottom hand when he has two hands on his stick (figure 11.22b-c); aim across the ball carrier's numbers to the head of the stick when he has one hand on the stick.
5. Do not extend the feet or upper body. Stepping in toward the ball carrier gives him a chance to dodge the defender.

a

b

c

Figure 11.22 Poke check. *(a)* Push stick through thumb and forefinger, *(b-c)* aim pole at ball carrier's bottom hand.

Error Detection and Correction for the Poke Check

Timing and technique are critical to a safe, effective poke check. Make sure your players square up and use good footwork when checking.

ERROR   Lunging and overextending when poke checking

CORRECTION

1. Keep feet parallel when poking. Do not step toward the ball carrier.
2. Keep a cushion between the defender and the ball carrier.
3. Slide the stick through the top hand.

Slap Check

In the slap check, the defender brings the head of his stick from in front of the ball carrier back into the ball carrier's stick hand and glove.

Players must learn the following skills to slap check:

1. Assume the defensive ready position and hold the stick out in front of the ball carrier at a 45-degree angle (figure 11.23).
2. Time the delivery of the slap check to coincide with a pass or shot attempt.
3. As the ball carrier places two hands on the stick in preparation for his pass or shot, bring the head of the stick down on his bottom hand.

Figure 11.23   Slap check.

Checking Games

STICK CHECK

Goal

To develop poke check and stick check skills

Description

Conduct this drill without a ball. Two parallel lines of players stand at the top corner of the attack box. The line closest to the midline is offense, and the line inside the attack box is defense. Signal the first pair of players to step out. The offensive player faces the cages, his stick in his left hand. The defender assumes the defensive ready position, with his stick ready to practice the poke or stick check. The offensive player jogs across the field as the defender shuffles with him and poke or stick checks. Players continue to the opposite top corner and stop. On your signal, the second pair begins. When all players have gone in one direction, repeat the drill in the opposite direction.

Variation

The offensive players carry a ball to work on stick protection. The ball carrier alternates between a jog and a run to give the defenders practice in shuffling and running hip to hip.

TURN IT OVER

Goal

To develop defensive checking skills (poke and slap)

Description

Play 3 v 3 with the goalie in the goal (figure 11.24). The offense works for a shot and the defender tries to force a turnover by using one of the two basic checks. Award the offense one point for a goal and the defense two points for each check that results in a turnover.

To make the game easier

⊙ Play 1 v 1.

To make the game harder

⊙ Remove the goalie and shooting option. Have the offense try to maintain possession in the penalty box while the defense tries to force a turnover.

(continued)

Turn It Over *(continued)*

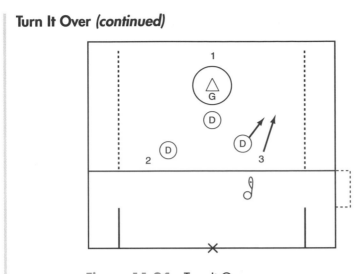

Figure 11.24 Turn It Over.

Body Check

Body checking is part of lacrosse, and, when it's combined with good stick skills and sound tactics, it adds another component to team play. (*Note:* No body checking is allowed in the Lightning and Bantam Divisions.) Lacrosse is a physical game, but never let physical contact overshadow stick skills and team play. Be sure to make clear to your players from the start that spearing—leading with the head to make contact with another player—is illegal and very dangerous to both players.

A player carrying the ball or one within five yards of a loose ball may be legally body checked from the front or side, above the knees and below the shoulders.

A legal body check in lacrosse is most effective in two situations:

- In a loose ball situation, where one defender takes the "ball" and one takes the "man."
- When sliding to a dodger who is closing in on the goal for a shot.

A legal body check in lacrosse is similar to a shoulder block in football. A player body checks by running, shoulder down, into an opponent. He makes contact with his shoulder and upper body, never with his head or stick.

Holds

As the ball carrier drives to his goal, the defender must prevent him from moving into a prime shooting area. Proper hold techniques make it possible for the defender to remain in good body and stick position while forcing the ball carrier away from the goal. Defensive players listen for their goalie to yell, "Hold." The goalie makes this call when the ball carrier runs into the prime scoring area in front of the goal—the hole. The hole area extends 7 yards from the goalposts out to the sideline and 12 yards forward toward the restraining lines.

The goalie calls, "Hold," when the ball carrier is slightly outside of these parameters to allow the defender to hear and react to the call. The defender always keeps the head of his stick in front of the ball carrier so that he's in position to block a pass or shot.

Forearm Hold

A right-handed defender plays a right-handed ball carrier this way:

1. Hold the right arm with the elbow bent at a 90-degree angle (figure 11.25).
2. Establish a wide base of support. Bend at the knees.
3. Hold the stick at chest level, parallel to the ground.
4. Apply pressure to the ball carrier's upfield-shoulder side at a point below the armpit. Keep space between the forearm and chest.
5. Use steady pressure to prevent the ball carrier from moving to the goal. Separate from the ball carrier when he moves out of the hole area.

Figure 11.25   Forearm hold.

Fist Hold

A right-handed defender plays a left-handed ball carrier this way:

1. Extend the hands completely away from the body as the defender prepares to apply pressure to the ball carrier. Slide the hands together by bringing the top hand down to meet the bottom hand.
2. Establish a wide base of support. Bend at the knees.
3. Hold the stick at waist level, parallel to the ground.
4. Apply pressure to the ball carrier's upfield-shoulder side at the point below the armpit, applying pressure with the fists. Keep the arms fully extended to keep a cushion between the defender and the ball carrier.
5. Move away from the ball carrier after the defender has pressured him away from the goal.

Error Detection and Correction for Holds

A defender must always keep his stick in front of the ball carrier in the passing and shooting lane.

ERROR   Incorrect hold technique

CORRECTION

1. When the ball carrier reaches the hole area, assume the defensive ready position: bend the knees, "sit," and keep the feet parallel to each other.

2. Keep the stick in the ball carrier's passing and shooting lane.

3. Keep the hands extended from the body on the forearm and fist holds as you apply pressure to the upfield-shoulder side below the armpit.

4. Do not step forward with the back foot and open up space when executing a hold; doing so invites the ball carrier to roll inside.

Holding Game

DEFENSIVE HOLD GAME

Goal

To develop correct hold techniques

Description

Two parallel lines of players stand at the top corner of the penalty box. The line closest to the midline is offense, and the line inside the attack box is defense. On your signal, the first pair of players steps out. The offensive player faces the cage, with his stick in his left hand, and the defender assumes the ready position. The offensive player jogs across the field and steps up to the attack box every six to eight yards. As the offensive player steps up to the line, the defensive player steps up to execute the correct hold technique. After the first pair has completed its second step up and hold, the next pair begins. Pairs continue across the box to the opposite corner. No offensive or defensive player should cross over the attack box line. Check that the defender places his feet and shoulders parallel to the attack box line, drops his center of gravity, and extends his hands during the hold.

Playing the Cutter

When an off-ball offensive player makes a cut to the ball, cover him tightly by

1. holding the stick up, running hip to hip with the cutter, and
2. checking down on the cutter's stick if his teammate feeds him the ball.

Defenders playing the cutter must communicate because a defender may not see the ball. He depends on the goalie to yell, "Check," to signal him that a feed is being made to his man. Cutters instinctively raise their eyes and hands as the ball arrives. When a defender sees that move, it is time to check.

Playing the V-Cut

When an offensive player breaks away from the goal area to receive a pass on the perimeter, the defender moves out to cover the receiver. As the ball is in the air, the defender moves out and breaks down (bends at the knees and partially sits) at least one stick's length away from the receiver. He keeps his stick parallel to the ground and ready to poke check. He can now move easily in any direction.

Team Offense

Here we discuss the offensive team tactics for transition, settled (6 v 6) play, clearing, and the extra-man offense.

Offensive Team Tactics for Transitional Play

The offensive team's primary objective is to advance the ball to the offensive half of the field and to then work together to create a scoring opportunity. When the goalie, defenders, or midfielders gain possession of the ball, all players become involved in the transition to offense in an attempt to move the ball from the half of the field they are defending to the half they're attacking.

Many great scoring opportunities arise during the transitional component of the game. Fast-break opportunities and uneven situations create many exciting and productive scoring chances for the offense. This phase of the game is fun for players to practice and incorporates many of the skills and tactics they need for playing lacrosse.

The Fast Break

In the traditional lacrosse fast-break situation, the offense outnumbers the defense four players to three. Three attackers and a midfielder (or defender) usually carry the ball upfield against three defenders and the goalie. The defense usually slides to the ball carrier. With accurate passing and proper positioning, this situation provides a great chance for a goal.

When the attackers recognize the four-on-three situation developing, they call out, "Fast break," and begin to move away from the midline by angle running toward their goal. In angle running, the attackers sprint toward their goal while watching the ball carrier.

The attackers (A1, A2, and A3) position themselves in an L formation (see figure 11.26) as the ball carrier pushes the ball toward the goal. The ball carrier must be ready to pass the ball when one of the defenders moves toward him to stop his movement to the goal.

When the defender commits to the ball carrier, the ball carrier passes the ball to an uncovered attacker. The defense usually will slide from the top, or point, attacker, who is positioned at the top of the attack box. The point attacker moves to the pass to position himself in the middle of the cage. If a defender slides to him, he quickly makes another pass. If no defender slides, the attacker goes to the cage and shoots. The original ball carrier stops at the top of the attack box after he has passed the ball. He is the top corner of the offensive box formation and stands ready to receive a pass.

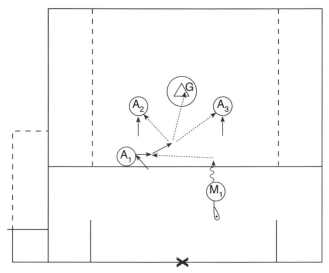

Figure 11.26   Fast break.

Fast-Break Games

HALF-FIELD FAST BREAK

Goal

To develop offensive and defensive transitional skills and tactics

Description

Players form two lines—one line of attackers and one line of defenders. Three attackers from these lines stand ready just outside the attack box. A line of midfielders stands just inside the midfield line. A goalie is optional for this game. Roll the ball for one player from the midfield line to scoop; then the player runs the four-on-three fast break. As the fast break begins, the ball carrier or goalie yells, "Fast break." The point defender yells, "Ball," and moves to defend the ball carrier as he crosses the restraining box. Remind the offense to set up in an L formation, the defense to form a triangle, and both teams to watch the ball as they funnel toward the goal.

Variation

The first player in the attacking line scoops up the ball; and the first player in the defensive line delays, then chases. This may end in a 4-v-4 situation.

BREAK AWAY

Goal

To learn to recognize and execute the fast break in game situations

Description

Play 4 v 3 with a goalie in the goal (figure 11.27). Start play by rolling the ball out to one of the offensive players between the restraining line and the midline. The offensive player then uses the 4-v-3 advantage to attempt a goal. Award the offense one point for every goal and the defense one point for every stop.

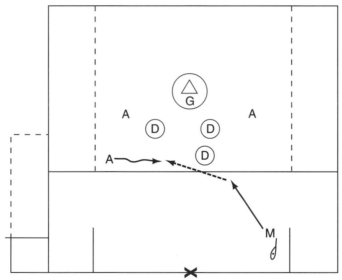

Figure 11.27 Break Away.

The Slow Break

When the offensive team is in a transitional situation and does not have a clear numerical advantage, the team continues to advance the ball toward its goal by passing. The ball moves much more quickly toward the offensive goal area when players pass than when they run with the ball.

The slow-break pattern attempts to create a scoring opportunity by moving the ball as quickly as possible to the X spot behind the goal and then cutting to the crease area. The slow-break pattern develops best when players pass the ball down the side of the field and then pass to X. Moving the ball quickly to the X spot stretches the defense out and then forces the defense to turn toward the X spot to locate the ball. When the ball arrives at X, midfielders have an opportunity to cut toward the crease. The ball carrier at X then feeds the cutting midfielder for an easy shot. Figure 11.28a identifies a full-team, slow-break pattern. Figure 11.28b shows what can be done when the ball reaches the X spot.

The slow break continues as the remaining midfielders arrive in the offensive half of the field. The midfielder who arrives at the point position first cuts toward X, and the remaining two midfielders fill in at the top of the attack box to back up any feeds and to be in position to get back on defense if the team loses possession.

The attackers break to receive the ball in the following pattern: The wing attacker on the ball side breaks out to receive the ball, and the opposite wing man breaks to X. The point man always remains in position for the fast break and moves to the opposite wing on the slow break.

The triangle positioning of the attackers as the ball approaches the offensive half of the field enables them to be in position to react to a fast break and a slow break. The attacker in the offensive half of the field must always be in position to become an outlet for the ball carrier and V-cuts to create open passing lanes. The key in transitional offense is for the ball carrier to draw a defender to him and then pass to an open teammate.

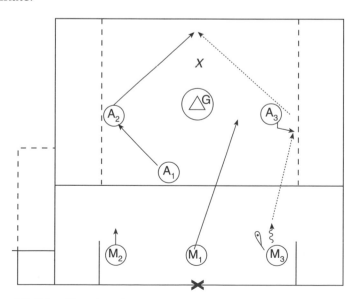

Figure 11.28 Slow break.

In the transitional situation, offensive players continue to pass the ball around the perimeter of the offense looking for cutters before the defense becomes settled. When the defense does become settled, the offense moves from the transitional situation to the settled offense. It is true that transitional situations can create good scoring opportunities, but scoring opportunities don't always materialize; so a team must know how to handle the ball during its entire offensive possession.

When all potential opportunities for fast-break and slow-break situations have passed, a team flows from its transitional offense to its six-on-six game. Encourage players to pass the ball, but consider the age, skill, and experience of the players as you coach transitional lacrosse. For example, a player with a weaker nondominant hand will most likely cause loss of possession. Since possession of the ball is key, have players put extra focus on improving left- and right-handed passing abilities prior to introducing a situation that requires these skills. It is crucial to stress passing and stick-handling drills during every practice. Otherwise, the team will be forced to rely heavily on the players who have both left- and right-handed skills, which creates negative team dynamics.

MAKING A BREAK

Goal

To recognize and execute the slow break in game situations

Description

Play 5 v 4 with a goalie in the goal (figure 11.29). Set up three attack and three defense players inside the box, with three midfielders at midfield (two on offense, one on defense). Begin play by rolling the ball to one of the offensive players at midfield. Once the ball has been picked up, the defensive players run downfield, cutting off the fast-break opportunity and forcing the offense to run a slow break. Award one point to the offense for each goal and one point to the defense for every stop.

Variation

Periodically hold the defensive midfielder to create a 5-v-3 situation. A second defensive midfielder delays and sprints into the defensive area, creating a 5 v 5.

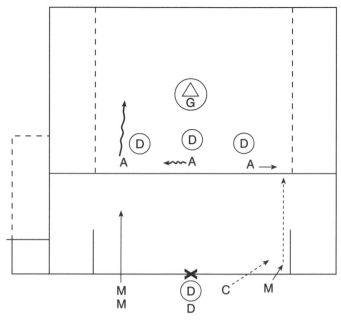

Figure 11.29 Making a Break.

SCRAMBLE

Goal

To develop offensive and defensive transitional skills and tactics

Description

All defensive players are outside of the penalty box in a straight line at the goal line extended. The offensive players are diagonally oppo-site the defense, 15 yards outside the corner of the penalty box. Call out a number from two to six. The offense sends out that number of players, and the defense sends out one less player. This always gives the offense a man-advantage situation. You can create a 2-v-1, 3-v-2, 4-v-3, or 5-v-4 situation (see figure 11.30a-d). Rolling the ball out to the offense begins play. You can allow play to continue until a shot is taken, the defense or goalie gains possession, or the defense clears the ball out of the box.

(continued)

Scamble *(continued)*

Variations

⊙ To allow for clearing over the midline, set up the drill from the sideline, with both the offense and defense on the same side. The defense can send in an extra defender to clear when the defense gains possession. The extra defender combined with the goalie gives the defense the man advantage and simulates game clearing situations.

⊙ To practice moving from an unsettled to a settled situation, send in an additional defender to "even up" the situation after a specified number of passes or time.

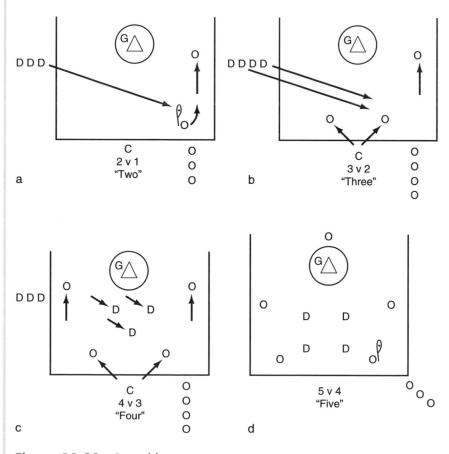

Figure 11.30 Scramble.

Six-on-Six Settled Game

The settled game is composed of six offensive players trying to score against six defensive players and the goalie.

Offensive Team Concepts

You can use several offensive team concepts to create scoring opportunities when the offense does not have a numerical advantage:

1. *Develop field sense.* First, offensive players should watch their teammate with the ball and also the teammate's defender. Second, when an off-ball defender turns his head or back and removes his attention from the man he is covering, that offensive player has an excellent opportunity to cut to his teammate for a feed or shot. (Viewing videos is helpful for both you and your players to help develop field sense.)

2. *Stay balanced.* The six offensive players work together to ensure that the field is balanced. Field balance prevents crowding, places players in position to back up shots, and positions players to make the transition to defense should the team lose possession.

3. *Give-and-go, or backdoor cut.* Players pass and then cut to receive a return pass. This tactic creates space for the ball carrier and often sets up a scoring opportunity.

4. *Dodge.* When the ball carrier receives a pass, he looks for an open area, dodges toward it, and goes to the goal for a shot or pass. The ball carrier doesn't dodge unless a teammate has cleared space. If an off-ball defender slides to the ball carrier, the ball carrier passes to an open teammate.

5. *Create space for the dodger.* Players adjacent to the ball carrier cut through and away from the ball carrier to create an open area for the dodger. When the ball carrier approaches a teammate, the teammate cuts through and creates space.

6. *Set a pick for a teammate.* Two teammates can work together by picking and cutting to create a scoring opportunity. If a player cuts off of a pick and does not receive the feed, he rounds out the cut and goes back to his original position to avoid crowding the ball carrier.

7. *Screen the goalie.* When a player is dodging from the midfield, a teammate—usually a crease attacker—screens the goalie to obscure the goalie's ability to see and block a bounce shot.

8. *Exchange places.* Two attackers or midfielders change places on the field. This simple maneuver occupies defenders and prevents potential defensive slides.

When a six-on-six situation exists, all six offensive players must work together to create scoring opportunities. The defense usually focuses on protecting the immediate goal area, and the offense needs a coordinated plan to involve the ball carrier and off-ball players to penetrate the defense.

A sample offense is the 3-1-2, which places two attackers behind the goal, one on each side; one attacker on the crease; and three midfielders at the top of the attack. This formation provides opportunities for the offense to

⊙ feed and dodge from behind the goal;

⊙ shoot, screen the goalie, and set picks from the crease position;

⊙ dodge from the midfield positions; and

⊙ cut without the ball.

These options are discussed in the next section.

Offensive Options

A number of basic options are available to offensive players who want to initiate a scoring opportunity. Coach all options equally.

Dodge From Behind

When an attack player (A₁) dodges from behind the goal (figure 11.31), the adjacent midfielder (M₄) cuts through to create dodging space. The opposite behind attacker (A₂) moves to a position where he can back

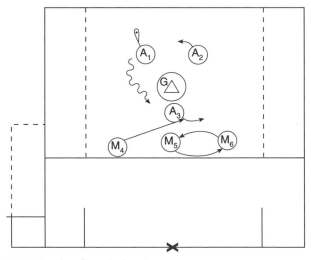

Figure 11.31 Dodge from behind.

up a shot. The crease attacker (A_3) moves away from the dodger to a high crease and to the far pipe. The two midfielders away from the ball (M_5 and M_6) can exchange places. The off-ball movement of these five players occupies defenders and creates an excellent dodging opportunity for the ball carrier.

Midfield Sweep

As shown in figure 11.32, the wing midfielder (M_1) passes to the center midfielder (M_2) and cuts to receive a return pass and to create dodging space. The center midfielder dodges to the vacated area. The crease attacker (A_1) screens the goalie, and the two attackers behind the goal (A_2 and A_3) exchange places as they stand ready to back up a shot. The remaining midfielder up top (M_3) is in position to get back on defense if the team loses possession.

Each player without the ball must watch his teammate who has the ball. If the defender covering the off-ball player "ball watches" (focuses only on the ball carrier), the player should cut to the ball carrier for a feed.

Cutting and Picking With the Ball Behind

When two attackers (A_1 and A_2) are handling the ball behind the goal (figure 11.33), the crease attacker (A_3) can move to a high crease, facing the midfielders, and set a pick for the midfielders to cut off of. He must be ready to follow or spin opposite the cutter and become a potential shooter. For example, attacker A_3 sets a pick for midfielder M_4, who

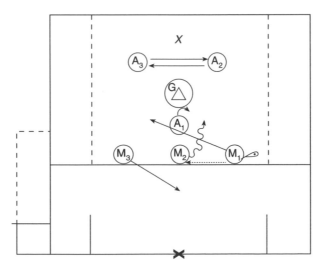

Figure 11.32 Midfield sweep.

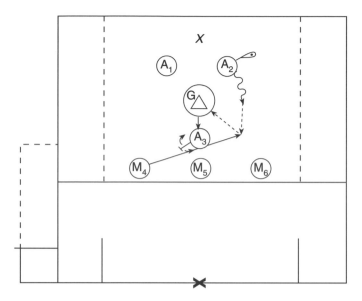

Figure 11.33 Cut and pick behind.

cuts to receive a pass from attacker A_2; midfielder M_4 may have a shot opportunity. The movement by the crease attacker and midfielders also creates dodging opportunities for the attacker behind the goal by occupying off-ball defenders.

Error Detection and Correction for Team Offense

Players without the ball must cut through (in toward the crease) to create space when the ball carrier comes toward them. Teach your players never to cut outside the ball.

ERROR Moving outside the ball carrier in the team offense

CORRECTION

1. The player without the ball should cut behind the defender to force the defender to turn and look away from the ball carrier.

2. Practice the timing of the cut to maximize offensive opportunities for the ball carrier.

Cutting and Picking Games

CUT AND PICK

Goal

To learn proper cutting and picking when the ball is behind the goal

Description

Play 4 v 4 inside the box with a goalie in the goal (figure 11.34). One attacker and one defender are behind the goal, and the other players are in front of the goal. The three offensive players in front of the goal pick for each other and cut to get open to receive a pass from the attacker behind, who is trying to get open to feed the ball. Award the offense one point for a goal; award the defense one point for a stop. Restart play by throwing the ball to the attacker behind the goal.

To make the game easier

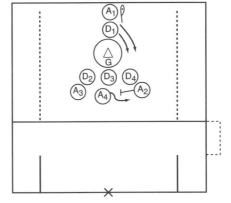

- Play 4 v 3, leaving the attacker behind the goal unguarded.

Figure 11.34   Cut and Pick.

EVEN NUMBERS

Goal

To develop settled offensive and defensive skills and tactics

Description

Create 1-v-1, 2-v-2, 3-v-3, 4-v-4, 5-v-5, or 6-v-6 setups in a half-field situation. All defensive players are out of the restraining box at the goal line extended. The offensive players are positioned 15 yards outside of the top of the penalty box, diagonally opposite the defense.

(continued)

Even Numbers *(continued)*

You are in the center at the top of the box with a supply of balls. Call out a number from one to six, and that number of offensive and defensive players enter the box to attack and defend. Roll the ball to the offense and begin play. Allow the drill to continue until a goal is scored, the defense gains possession, or the ball is cleared outside the penalty box (see figure 11.35a-b).

The offense should balance the field in the same alignment as in uneven numbers:

- ⊙ Two: one at the midfield and one at attack
- ⊙ Three: triangle
- ⊙ Four: box
- ⊙ Five: 1-2-2
- ⊙ Six: 1-3-2, 2-2-2, or 1-4-1

The defense must get in and defend from the inside out. All defenders must be between their man and the goal. They must match up and communicate by calling out, "Ball," and "One" and "Two" slides.

Variation

- ⊙ *Practicing in-bounds riding and clearing.* Set up the drill on the sideline with both the defense and the offense on the same side of the field. The defense must now attempt to clear over midfield when they gain possession. The offense must try to regain possession when they lose the ball.

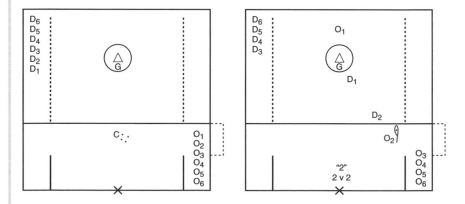

Figure 11.35 Even Numbers. *(a)* Set-up and *(b)* example of 2-v-2 situation.

Clearing

Clearing the ball means advancing the ball from the defensive half of the field to the offensive half. When a team gains possession of the ball in its defensive half of the field, all players become involved in the clear.

The defensive team has a numerical advantage in a clearing situation. The advantage occurs because of the offside rule that requires each team to keep four people in its defensive half of the field and three in its offensive half. With the addition of the goalie, the clearing team has seven players (three defenders, three midfielders, one goalie), and the riding team has six players (three attackers and three midfielders). The clearing game comprises the in-bounds clear and the dead-ball clear.

In-Bounds Clear

The in-bounds clear occurs when the ball is in play. It usually results from the goalie making a save or a defender scooping up a loose ball. The team now possesses the ball, and everyone becomes involved in clearing the ball to their offensive half of the field. In this situation, the defensive team instantly moves from defending to attacking.

When the goalie makes a save, he immediately yells, "Clear," to let his teammates know that their team has possession and a clear is developing. He looks to immediately pass the ball to the defender who was covering the shooter because this defender is in position to quickly break out.

The goalie has four seconds in the crease, which allows him ample time to scan the field for an open teammate (figure 11.36). The

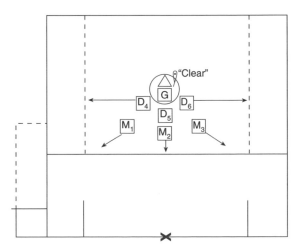

Figure 11.36   In-bounds clear.

midfielders (M_1, M_2, and M_3) break out to the open area between the attack box and the midfield line, looking for an over-the-shoulder pass.

The wing defender (D_4 or D_6) breaks out on the goal line extended toward the sideline, watching the goalie at all times. The goalie can safely pass the ball to the wing defender if all midfielders are covered. The defenders back out with their backs to the sideline.

To protect against a broken clear, the crease defender remains in the hole area until he sees the goalie pass the ball out. When the goalie passes the ball out, the crease defender moves to an open area to receive a pass.

Dead-Ball Clear

A dead-ball clear results when the ball goes out of bounds and an official awards it to the defensive team or when a technical foul awards the ball to the defense. The clearing team spreads the riding team and takes advantage of its seven-on-six advantage.

Dead-ball clears are based on two concepts: to spread the riding team and to create overload situations that place more clearing players than riding players in an area. The three defenders and the goalie position themselves in a line along the goal line extended, while the midfielders spread evenly along the midfield line (figure 11.37). The goalie has the ball and all players (defenders and midfielders) work together to slowly advance the ball to create a two-on-one situation. A midfielder—who has a shorter stick and therefore better stick-handling and ball-control abilities—may switch positions with a corner defender to increase stick handling on the clear. The ball carrier tries to draw a rider to him and then to advance the ball by passing ahead to an open man. Players off the ball move into open spaces to provide the ball carrier with passing possibilities. Communication is very important. The ball carrier often locates open teammates by hearing their "Help" call.

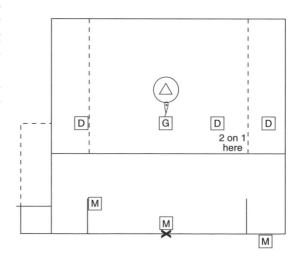

Figure 11.37
Dead-ball clear.

Clearing Game

CLEARING

Goal

To develop stick skills and clearing tactics

Description

Remove the goal from the attack box area and position two teams of four players each and a neutral player in the area (figure 11.38). The neutral player always plays offense, providing a 5-v-4 advantage to the team with the ball. Each team tries to maintain possession by running and passing the ball. The defensive team plays zone defense, with one player covering the ball and the remaining three players splitting the four remaining offensive players. The offensive players spread the defense by moving to open areas and calling, "Help," when they are open to receive a pass.

Variation

Set up two 4-v-4 neutral games.

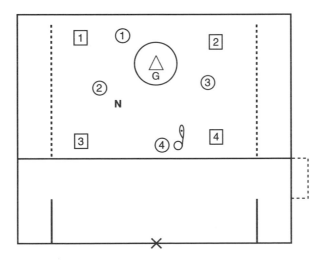

Figure 11.38   Clearing Game.

Extra-Man Offense

Extra-man offensive situations provide the offense with an excellent scoring opportunity. The offensive team has a one-man advantage, with six offensive players against five defenders and a goalie (who only covers the goal).

Here are the general concepts of the extra-man offense:

1. Select six offensive players to work as an extra-man unit. Teach the plays and formations for each position to substitutes.
2. Quickly pass the ball and cut rather than dodge against the man-down zone defense.
3. Combine simple plays that change the offensive formation with quick passing for good shooting opportunities.
4. Always force a defender to commit to the ball carrier. Each player receives the pass, squares up to the goal, draws a defender to him, and then makes the next pass. Attempt to create a two-on-one advantage.
5. Always have one player in position to back up shots and one player who can get back on defense if the team loses possession.
6. Reverse the direction of the passes often.
7. Be patient. Pass the ball frequently to create a good shot against an organized man-down defense.
8. Have off-ball players cut to receive a pass when the defense focuses only on the ball carrier.

Wide 2-2-2 Formation

Teach beginning players the 2-2-2 extra-man offensive formation. With all six offensive players positioned on the perimeter, the extra-man offense creates many passing, cutting, and shooting opportunities (figure 11.39). This is basic "draw-and-dump" lacrosse, focusing on the offensive players passing the ball quickly, drawing a defender to them, and moving the ball to the next open man. The offense passes the ball around the perimeter until the defense fails to make a slide, freeing the shooter for an uncontested shot. As the offense becomes skilled in draw-and-dump lacrosse and creating the 2 v 1, they can progress to looking for the skip pass (skipping the adjacent man and passing to the man two passes away from the ball). As the defense extends out on their slides, the skip pass becomes a good option.

The offense passes the ball quickly around the perimeter to create a two-on-one advantage (figure 11.40). Cutting opportunities for off-ball

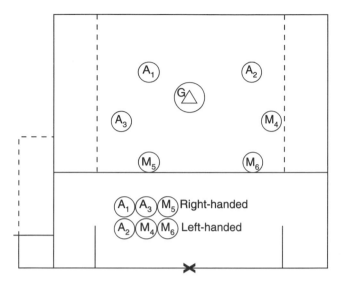

Figure 11.39 Wide2-2-2 extra man.

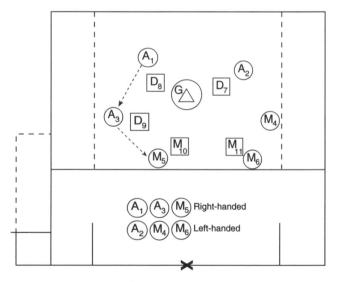

Figure 11.40 Two-on-one advantage.

players arise as teammates pass the ball and defenders focus on only the ball. The off-ball offensive players (A_2, M_4, and M_6) watch the ball and the defenders. When a defender turns his back to focus on only the ball, an off-ball offensive player cuts to the ball carrier for a feed. He circles back to the perimeter if he doesn't receive the pass.

3-3 Formation

Intermediate players use a 3-3 formation, in which all players are in front of the goal in shooting position. The 3-3 is a good offensive formation for teams that have strong outside shooters. The basic concept in the 3-3 is for the offense to quickly pass the ball around the perimeter to the next open man, always trying to draw a defender. The inside crease player (A_2) continuously moves as the ball is passed around the perimeter to receive a pass for an inside shot (figure 11.41). Advanced players may skip pass.

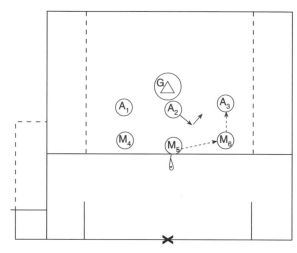

Figure 11.41   3-3 extra man.

1-3-2 and 1-4-1 Formations

Advanced players use the 1-3-2 and 1-4-1 formations. A cutting play begins in a 1-3-2 formation, and players cut into a 1-4-1. This combination affords opportunities for outside shooting and positions a feeder and two inside crease players for inside shooting opportunities.

At a predetermined signal (verbal, ball location, or number of passes), the two top midfielders cut toward the crease, and the crease man moves up to the point position. As the attacker at

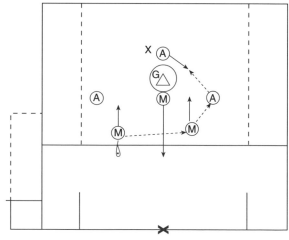

Figure 11.42   1-3-2 cut to 1-4-1.

X receives the ball, he looks for the cutting midfielders (figure 11.42). The players then shift into a 1-4-1 formation.

The inside players in the 1-4-1 work together, with enough space between each other so that one defender cannot cover both players. Players continue to pass the ball around the perimeter as they try to draw a defender, and then pass to the open man. All perimeter players continuously look to the crease for the inside players. The best feeding position is at X. When the ball is behind the cage, the defense must divert its attention from the ball behind the cage to the players in front.

Extra Man Offense Game

MONEY, OR MONEY IN THE BANK

Goal

To develop extra man offense and man-down defense skills and tactics

Description

Play 4 v 3 in the penalty box with a goalie in the goal (figure 11.43). The offense passes the ball around the perimeter, looking to create a shooting opportunity. The defense must play a zone and rotate to the ball carrier (this rotation is the same as the 4-v-3 fast-break defense). The offense is awarded one point for each goal scored, and the defense scores one point each time they gain possession.

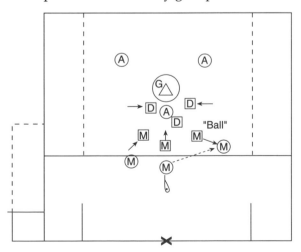

Figure 11.43   Money in the Bank.

To make the game easier

- Play 3 v 2.
- Play 4 v 2.

To make the game harder

- Have offense shoot only with their nondominant hand.
- If a shot has not been allowed within five passes, the defense is awarded a point.

Team Defense

Players need to know defensive team tactics for playing transition defense, settled defense (6 v 6), man-down defense, and riding defense.

Defending in Transition

Transitional situations occur often in a game, and the defense needs a coordinated plan to protect the crease area until the number of defensive players at the crease matches the number of offensive players.

Defending Against the Fast Break

When the defense recognizes that a four-on-three fast-break situation exists, they angle sprint to their defensive goal area and form a tight triangle. The top point of the triangle is five yards inside of the attack box.

As the ball approaches one defender (figure 11.44), the point man (D_1) slides across to stop the ball. The point man extends out just far enough to force an initial pass. The point man (D_1) must not extend too far from the goal because he must be able to slide back to help defend the player who received the pass.

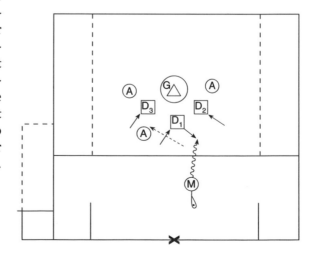

Figure 11.44
Fast Break defense.

The remaining defenders (D_2 and D_3) slide as subsequent passes are made. By positioning themselves in a tight triangle and reacting quickly to the offense's passes, three defenders can stop the fast break until more defenders arrive.

Fast-Break Game

STOP THE BREAK!

Goal

For the defense to learn to properly defend against the fast break

Description

Play 4-v-3, in the box, with a goalie in the goal (figure 11.45). Start play by rolling the ball to one of the offensive players between the restraining line and midline. The offense uses the 4-v-3 advantage to try to score, while the defense tries to stop the ball using defensive tactics. Award two points to the defense for a stop and one point to the offense for a goal.

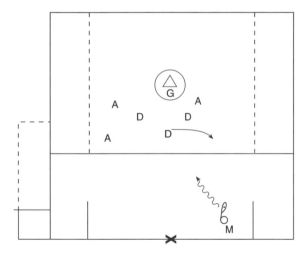

Figure 11.45
Stop the Break.

Midfielders in Defensive Transition

Each midfielder sprints back to his defensive goal area when his team loses the ball. Instruct each player to first get into the hole and then to match up man-to-man with his offensive opponent. The best way to stop offensive transition is for all six defenders to be in the defensive hole area before the ball arrives.

Transition Game

HIGHWAY 66

Goal

To develop transitional skills and concepts and overall stick work

Description

Place the goals at the top of each attack box to shorten the field (figure 11.46). Two teams, each consisting of three attackers, two defenders, and a goalie, stand around their respective goals. Each team is short one defender, which results in a continuous transitional opportunity for the offense. Two midfielders for each team stand across the midfield line. Use offside rules (three players must stay in the defensive half of the field). Each goalie has an ample supply of extra balls in the cage, and when a goal or missed shot occurs the goalie quickly scoops up a ball out of the cage and initiates the clear. Remember to help players recognize their fast- and slow-break opportunities.

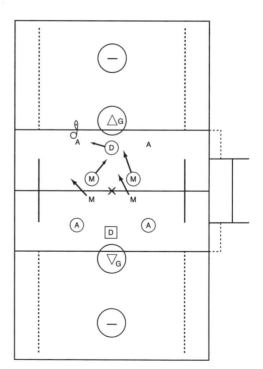

Figure 11.46
Highway 66.

Six-on-Six Defense

When all six defenders (three defense and three midfield) are in the defensive box area and are matched up man-to-man on the six offensive players (three attackers and three midfielders), the defense can coordinate their efforts.

Each off-ball defensive player moves into the hole area and uses the "head on a swivel" technique to constantly look back and forth from the man he is covering to the ball carrier. When the ball carrier gives up the ball, his defender now becomes an off-ball defender and must sink back into the hole area because he does not have to cover his man as tightly when the ball is elsewhere. Then a teammate quickly moves out to the new ball carrier and yells, "Ball." The piston motion of one player moving out to play the ball and one pinching in helps to keep the defense from becoming overextended (figure 11.47).

When the ball is in front of the goal and offensive players are behind the goal without the ball, the off-ball defenders stay above the goal line extended. No defensive player should go behind the goal to guard a man without the ball because this prevents him from being in the hole area to provide backup. Instead, he remains just above the goal line extended until a teammate passes the ball to an attacker behind the goal or until he must slide to cover another player.

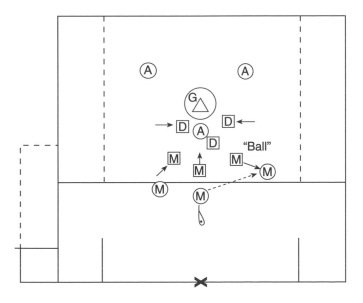

Figure 11.47   6-v-6 defense.

Defensive Team Concepts in the Six-on-Six Game

For effective team defense, combine individual skills on and off the ball with these team defensive concepts:

1. *Matching up*. Every offensive man must be covered! Each defender should call out loudly the number of the player he is guarding.

2. *Pressuring the ball*. The defender covering the ball puts pressure on the ball carrier by mirroring his movement with good footwork and by poke checking to disrupt his concentration.

3. *Communicating and providing backup*. Team defense is a collective effort of six defenders and the goalie. The defender covering the ball must loudly call, "Ball," signaling that he is covering the ball carrier. His teammates off the ball must communicate "One" and "Two" slides. If the defender covering the ball carrier is dodged, a teammate must slide to stop the immediate threat to the goal. This is the one slide. The sliding defender leaves his man to stop the ball carrier and prevent a shot. As he leaves his man, a second slide (two) moves to cover for him. The man who was initially dodged must "recover back" to the crease area and find the man left open by the second slide. The coordinated effort of first slide, second slide, and recovery back is the core of team defense. The goalie is quarterbacking the defense and is calling out the location of the ball, sliding, and providing feedback to the ball defender (see chapter 13 on goalkeeping).

4. *Pinching the crease*. When in an off-ball position, five players pinch to the hole area, and one player plays the ball carrier on the perimeter. Off-ball players help protect the most dangerous area, which is the hole.

Defensive Team Tactics

A defense player slides to a dodger if the dodger has clearly beaten a teammate and is within shooting range of the goal. Defensive play requires quick reactions, so all players pinch in toward the crease area with their heads on a swivel.

Slide From the Crease When the Ball Is Up Top

As shown in figure 11.48, when an offensive player (M_1) beats a midfield defender (M_7), a teammate (D_{11})—who is playing between a crease offensive player and the ball) slides to stop the dodger. An adjacent diagonal defender (D_{12}) slides in to cover the crease. The second slide prevents the easy pass into the crease area. The defender who started on the ball and was beaten must recover back to the crease and find the

Figure 11.48
Slide crease.

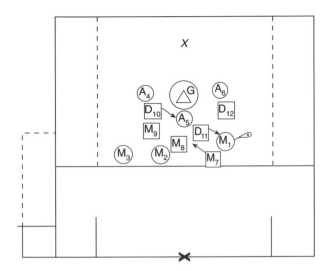

man left open by the second slide. Each time a player is dodged and the defense slides, there will be a first slide to stop the dodger, a second slide or fill to cover for the first slide, and the initial ball defender who was dodged recovers back to find the man left open by the second slider.

Slide Across and Down When the Ball Is Behind

When the ball carrier (A_1) beats a defender (D_7) from behind the cage, another defender (D_9) slides across the goal mouth to stop the dodger, and an adjacent player (M_{12}) slides down to cover. The second slide usually comes from a midfielder (figure 11.49). The initial ball defender who was beaten on the dodge must slide back to find the man left open by the second slide.

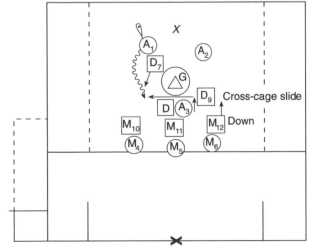

Figure 11.49
Slide across.

Defensive Game

BINGO

Goal

To teach team defensive concepts

Description

Five offensive players in the attack box arrange themselves in a 2-1-2 formation, with five defensive players matching up on them (figure 11.50). The offensive team passes the ball around the perimeter while you check each player's on-ball and off-ball positioning. Instruct the offensive players not to pass until you have corrected the position of all the defensive players.

Be sure the defensive players use the piston concept as the offensive team passes the ball: One defensive player moves out to the ball and one moves back in. Make sure that the defensive player moves out to the ball in a controlled manner, otherwise the ball carrier will just run past the charging defender and have an open shot. Make sure players understand that if a defender runs out, there is no way he can change directions if the ball carrier decides to dodge. Emphasize the pinch concept: Four defenders play in the defensive hole and one plays the ball outside the hole.

Variation

When the ball is in the air on an offensive pass, call, "Dodge." To create a slide situation, the defensive player allows himself to be beaten as the ball arrives. Defenders must then make correct slides.

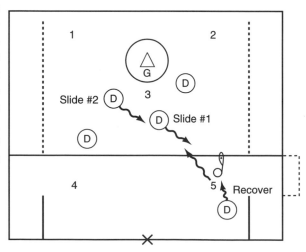

Figure 11.50
Bingo.

Communication on Defense

Communication by the defense is critical to success. As each defender's man receives a pass, the defender moves out and yells, "I've got ball." The defender responsible for the initial backup calls, "I've got your help," or "I'm one." The second slide defender calls, "I'm two," indicating he has the second slide.

Playing Picks and Cutters

Off-ball defenders call, "Pick," to give a teammate time to react to an offensive pick and to slide over the top or behind the pick. Again, communication is important. The man covering the pick man calls a "switch" only if the man playing the cutter is picked off. For example, in figure 11.51, attacker A_9 sets a pick on defender M_4. The off-ball defender M_5 calls, "Pick," to alert defender M_4, while defender D_3 calls, "Switch," to cover the midfielder M_{10} as he cuts through. Defender M_4 is now responsible for covering attacker A_9.

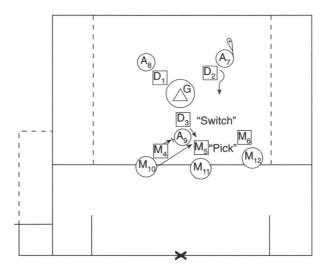

Figure 11.51   Switch.

Covering a Crease Player

When an offensive player (A_3) positions himself in the hole area directly in front of the goal, the defender (D_9) employs one of several different techniques to defend this immediate scoring threat (figure 11.52).

Figure 11.52
Face-to-face position.

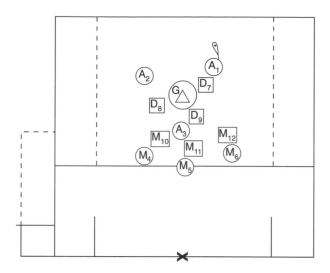

When the ball is behind the goal, the crease defender plays face-to-face with his offensive opponent. He maintains a position between the ball and the offensive player. He holds his stick up straight, ready to check. Holding the stick up straight also enables his teammates to move freely through the crease area without being encumbered by their own crease defender's stick. He does not look for the ball when he's in this position because any momentary inattention can result in a goal.

When the ball is in the midfield area (figure 11.53), the crease defender (D_8) again positions himself between the ball and his man. He now keeps his head on a swivel, as he acts as the primary backup de-

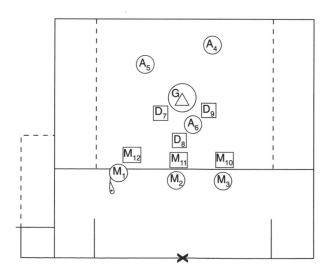

Figure 11.53
Topside position.

fender if the ball carrier (M$_1$) dodges past his teammate (M$_{12}$) in the midfield. As he quickly looks away from his man to locate the ball, he uses the head of his stick to maintain slight contact with the offensive player. This "topside" position places the defender in good position to slide to a midfield dodger.

Error Detection and Correction for Team Defense

When sliding on a dodger who has penetrated the defense, the backup (sliding) defender breaks down to a position in which his stick is down and he is partially sitting. If he does not meet the dodger in a body-on-body and stick-on-stick position, he risks being dodged.

ERROR   Failing to establish a good defensive position when sliding

CORRECTION

1. Never lunge at the dodger.

2. Slide in a controlled manner to ensure sound defensive positioning.

Man-Down Defense

The man-down defensive unit plays a zone defense to compensate for the extra-player advantage of the offense:

1. Select five defensive players (generally three defenders and two midfielders) to work together as a man-down unit. Prepare two substitutes, one long stick and one midfield, to play if a member of the man-down unit must serve the penalty.

2. The defense works together to protect first against the inside shot and then against the outside shot.

3. Off-ball players sag to the crease to help on the inside.

4. Players who move out to play the ball yell, "Ball." Teach players not to extend too far out so that they can quickly move back inside when the offensive player passes the ball. The concept of moving out and quickly back is critical in preventing the defense from becoming overextended and creating passing lanes through the zone.

5. Emphasize the pinch concept. As one player moves out to play the ball, the four remaining players pinch into the crease area.

6. Hustle! The defense has one less player.

The man-down defense faces the challenge of covering six offensive players with five defenders and a goalie. They must use a zone defense, and each defender must work "double time" to compensate for being a man short. A 2-1-2 zone, similar to a basketball zone defense, is a basic approach to man-down defense (figure 11.54).

For example, in figure 11.55, midfielder M_4 covers attacker M_5, who passes to attacker A_3, which leaves an attacker (A_1) open. Defender D_3 must slide across the crease to cover attacker A_1.

Each perimeter player tries to play two offensive players. When none can, the defense slides (rotates) toward the open player in a maneuver similar to the one used in six-on-six defense when a player is beaten.

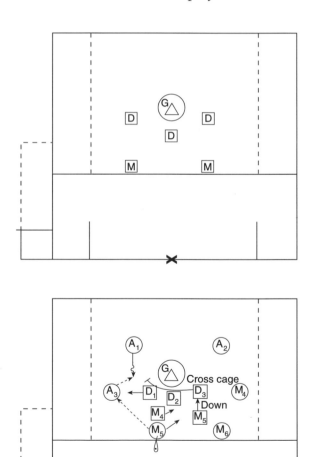

Figure 11.54
2-1-2 zone.

Figure 11.55
Man-down defense.

Man-Down Game

DOUBLE TIME

Goal

To develop man-down skills and tactics

Description

Play 5 v 4 with the goalie in the penalty box area (figure 11.56a-b). The offense attempts to pass the ball to create a shooting opportunity while the defense works "double time" to prevent a shot. The offense aligns in a 2-1-2 and the defense in a box. The defense stays compact in a tight box attempting to force a shot from the outside. All ball players pinch to the crease man trying to deny a pass to the inside. All defenders should apply a basic man-down tenet of "sticks in and bodies out." Defenders should position their sticks to the inside (pointing to the crease), cutting down passing lanes to the crease area. The defense should be ready to rotate if the offense creates a 2-v-1 situation.

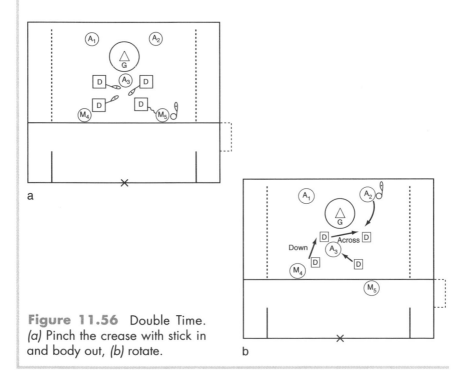

Figure 11.56 Double Time. *(a)* Pinch the crease with stick in and body out, *(b)* rotate.

Riding

Similar to a press defense in basketball or a fore check in hockey, riding involves the six players who have lost possession of the ball in their offensive half, who must now work together to regain possession.

The riding team has only six players (three attackers and three midfielders), and the clearing team, including the goalie, has seven. Working together, the riders must "hustle" extra hard to compensate for their numerical disadvantage. Much of riding falls on the attackers, but all midfielders, defenders, and the goalie have some riding responsibilities.

In an in-bounds ride situation, the attacker closest to the ball immediately goes to the ball carrier and applies pressure. The remaining five riders begin to drop toward their own goal area to defend the open area behind them. Their first priority is to delay the ball from advancing quickly, avoiding a possible fast-break situation.

The two remaining attackers drop diagonally toward the midfield line and favor the ball side of the field. The attack works together in a triangle zone to regain possession of the ball (figure 11.57). For example, the goalie yells, "Break," and passes the ball to a wing defender (D_1). The crease attacker (A_7) is the closest to the defender (D_1) and rides him. Midfielders (M_4, M_5, and M_6) drop back to get into defensive position. The attacker (A_8) can get into position to create a 2-on-1 situation with A_7, or he can find an opponent to defend.

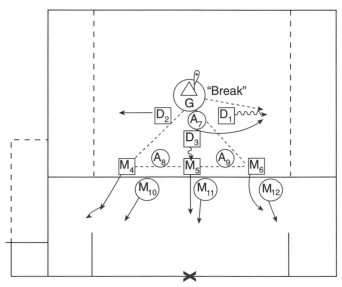

Figure 11.57 Riding.

As the attackers work together to regain possession of the ball, the midfielders immediately make the transition to their defensive end. They do not slide up the field to stop the ball because that may allow the ball carrier to throw the ball over their heads.

Dead-Ball Ride

A 3-3 zone ride, which places three attackers and three midfielders in a zone formation covering the area between their attack box and their defensive box, is one of the most basic and effective rides.

The attackers (A_1, A_2, and A_3) work in a rotating triangle, while the three midfielders (M_4, M_5, and M_6) defend one third of the field in the midfield area (figure 11.58). In the 3-3 zone, the wing midfielder farthest from the ball (M_4) plays the role of a football free safety and, when the ball is advancing up the side of the field opposite him, drops into his defensive zone area to stop any fast breaks. The attacker who is closest (A_3) must play the defender (D_8), who receives a pass from the goalie.

Riding midfielders (M_5 and M_6) do not slide up the field toward the ball carrier unless they can get to a loose ball—or arrive at a pass receiver immediately after the ball does—to dislodge the ball by stick checking or body checking.

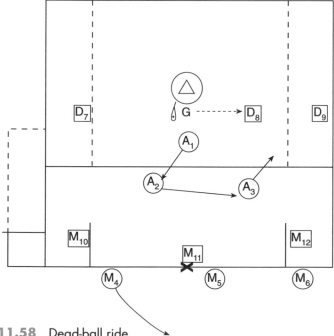

Figure 11.58   Dead-ball ride.

Error Detection and Correction for Riding

It is important for midfielders to get back on defense when they lose the ball on offense.

ERROR   Midfielders and defenders who slide up the field to the ball carrier create excessive two-on-one passing situations (a two-on-one passing situation works to the advantage of the clearing team).

CORRECTION

1. Players should play man-to-man defense until the ball carrier is in a critical scoring area.

2. Defenders need to communicate with each other. For instance, a defensive player should only leave his offensive player if he has help from a teammate.

chapter 12

Boys' Lacrosse Season Plans

Up to now you've been introduced to the basic skills of coaching: what your responsibilities are as a coach, how to communicate well and provide for safety, how to use the games approach to teach and shape skills, and how to coach on game days. But game days make up only a small portion of your season. You and your players will spend much more time in practice than in competition. How well you conduct practices and prepare your players for competition will greatly affect both your and your players' enjoyment and success throughout the season.

In this chapter, we present three levels of season plans: one for Level C, one for Level B, and one for Level A. Use these plans as guidelines for conducting your practices. These plans are not the only way to approach your season, but they do present an appropriate teaching progression.

For safety reasons, be sure the basic skills have been taught, drilled, and practiced under competitive practice situations before introducing a game. Remember to incorporate the games approach as you use these plans, to put your players in a gamelike situation that introduces them to the main tactic or skill that you want them to learn that day. Then guide your players through a short question-and-answer session that leads to the skill practice.

Some coaches may face the added challenge of very limited practice meetings and times. Take what information you can and adapt it to your situation. Each practice, regardless of your daily purpose and practice length, should include

1. a warm-up and stretching;
2. stick work, both stationary and on the move;
3. conditioning;
4. small-game situations (1 v 1, 2 v 2, 3 v 3, with and without goalie);
5. large-game situations (7 v 7 and larger);
6. time for discussion, question and answers, and reinforcement of successes;
7. fun.

Refer to chapter 5 (pages 45-47) for how to run a practice. In chapter 8 you will find descriptions of all the skills and tactics and games you can use to practice them. Throughout the season plans, we refer you to the appropriate pages for those skills and tactics and games.

Remember to keep the introductions, demonstrations, and explanations of the skills and tactics brief. As the players practice, attend to individual players, guiding them with tips or with further demonstration. Good luck and good coaching!

Season Plan—Level C (Bantam Division/Beginner)

Beginning players should learn the basic skills of the game (cradling, throwing, catching, scooping, dodging, and defense.) They should also be introduced to basic team tactics through small group games that allow for practice through play. A balance of drill work and small-sided games will assist coaches in helping their players develop the basic skills and expose them to the excitement of the "fastest game on two feet."

Practice 1

- ⊙ **Purpose:** To learn the basics of cradling, throwing, and catching
- ⊙ **Games:** Partner Passing—Dominant Hand (p. 187), Right-on-Right Passing and Catching (p. 188), Creative Cradling (p. 183)
- ⊙ **Skill development:** Cradling, throwing, and catching

Practice 2

- ⊙ **Purpose:** To learn the basics of scooping and review cradling, catching, and throwing
- ⊙ **Games:** Cradling Game (p. 182), Partner Scooping and Cradling (p. 194), Hot Rock (p. 191)
- ⊙ **Skill development:** Scooping, cradling, throwing, and catching

Practice 3

- ⊙ **Purpose:** To learn the basics of dodging (introduce inside-and-out dodge, roll dodge, and face dodge)
- ⊙ **Games:** Creative Cradling Game (p. 183), Show Time (p. 198), Go For It (p. 199)
- ⊙ **Skill development:** Dodging

Practice 4

- ⊙ **Purpose:** To develop shooting skills
- ⊙ **Games:** Drive From the Center and Shoot (p. 207), Shoot Away (p. 207)
- ⊙ **Skill development:** Shooting skills

Practice 5

- ⊙ **Purpose:** To introduce man-ball, and ground ball situations
- ⊙ **Games:** 1 v 1 Scooping With Outlet (p. 193), 2 v 1 Ground Ball (p. 194)
- ⊙ **Skill development:** Scooping, catching, throwing, 2 v 1 ground ball tactics, body checking

Practice 6

- ⊙ **Purpose:** Introduce stick checks and holds
- ⊙ **Games:** Stick Check (p. 217), Defensive Hold Game (p. 221), Turn It Over (p. 217)
- ⊙ **Skill development:** 1 v 1 defensive skills

Practice 7

- ⊙ **Purpose:** To develop skill and tactical understanding in unsettled situations
- ⊙ **Game:** Scramble (p. 227)
- ⊙ **Skill development:** Transition skills and tactics

Practice 8

- ⊙ **Purpose:** Introduce 4 v 3 fast-break offense and defense
- ⊙ **Games:** Shoot Away (p. 207), Break Away (p. 224), Stop the Break! (p. 243), Money in the Bank (p. 241)
- ⊙ **Skill development:** Draw-and-dump skills

Practice 9

- ⊙ **Purpose:** To develop 1 v 1 offensive and defensive skills
- ⊙ **Games:** Agilities (p. 213), Defensive Hold Game (p. 221), Even Numbers (p. 233), Turn It Over (p. 217)
- ⊙ **Skill development:** 1 v 1 and 3 v 3 team offensive and defensive skills and tactics

Practice 10

- ⊙ **Purpose:** Introduce riding and clearing skills and tactics
- ⊙ **Games:** Hot Rock (p. 191), Clearing (p. 237)
- ⊙ **Skill development:** Clearing and riding skills

Practice 11

- ⊙ **Purpose:** Introduce 6 v 6 settled offense and defense
- ⊙ **Games:** Even Numbers (build up to 6 v 6) (p. 233), Bingo (p. 248)
- ⊙ **Skill development:** Team offensive and defensive tactics

Practice 12

- ⊙ **Purpose:** Introduce man-up and man-down skills and tactics
- ⊙ **Games:** Double Time (p. 253), Scramble (p. 227)
- ⊙ **Skill development:** Stick work, extra-man offense and man-down defense skills and tactics

Season Plan—Level B
(Lightning Division/Intermediate)

As players master basic skills they can apply them in small-group games. The opportunity to use skills in gamelike situations will expedite their mastery of basic skills and tactical development.

Practice 1

- ⊙ **Purpose:** To develop throwing and catching skills using both hands
- ⊙ **Games:** Over the Shoulder (p. 190), Four Corner Passing (p. 188), Hot Rock (p. 191)
- ⊙ **Skill development:** Throwing and catching

Practice 2

- ⊙ **Purpose:** To develop scooping and passing skills
- ⊙ **Games:** Scooping and Passing (p. 194), 1 v 1 Scooping with Outlet (p. 193), 2 v 1 Ground Ball (p. 194)
- ⊙ **Skill development:** Scooping, man-ball tactics, throwing and catching, body checking

Practice 3

- ⊙ **Purpose:** To develop dodging and shooting skills
- ⊙ **Games:** Same-Side Shooting (p. 206), Money In The Bank (p. 241), Line Dodging (p. 197), Go For It (p. 199), Shoot Away (p. 207)
- ⊙ **Skill development:** Catching and shooting, shooting off the dodge

Practice 4

- ⊙ **Purpose:** To develop offensive and defensive transitional skills and tactics
- ⊙ **Game:** Scramble (p. 227)
- ⊙ **Skill development:** Stick work, transitional skills and tactics

Practice 5

- **Purpose:** To develop quick clear skills, and transitional offensive and defensive transitional skills and tactics
- **Games:** Highway 66 (p. 244), Break Away (p. 224), Stop the Break! (p. 243)
- **Skill development:** Stick work, transitional skills and tactics, clearing

Practice 6

- **Purpose:** To develop settled and defensive skills and tactics
- **Games:** Defensive Hold Game (p. 221), Stick Check (p. 217), Bingo (p. 248), Go For It (p. 199)
- **Skill development:** V-cutting, offensive and defensive skills and tactics

Practice 7

- **Purpose:** To develop off-ball offensive and defensive skills and tactics
- **Games:** Cut and Pick (p. 233), Even Numbers (p. 233)
- **Skill development:** Cutting, picking, off-ball defensive skills

Practice 8

- **Purpose:** To develop slow-break skills and tactics
- **Games:** Making a Break (p. 226), Scramble (5 v 4) (p. 227)
- **Skill development:** Stick work, transitional skills and tactics

Practice 9

- **Purpose:** To develop riding and clearing skills and tactics
- **Games:** Hot Rock (p. 191), Clearing (p. 237)
- **Skill development:** Stick work, riding and clearing skills and tactics

Practice 10

- **Purpose:** To develop extra-man offense and man-down defense skills and tactics
- **Games:** Scramble (p. 227), Double Time (p. 253)
- **Skill development:** Stick work, shooting and defensive skills

Season Plan—Level A
(Junior or Senior Division/Advanced)

Players who have mastered basic and intermediate skills and tactics can continue to develop their game by improving their nondominant hand and learning the finer points of team play (such as playing without the ball on offense and defense) and transitional offense and defense skills and tactics. Continual work on fundamentals should not be neglected and can be incorporated into practices in transition games and drills. These drills and games allow players to practice fundamentals in gamelike situations.

Practice 1

- **Purpose:** To develop throwing and catching skills (using both hands)
- **Games:** Right-on-Right and Left-on-Left Passing and Catching (p. 188), Diamond Passing (p. 189)
- **Skill development:** Throwing and catching

Practice 2

- **Purpose:** To develop change-of-direction dodge
- **Games:** Four Corner Passing (p. 188), Diamond Passing (p. 189), Clearing (p. 237)
- **Skill development:** Throwing and catching, change-of-direction dodge

Practice 3

- **Purpose:** To develop transitional skills and tactics
- **Games:** Scramble (p. 227), Break Away (p. 224), Highway 66 (p. 244)
- **Skill development:** Stick work, transitional skills and tactics

Practice 4

- **Purpose:** To develop shooting skills with both hands
- **Games:** Same-Side Shooting (p. 206), Drive From the Center and Shoot (p. 207), Shoot Away (p. 207)
- **Skill development:** Throwing and catching, shooting

Practice 5

- ⊙ **Purpose:** To develop scooping skills and tactics
- ⊙ **Games:** Scooping and Passing (p. 194), 1 v 1 Scooping With Outlet (p. 193), 2 v 1 Ground Ball (p. 194)
- ⊙ **Skill development:** Scooping, man-ball tactics, throwing and catching, body checking

Practice 6

- ⊙ **Purpose:** To develop transitional skills and tactics
- ⊙ **Games:** Scramble (p. 227), Break Away (p. 224), Highway 66 (p. 244)
- ⊙ **Skill development:** Stick work, transitional skills and tactics

Practice 7

- ⊙ **Purpose:** To develop settled offensive and defensive skills and tactics
- ⊙ **Games:** Even Numbers (p. 233), Turn It Over (p. 217), Go for It (p. 199), Bingo (p. 248)
- ⊙ **Skill development:** Stick work, dodging, settled offensive and defensive skills and tactics

Practice 8

- ⊙ **Purpose:** To develop in-bounds clearing and riding skills and tactics
- ⊙ **Games:** Highway 66 (p. 244), Clearing (p. 237)
- ⊙ **Skill development:** Stick work, riding and clearing skills and tactics

Practice 9

- ⊙ **Purpose:** To develop off-ball skills and tactics
- ⊙ **Games:** Playing the Cutter (p. 209), Cut and Pick (p. 233)
- ⊙ **Skill development:** Picking, cutting, feeding, shooting, crease defense play

Practice 10

- ⊙ **Purpose:** To develop extra-man offensive and defensive skills and tactics
- ⊙ **Games:** Scramble (p. 227), Double Time (p. 253), Money In The Bank (p. 241)
- ⊙ **Skill development:** Stick work, shooting, extra-man offense and man-down defense skills and tactics

chapter 13

Lacrosse Goalkeeping

Goalkeeping is the most mentally demanding of all the positions on a lacrosse team. Goalkeepers enjoy the special privileges of playing the ball with their hands, playing on the field, and having a crease that is designed especially for them. Goalkeepers also may use an extra-large stick head (it measures 16 inches across at its widest part) to play the ball.

This position needs extra coaching and specialized warm-up sessions to ensure the players' success. Goalies are the last line of defense and are constantly pressured to make a big play. They must play with confidence to be successful.

What About Goalkeeping?

An aspiring goalkeeper must have the skills of a good athlete first—hand and foot speed, quick reactions, and excellent eye–hand coordination. The player should possess very good stick skills and be strong enough to handle the larger and heavier goalkeeper's stick. Most of all, goalies need to be courageous to move the stick and their body behind each shot. Goalkeepers must also be able to communicate with their teammates throughout the game, while remaining calm, poised, and in control. The ability to concentrate and focus on the ball and the situation on hand is challenging for any young athlete; however, this is also a mental trait to look for and to develop in young goalkeepers.

The Goalkeeper's Team Role

Goalkeepers should be leaders on their teams; they are asked to be the "quarterback" of the defense. As goalies develop within a defensive unit, they have an increasing responsibility to communicate to their teammates. The goalkeeper's verbal commands are more extensive in the boys' game, but all goalkeepers must make specific decisions and communicate them to their team. Because goalkeepers are considered the last line of defense, they are also often the players that initiate the attack. Their ability to clear the ball accurately and quickly is key to developing an offensive fast break.

Girls' and Boys' Goalkeepers

The girls' and boys' games of lacrosse differ to some degree, yet they are similar in many ways. The methods and movements of a boys' and girls' goalkeeper to save a shot are very similar. The shots received are different because of the pocket size of the shooters' sticks. The release of the shot comes from a deeper pocket in a boys' stick. The skills necessary to be a successful goalkeeper, particularly the method for stopping a shot, are the same in both games. There are, however, a few minor rule differences that govern what a goalie may do in the crease with the ball in his or her stick.

Goalkeeper Equipment

A goalkeeper should be properly fitted with protective equipment to prevent serious injury. Major lacrosse manufacturers make goalkeeper equipment in youth sizes. All goalkeepers must wear a mouthguard, as well as a helmet with a face mask properly attached. Fit all helmets for the size of the player's head and make sure they have a chin strap and a separate throat protector. The rules require a chest pad or a protective upper-body piece. Groin protection for both boys and girls is essential. Recommend that your goalkeepers wear protective equipment for their hands (goalie gloves with reinforced thumb padding) shins, elbows, and thigh areas as well. A soft mesh pocket is recommended for beginners, along with a shorter handle or shaft.

Where to Start?

First of all, you must spend extra time working with goalkeepers, especially in the beginning. Develop a rapport by encouraging and building the confidence of new goalies. Do not test new goalkeepers with hard shots until they have learned the basic movements. Instruct goalkeepers in the fit, use, and care of their equipment, especially working to ensure that the stick pocket is broken in and adjusted to throw properly. Begin by teaching the ready position, then the body and stick movement behind a shot. Consider teaching goalkeeping skills by having the player follow or shadow you as you go through the basic movements, starting with the ready position, stick movement, and body movement through various positions.

Goalkeeper Skills

Young goalkeepers need a high level of inspiration and positive influences. Developing the fundamental goalkeeping skills gives young goalies a solid base. In your instruction, emphasize the development of both the mental and physical skills of goalkeeping.

Ready Position

The ready position should be the home base for every goalie just before he or she makes a save. A good ready position in the goal is a lot like the ready position of the middle linebacker in football. The keeper stands with hips and shoulders square to the ball carrier, hands always away from the body, and a strong focus on the ball. No matter how much movement the goalkeeper may be required to make during play, you should emphasize the need to be ready or set to receive a shot.

Goalies in the ready position stand with their feet shoulder-width apart, weight on the balls of their feet, and toes pointed toward the shooter (figure 13.1). They should remain balanced at all times, while

Figure 13.1 Goalie ready position.

leaning slightly forward with their knees and hips flexed. The head stays level, with the eyes focused on the ball. The arms extend partially, holding the stick away from and diagonally across the body, with the dominant hand positioned at the uppermost part of the shaft. The grip rotates slightly to the right, or counterclockwise, so that the goalie can move the stick to the opposite shoulder without changing the grip. A young goalie must not squeeze the shaft; the tighter the grip, the slower the reaction speed. Stress the idea of "soft" hands.

Teach goalies these skills, so they will execute the ready position correctly:

1. Grasp the stick at the base of the head with the top hand and a firm, yet relaxed, grip.
2. Keep the arms extended away from the body and on a slight diagonal.
3. Place the top hand at shoulder level, the bottom hand between chest and waist level.
4. Flex the knees and hips, and be ready to move.

The Save

The key to making a save on a shot is to track, or see, the ball all the way into the goalkeeper's stick head. We will present several visual ball drills later in the Teaching section (page 277). Incorporate them into your daily practice to improve eye-tracking skills. After your goalies can see the ball in flight, teach them how to move their sticks and bodies into a position behind the ball.

Feet

Be sure you teach goalkeepers to move toward the ball as it is released by stepping to one side on a 45-degree angle toward the ball (figure 13.2). This step is toward the side of the goalie that the ball is heading. For example, if the ball is coming to the right side of the goalie, then the goalie steps with the right foot. The toe of the lead foot points to the shooter. Discourage the goalie from pointing the toe toward the side-line and opening up the hips. The weight should transfer to the lead foot as the trail foot moves next to the lead. Goalkeepers always should strive to bring the trail foot back parallel to the lead foot to enable the hips to remain square to the shooter.

Teach goalies these footwork skills for executing a save:

1. Step forward on a 45-degree angle toward the ball.
2. Transfer the weight to the lead foot from a balanced position.
3. Keep the toe pointing at the shooter.
4. Bring the feet back side by side in a parallel stance after the save.

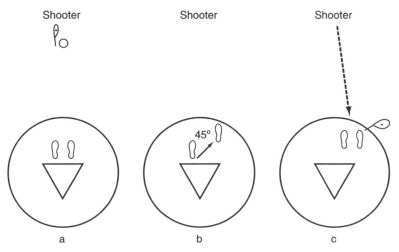

Figure 13.2 Goalie feet position. *(a)* Set position, *(b)* first step with right foot, *(c)* second step with left foot pointed at shooter.

Body

Because the body provides a backup to the stick in making a save, goalies should try to position as much body area behind the shot as possible. A forward step at a 45-degree angle to the goal line initiates this body movement. The shoulders and hips move together behind the shot and remain square to the shooter. If a shot hits the ground and bounces upward, goalies must keep their upper body leaning forward slightly to keep the rebound in front of them (by bending at the knees more than at the waist).

To position the body correctly during a save, goalies should follow these instructions:

1. Align the shoulders with the hips to remain square to the shot, and move the body over the lead foot.
2. Bend at the knees instead of the waist and lower the center of gravity to save a low shot (figure 13.3).

Stick

If goalkeepers hold the stick in the correct position when they're ready to receive a shot, then the only movements necessary are to move the stick behind the shot and to give with the shot. Basically, the arms move the stick to the correct position behind the shot, and the top hand, wrist, and arm give with the shot to keep the ball in the stick pocket. Often, beginners are tempted to reach or to push the stick head at the ball, which creates a hitting motion. Remind players to give with the ball as it reaches the mesh pocket. Emphasize that a good goalie is simply trying to block the ball.

The stick moves within a plane that is parallel to the shoulders and hips but that is 8 to 14 inches away from the body. (The distance from the body depends on the arm length of the goalie.) In any movement of the stick, the hands do not move toward or away from the body before the shot (figure 13.3). The top hand guides the stick head to meet the ball in front of the body as the body moves forward with a step. The stick head travels a straight line from the set position to the save position, and it doesn't rotate around the body.

Goalies execute these steps with the stick during the save:

1. Keep both hands in front of the body to move the stick head directly behind the shot.
2. Give with the arms, wrists, and hands to keep the ball in the stick's pocket.

Figure 13.3   Goalie body and stick position.

Ground Shots

Shots that hit the ground in front of the goalkeeper are often the most difficult to receive. As you teach the positioning for all shots, emphasize how to play a ground shot. If a shot hits the ground and bounces upward, the goalie needs to keep his or her upper body leaning slightly forward from the waist to keep any rebound in front of him or her. Teach goalies to lower their center of gravity or to semi-squat, rather than just bending at the waist, as the bounce shot approaches. Squatting allows them to see the ball and to react to any crazy bounce. It also allows goaltenders to react to rebounds.

The stick moves to an inverted position of the ready position when the shot is released (that is, the left hand over and the right hand below for right-handed goalkeepers). Once the stick is inverted, it angles away from the body so that the left hand is extended farther out from the body than the right. Encourage the goalie to "punch" with the left hand to trap the ball or deflect the ball down in front of the stick (figure 13.4). If the stick is not properly angled this way, a ball may be deflected up the shaft or over the goalie's shoulder.

Figure 13.4 Goalie stick in the ground position.

Only after goalies understand and have practiced these foot, body, and stick movements without a ball coming toward them should you begin to throw a ball to represent a shot. Throw a lot of balls to a specific area to develop a pattern of correct movement with a young goalie (see the "Spot Shooting" section, on page 277).

Positioning Within the Crease

After goalies have the proper technique to save a shot from a stationary shooter, they must begin to understand the importance of angles relative to their positioning in front of the goal. It is important to teach goalies to align their body position off of the stick of the shooter, not off of the shooter's body. When a ball carrier changes hands from left to right as he or she looks to shoot, the goalkeeper makes a small, but very necessary, adjustment to his or her positioning to reduce the player's angle for a shot. Remind all goalkeepers to step up on a shot to reduce the available scoring area.

As a ball carrier moves across the goal mouth, the goalkeeper moves to maintain the angle in the middle of the shooting space. Visually check after each shot to see that the goalkeeper has covered the shot with equal space to either side. Although the goalie takes smaller steps than a field player circling the cage, the steps must be quick, balanced, and precise to maintain good body positioning. These small lateral steps allow the goalie to be ready to step toward the shot at any time.

One common method of teaching young players how to understand movement in the crease is called the *arc method* (figure 13.5). In the arc method, goalies create an imaginary arc that goes from one goalpost to the other and follows the same path as the crease. They try to keep their heels on the arc as the ball moves around the goal. The top of the arc should be 18 to 25 inches from the goal line. You can help goalies learn their positioning by marking the arc with any safe material such as chalk, powder, or laundry soap. Also helpful for young goalkeepers is to make additional marks on the crease at center (90 degrees) and both 45-degree angles to the goal line.

When a player passes the ball to a teammate in front of the goal, the goalkeeper moves while the ball is in the air and tries to be set in the new alignment when the opposing player catches the ball. Remind goalkeepers to always "see the ball in the air," and with practice they will learn to position themselves in the correct angle as they move.

The most difficult situation for a goalkeeper to defend is a pass from behind the goal cage to a player in front. Instruct the keeper to drop-step the foot that's on the same side as the shoulder the ball is moving

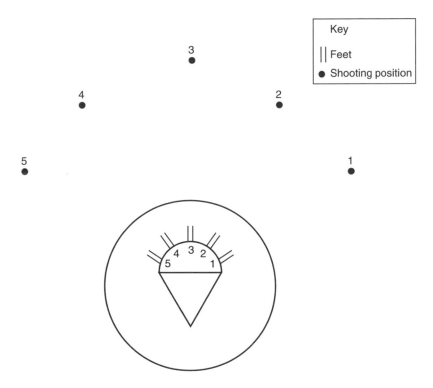

Figure 13.5 Arc method of movement for goalie.

past. The drop step allows the hips to rotate around and the goalie to step up to the new position (figure 13.6, a-c). When the ball is directly behind the goal, the keeper moves to the middle of the arc and is ready to move to either goalpost, depending on the next movement of the ball. The goalie should be alert to intercept a pass, with the stick near the top of the goal cage. The goalkeeper can increase his or her reach by pushing the butt of the stick, held with the bottom hand, up through the top hand. Warn young goalkeepers against being tempted to over-commit themselves to intercept a pass; they'll be left way out of position for defending the shot if the interception is unsuccessful.

Play Outside the Crease

On some occasions, the goalkeeper must come out of the crease to play the ball or an opponent. If she or he makes a mistake in her or his decision, the opponents usually score on an open net. However, nothing is more enjoyable and exciting for a goalkeeper and the team than the goalkeeper intercepting a pass on the field and starting a fast break.

A goalkeeper proficient in ground ball pickups is an asset to the team because any loose ball that she or he can get to and play first results in a possession. On a fast break against a goalkeeper, the opposing team is taught to slide and pressure the ball, which results in an extra, unmarked opponent close to the goal. An experienced goalie seizes the opportunity to intercept the last pass to the free player. Often the goalkeeper plays a shooter who is very close to the crease by stepping forward and blocking the ball as it comes out of the shooter's stick. With further experience, a goalie may choose to come out of the crease and check the ball carrier in a surprise tactic. A common mistake that a young goalie makes, however, is to be too quick to leave the goal. Constantly remind your goalie to be a goalie first and a field player second.

Clearing the Ball

A goalkeeper should be able to handle the stick in such a way as to dodge opponents and throw a clearing pass while on the move. Instruct the young goalie how to throw with the extra-large stick because the technique is different from throwing with a regulation field stick and the goalie needs more time and space to prepare the stick for the throw. Instruct the players to take the head of the stick back behind and above the throwing arm's shoulder. From here, the stick head travels up and then out to the target. Often young goalies have more success with longer passes if they slide the top and bottom hands down the shaft about 6 to 12 inches.

Figure 13.6 Crease challenge. *(a)* Stick is up to intercept, *(b)* goalie moves to the post as player comes around crease, *(c)* goalie drop steps to position for stopping a shot from player receiving pass in the front of the goal.

Note: Though legal in boys' lacrosse, in girls' lacrosse neither the defender nor her stick are allowed to enter the crease unless she is serving as deputy goalie.

The boys' and girls' games differ significantly in the goalkeeper's privileges and time of possession. In the following paragraphs, we summarize the rules and how they affect the goalkeeper's role in clearing the defensive end of the field.

Clearing Strategies in Girls' Lacrosse

A goalkeeper in the girls' game may use her hands while playing a ball in her crease. After the ball enters the crease, she has 10 seconds to remain in this area and look for a pass to a teammate. By the end of the 10-second count, she must have passed the ball or moved outside of the crease with the ball in her stick. Once she is out of the crease, the goalkeeper becomes a field player and may be checked by her opponent. She may roll the ball back into the crease to accrue another 10 seconds to decide what to do with the ball, but only after the ball has been played, as when the ball is touched by another player or an opponent checks the goalie's stick.

Your goalkeeper's throwing ability determines what options are available for your team. Young goalies may not have enough upper-body strength or accuracy to throw the ball very far. Therefore, coach your defensive unit on making short passes and controlling the ball up the field. Discourage a goalkeeper from clearing toward the center of the field. If a goalkeeper can pass accurately over 30 yards or more, the team has the option to go for a longer clear directly to the attack.

Clearing Strategies in Boys' Lacrosse

After the goalie gains control of the ball or makes a save, he has four seconds before he needs to vacate the crease. Remind young goalies that four seconds is a long time. Teach them not to rush the pass or to run the ball out of the crease into traffic.

Teach your goalies this four-point checklist for clearing:

1. Always look to where the shot came from. The defensive players should have a step on the offense, so try to push the transition.
2. Look high and away first; if the goalie determines that the first look is not there, look to the other midfielders, who are breaking upfield.
3. Look to the wing defenders. By now, the count should be 2 1/2 seconds. Find an open teammate whom the goalie feels confident he can get a pass to.
4. Look for a safe alley to leave the crease. If everyone is covered, then the goalie is the open player. Exiting at the back of the crease allows the goalie to use the crease as protection from opponents and provides some time to decide on a pass.

Here are some key coaching points:

- Goalies are protected while in the crease and are allowed an unimpeded outlet pass. They should not be intimidated by opponents standing near the crease.
- The pass to any teammate in the middle of the field is a risky pass; encourage a pass to one side of the field or the other.
- Count out loud to help the goalie learn to keep possession for at least 3 1/2 seconds. Young goalies usually force the clear in 2 1/2 seconds. Four seconds is really cutting it close.
- To prevent goalkeepers from scoring on themselves by losing the ball out of their sticks while making a pass, have the goalie move outside the goal mouth area to their top-hand side of the crease to make a pass.

Goalkeeper Teaching Progression

The goalkeeping position combines a range of challenging skills for a young player. When teaching them, start with and allow your goalies to master the most fundamental and easy skills first. For beginners, use tennis balls instead of heavier lacrosse balls to allow the goalie a chance to learn the body and stick movements without fear of discomfort or injury. This allows the goalies' confidence to build and provides a solid base from which to progress.

Spot Shooting

Teach the goalkeeper the proper body and stick positioning for each of the following areas. Concentrate on correcting the technique in one area before you move on to the next (figure 13.7). Use a high repetition of tosses or shots to imprint correct movement for each area of the goal. Start with soft tosses to the dominant, top-hand high side. Teach the goalie to block, rather than catch, from this point on.

1. High right
2. High left
3. Middle right
4. Middle left
5. Low right
6. Low left
7. Bounce shots
8. Between the feet

Figure 13.7 Spot shooting to high right.

Use this progression to help warm up the goalkeeper and to practice keeping an eye on the ball. Low shots are the toughest to get to, so they should come later in the warm-up. Shoot 10 to 15 shots at each spot before moving to the next. Make up games toward the end of the warm-up. Challenge your goalie to save 70 percent of your shots.

Make sure that goalies, especially younger ones, are in the ready position before each shot. Teach this trick to help goalies with proper body positioning behind a shot: Make an imaginary line from the belly button to the nose, and try to split the ball in half with that line each time a shot is taken. If the goalie turns his or her hips and does not keep his or her shoulders square, it will be impossible to split the ball in half. If the ball is shot to the goalie's left, his or her whole body must stay square and move left to split the ball.

Angles Around the Cage

After going though spot shooting, instruct your goalkeepers about the importance of maintaining the correct angle to best defend and save a shot. To demonstrate how the body positions to cover the shooters angle, tie a rope to each goalpost that reaches out about 8 to 10 yards from the cage. As you walk around an arc with the rope pulled tightly around a stick handle, your goalkeepers can visualize the cone-shaped area they must cover, and they can see how one step to the left or right will cover the angle of a shot to that post. When the goalkeepers see the scoring space to either side, they transfer this visual cue into a feeling of being in the center of a shot on goal.

When the goalies understand the concept of positioning themselves in the center of the shooter's angle, you should begin to shoot at them. When shooting at an angle, stay stationary during the shot but move to a different spot around the cage after each shot. Before each shot, give feedback on the keepers' positioning ("Right side open," "Middle good," "Left side open"). Only after your keepers have learned to align correctly with a stationary shooter should they progress to a moving shooter.

Movement Before the Shot

The next step in the teaching progression is for the goalkeeper to move around the cage with the player before taking the shot. The simplest movement is straight across the goal or parallel to the goal line. Instruct goalkeepers to move in small, quick steps around the arc, keeping their shoulders and hips square to the shooter. Also remind the keepers to stay balanced on the toes of both feet, so they can be set and ready to step with either foot to make a save. Teach the goalkeepers to have patience and continue concentrating on the ball in the shooter's stick. This is especially important when the shooter is running in at the goal cage.

Shot From a Pass

The next skill to teach young goalkeepers is how to move and position when an attacker passes to a teammate, who then shoots at goal. In this situation, two players or coaches position themselves in front of the cage and pass a ball between them. On each catch, the player looks to shoot, checking the angle and set position of the keeper. Only after goalkeepers feel comfortable that they know where they are in the crease after each pass should a shot follow a catch. Eventually, change the shooters' location in front of the goal between each pass or after every shot.

Defending a Pass From Behind

Goalkeepers who are trying to defend a pass from behind and are trying to save a shot from in front of the goal should be instructed about correct movements of the feet, body, and stick. First, teach the proper footwork of turning as an opponent passes the ball over the goal cage: To rotate efficiently, the goalie turns to the side over which the ball is passed, then steps up with the trail foot. Make the goalies repeat the footwork to imprint the skill, so they can immediately react to the ball's movement. Next, teach keepers how to read the pass and to position on the turn so that they arrive on the correct angle to save the shot. Watch for the common fault of goalkeepers lowering their stick head as they turn around to face a shot. Finally, show them how to extend, or telescope, the stick through the top hand to try to intercept the pass. Remember to discourage keepers from jumping off the ground to try for an interception over the goal cage.

Goalkeeper Warm-Up

Goalkeepers need extra time and attention to prepare before other players shoot on them. Young goalkeepers should not just step into a goal cage and allow their teammates to shoot on them indiscriminately. Develop a warm-up routine to teach, supervise, and encourage young goalkeepers before they step into the crease to receive a shot. These routines help warm up the goalkeepers' bodies and improve their eye tracking, balance, conditioning, and concentration. We've outlined several warm-up suggestions in the following section, but there are many more possibilities. The goalkeepers should be fully dressed in all their equipment and have completed a series of stretching exercises before continuing to warm-up.

Daily Practices

To be successful, young goalkeepers must acquire agility, balance, confidence, quick reactions, and leadership. Daily practice of such skills as footwork, stick control, and body positioning will help goalies develop mentally and physically.

Footwork

Goalkeepers must be prepared to move quickly from one place to another within the crease. First, young goalies should develop foot speed and then gain knowledge of how and where to step.

Here are some footwork activities:

⊙ **Over and Around the Stick.** The goalkeeper's stick is on the ground. The goalkeeper steps, with one foot following the other, over and back, across the shaft of the stick as quickly as possible (figure 13.8a). Each time the goalie steps over the stick with both feet, the feet should be in the ready position. Next, starting at the bottom of the shaft, with toes perpendicular to the shaft, shuffle sideways toward the head (figure 13.8b). When the top of the head is reached, run forward to the other side of the head; then, with the back toward the stick, shuffle sideways back to the end of the stick. Finally, starting at the bottom of the shaft and facing the stick head, run forward to the top of the stick, shuffle sideways across the head, and run backward to return to the bottom of the shaft (figure 13.8c). Continue this for 15 seconds.

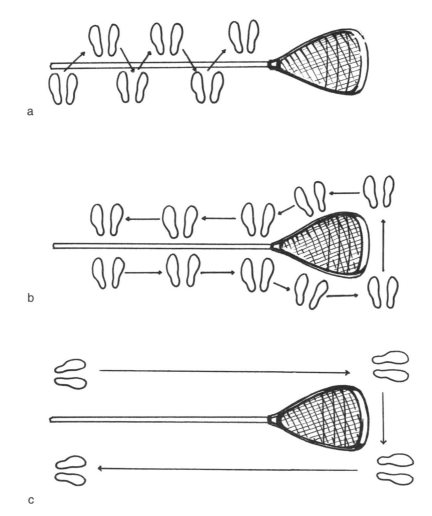

Figure 13.8 Goalie footwork (over and around the stick). *(a)* Over and back, *(b)* sideways shuffle, *(c)* run forward, shuffle, run backward.

⊙ **Box Drill.** Form a cross with two sticks on the ground. The goalkeeper moves from one corner of the box to the next. The keeper gets into the ready position with each move to a new corner (figure 13.9). The goalie may step only with the inside foot when changing boxes. Establish various patterns or changes of direction.

Stick

Young goalkeepers must orient themselves with the stick. Learning how to hold the stick, how to move the stick, and how to throw with the stick are all skills needed to save a shot on goal. These drills are also very important in teaching eye-tracking skills.

Here are some activities involving stick work:

⊙ **Quick Stick.** Stand with a ball about five yards away from the goalkeeper. Toss the ball underhanded to the goalkeeper's right shoulder. The goalkeeper steps forward with the right foot as he or she watches the ball enter the stick and gives with the catch. The goalkeeper

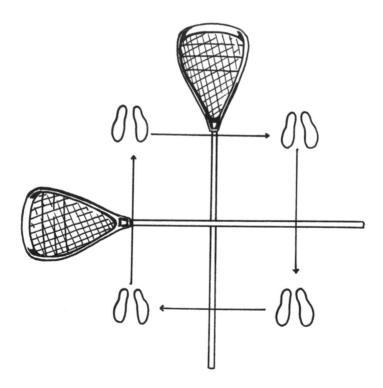

Figure 13.9 Goalie footwork (box drill).

returns the ball to you in a quick stick motion after the give. Back up one step as the goalkeeper advances one step on each throw. Emphasize the step to the ball and the give with the catch. Variations: Toss to different areas of the goalkeeper's body. Toss the ball from alternate hands so that the goalkeeper has to locate and then track the ball. Increase speed of delivery of the toss (not speed of the throw).

⊙ **Spot Shadow Tag.** The goalkeeper stands where he or she has space to move forward. The goalkeeper makes five imaginary saves to each area, returning to a ready position between each save. For example, the goalie makes five saves each to high right, to middle right, to low right, between the feet, overhead, to high left, to middle left, and to low left. Emphasize correct technique and stick, feet, and body movement. Eye movement should be from a shooter several yards away to the mesh pocket in the stick with each save. Variations: Call the spot for the goalkeeper to save to. The goalkeeper makes one save to each area five times through the cycle. Have the goalie turn 180 degrees before making the imaginary save, and check that his or her feet are set before stepping to make the save.

Body

The goalie always starts with his or her body in the ready position when the ball is in his or her defensive half of the field. A goalkeeper keeps his or her body between the goal and the ball as the attacking team approaches. Remind goalkeepers to always see the ball coming toward them or to track the ball in the air. They must anticipate a loose ball situation and decide if they can leave the crease to be the first player on it.

Here are some activities for body position:

⊙ **Step Up.** Use the same setup as in Quick Stick, except the goalkeeper doesn't use a stick. Toss the ball just outside of the goalkeeper's body. The goalkeeper steps to the ball and catches with two hands together, trying to move his or her body behind the ball. Emphasize stepping to the ball, keeping the toes pointing toward you, and keeping the shoulders and hips square behind the ball. *Variations:* Using a tennis ball, have the goalkeepers hold their hands behind their back and let the ball hit their body. Next, just give the goalies a shaft or broomstick handle to move for each shot and let the ball hit their body. Toss the ball with alternate hands. Decrease time between throws. Add fakes.

⊙ **Circle the Cage.** The goalkeeper stands in the crease near one post. Move along an arc about 10 yards from one post to the other and back.

While looking out toward you, the goalkeeper moves around the crease, following the arc. Emphasize moving at your speed; keeping shoulders and hips square; making small, quick steps; and staying balanced and in the ready position at all times. Check angles as the goalkeeper moves. *Variations:* Change speed and direction of the run or change the top hand the coach cradles with. Add fake shots to see if the goalie is set. Set up a pass from behind to check the goalkeeper's turning and angles.

After the preliminary warm-up, a goalkeeper should then continue to warm up with shots from you or a trained player. The object is to allow the goalkeeper enough time and practice in making saves in a controlled environment. Begin with shots at about 50 percent speed, and increase the speed as the warm-up routine continues. Don't progress in the warm-up until the goalkeeper feels comfortable at the speed you're using and with the activity itself. The goalkeeper must concentrate on seeing the ball out of the shooter's stick and into his or her own stick as the speed of the shots increases. Never allow your own or a player's ego to interfere with the warm-up of the goalkeeper. In other words, don't make scoring on a shot an objective as you help the goalie warm up.

Progress daily in the warm-up as in the teaching progression. Don't add players to a goalie's warm-up session until the goalie is ready and you have set up a controlled shooting drill. Remember to instruct the players that their purpose is to help warm up the goalkeeper; it's not to let loose and shoot uncontrollably. Be sure to include the skills of throwing and clearing for a goalkeeper at some point in the warm-up.

US Lacrosse - 113 W. University Parkway
Baltimore, MD 21210-3300
410.235.6882 / 410.366.6735 (fax)
www.uslacrosse.org   info@uslacrosse.org

US LACROSSE IS HERE TO HELP!

Founded on January 1, 1998 as the national, non-profit governing body of men's and women's lacrosse, US Lacrosse unites the national lacrosse community around one organization to effectively serve the sport. The mission of US Lacrosse is to ensure a unified and responsive organization that develops and promotes the sport by providing services to its members and programs to inspire participation, while preserving the integrity of the game. In addition to our national headquarters, over fifty regional chapter organizations around the country help to fulfill this mission. Please contact us for more information on how we can help you succeed as a lacrosse coach, official, or player.

US LACROSSE MEMBER BENEFITS

US Lacrosse is committed to improving and expanding services to our members. In addition to supporting and growing the sport, your membership dues entitle you to be a part of the growing US Lacrosse family that creates opportunities for all people to experience lacrosse. In addition, members receive direct benefits such as *Lacrosse Magazine*; insurance; a 10 percent discount on all purchases made from the Lacrosse Museum and online gift shop; a personalized membership card and sticker; free admission to the Lacrosse Museum and National Hall of Fame; monthly email newsletters; access to numerous programs and services; membership in and financial rebate dollar support to your local US Lacrosse chapter; access to National Partnership benefits such as special Positive Coaching Alliance programs, MBNA credit cards, and discounted Hertz car rentals; eligibility to participate in US Lacrosse sanctioned events; volunteer opportunities on the local and national level; knowledge of being a part of the lacrosse movement, and more!

A sampling of US Lacrosse operations...

- *Lacrosse Magazine*, the sport's premier feature magazine
- A comprehensive lacrosse insurance program for players, coaches, officials and events
- Developmental assistance for new teams and leagues including information resources, grants and stick loan kits
- Regional clinics and / or online education for coaches, officials and players
- Partnership programs offered in collaboration with the Positive Coaching Alliance
- Production of instructional videos, manuals and the *Parents' Guide to the Sport of Lacrosse*
- Development of BRIDGE Lacrosse (programs for children in traditionally underserved communities)
- Ongoing coordination of safety and injury research, including risk-management information
- Coordination of the US National Lacrosse Teams and special events such as the US Lacrosse National Youth Festival
- The Lacrosse Museum and National Hall of Fame, the national archives of men's and women's lacrosse

Injury Report

Name of athlete _____

Date _____

Time _____

First aider (name) _____

Cause of injury _____

_____

Type of injury _____

Anatomical area involved _____

Extent of injury _____

_____

_____

First aid administered _____

_____

_____

Other treatment administered _____

_____

_____

Referral action _____

_____

_____

First aider (signature) _____

Emergency Information Card

Athlete's name _____ Age _____

Address _____

Phone _____ S.S.# _____

Sport _____

List two persons to contact in case of emergency:

Parent or guardian's name _____

Address _____

Home phone _____ Work phone _____

Second person's name _____

Address _____

Home phone _____ Work phone _____

Insurance co. _____ Policy # _____

Physician's name _____ Phone _____

IMPORTANT

Is your child allergic to any drugs?_____ If so, what? _____

Does your child have any other allergies? (e.g., bee stings, dust) _____

Does your child suffer from____asthma, ____diabetes, or____epilepsy?

Is your child on any medication?_____ If so, what? _____

Does your child wear contacts?_____

Is there anything else we should know about your child's health or physical condition? If yes, please explain. _____

_____

_____

_____

_____

_____

Signature _____ Date _____

Emergency Response Card

Information for emergency call
(Be prepared to give this information to the EMS dispatcher)

1. Location _____

   Street address _____

   City or town _____

   Directions (cross streets, landmarks, etc.) _____

   _____

   _____

2. Telephone number from which the call is being made _____

3. Caller's name _____

4. What happened _____

   _____

   _____

   _____

   _____

   _____

5. How many persons injured _____

6. Condition of victim(s) _____

   _____

7. Help (first aid) being given _____

   _____

   _____

   Note: Do not hang up first. Let the EMS dispatcher hang up first.